FLORIDA STATE
UNIVERSITY LIBRARIES

DEC 20 2000

TALLAHASSEE, FLORIDA

Financial Decision-Making in Mexico

PITT LATIN AMERICAN SERIES

Billie R. DeWalt, General Editor
G. Reid Andrews, Associate Editor
Catherine Conaghan, Associate Editor
Jorge I. Domínguez, Associate Editor

Also by Sidney Weintraub

Free Trade between Mexico and the United States?

A Marriage of Convenience: Relations between Mexico and the United States

At the Crossroads: Mexican Migration and US Policy
(editor, with Frank D. Bean, Rodolfo O. de la Garza, and Bryan Roberts)

Integrating the Hemisphere: Perspectives from Latin America and the Caribbean
(editor, with Ana Julia Jatar)

NAFTA and Sovereignty: Trade-Offs for Canada, Mexico, and the United States
(editor, with Joyce Hoebing and M. Delal Baer)

NAFTA at Three: A Progress Report

Financial Decision-Making in Mexico

To Bet a Nation

Sidney Weintraub

University of Pittsburgh Press

Published by the University of Pittsburgh Press, Pittsburgh, Pa. 15261

Published in North America under license from Macmillan Press Ltd., Houndmills, Basingstoke, Hants. RG21 6XS, United Kingdom

Copyright © 2000 by Sidney Weintraub

All rights reserved

Printed on acid-free paper

10 9 8 7 6 5 4 3 2 1

ISBN 0–8229–4127–9 (cloth)

ISBN 0–8229–5731–0 (paper)

*To Gladys:
my decision-maker*

Contents

Preface	ix
Acknowledgments	xiii
List of Abbreviations and Acronyms	xvi
Chronology of Key Events	xviii

1 The Cultural Setting	**1**
The impact of history	3
Conclusions	20
2 Antecedents to the Decisions of 1994	**22**
The breakdown of the import-substitution model	22
Salinas' first five years	30
The commercial banks	35
Assessing the pre-1994 policy failures	38
3 The First Quarter of 1994	**40**
The mood of policy-makers as 1994 opened	40
The political–economic interplay	46
Colosio's assassination	56
4 The Second Quarter of 1994	**60**
Actions of the Bank of Mexico	62
The development banks and fiscal policy	71
The departure of Córdoba	74
Tesobonos and foreign investors	77
5 The Third Quarter of 1994	**79**
Pre-election economic policy	80
Post-election policy	82
Expert views on the policy model	88
Commercial bank fragility	91

6	**The Fourth Quarter of 1994 and Beyond**	93
	The public face of the authorities	94
	Behind the scenes	97
	The new administration	100
	"*El Error de diciembre*" (The Error of December)	108
	Mexico's immediate response	110
7	**Back in Washington and New York**	112
	Tracking events before the US and international rescue package	113
	The Mexican rescue package	138
8	**The Aftermath**	147
	The underlying policy principles	149
	Key elements of the adjustment program	150
	Strengths and weaknesses	154
	The NAFTA connection	158
	Final comment	161
9	**To Bet a Nation**	162
	The technical lessons	164
	The cultural explanation	167
	The disproportionate bet	170
	Concluding comment	172
Notes and References		174
Bibliography		194
Index		203

Preface

The crash of the Mexican economy in December 1994 attracted worldwide attention. Economists had long been concerned that earlier accepted wisdom, that the international financial system worked most efficiently when trade and capital movements were free, needed re-evaluation. The reason was that portfolio capital flows – purchases of stocks and bonds and government paper by foreigners and nationals alike – were becoming increasingly vast and mobile and could overwhelm the best-laid policies of small and medium economies. Such investment funds were moving increasingly to emerging countries, and Mexico became a prime destination. What became evident was that when investors in these instruments, whether foreigners or nationals of the country in question, collectively concluded that the economic or political stability of that country was endangered, the funds could move out even more quickly than they moved in. Spontaneous flight from the currencies of these countries could easily destroy prevailing macroeconomic policy.

The potential disrupting effects of capital movements on national economies was not new; in fact, this reality was built into the articles of the International Monetary Fund (IMF) when it was established after the Second World War. What was new, if not in concept but in size, was the speed with which portfolio capital investment decisions could be carried out and then reversed, and the immense quantities of capital that could be shifted out of a country.

Mexico became Exhibit One in demonstrating how these movements could have a devastating effect on a mid-sized, emerging economy. Mexico, from late 1988 through 1993, became the poster country for attracting these portfolio investment inflows. The president in these years, Carlos Salinas de Gortari, became the darling of the foreign investment community. He was admired for carrying out what was begun by his predecessor, Miguel de la Madrid, and bringing the Mexican economy out of its relative isolation. The Mexican market was opened and it became official policy to seek increasing amounts of foreign long-term and portfolio capital. The crowning achievement, at least for private market investors, was the conclusion of the North American Free Trade Agreement (NAFTA) with the United States and Canada, which went into effect on January 1, 1994. The United States had such a high regard for Salinas that it promoted his candidacy to head the newly-created World Trade Organization (WTO).

The sentiment toward Mexico began to change from the first day of 1994, when the Zapatista revolt erupted in the southern state of Chiapas. This, by itself, had little effect on capital flows into or out of Mexico – after declining for a few weeks, portfolio capital inflows increased after the uprising – but it brought home that Mexico, at its core, was a developing country with serious problems of poverty, inequality, and potential political instability. This was followed during the year by a series of external and internal shocks – the assassination of the presidential candidate of the Partido Revolucionario Institucional (PRI) or Institutional Revolutionary Party, which had governed Mexico uninterruptedly since 1929; a series of spectacular kidnappings for ransom; murders of other political figures and journalists; and successive increases in short-term US interest rates, which affected Mexico's ability to attract portfolio capital.

A consensus emerged within and outside Mexico that the exchange rate was becoming overvalued and that there was no high-level inclination to devalue the peso more rapidly until the presidential election of August 1994 was completed. Limiting the depreciation of the exchange rate, in fact, was the anchor around which the anti-inflation program was structured. Since 1987, the Mexican authorities had worked out a series of agreements between government, business, and labor – the *pactos* as they were called – to contain price and wage increases and to exercise control over government expenditures. This form of corporatist incomes policy was successful in bringing down the level of inflation, but at the cost of growing overvaluation of the peso. In addition, Mexico's economic growth was relatively anemic, a situation that had existed for 12 years.

Mexico decided, in these circumstances, to use its high level of foreign reserves, which were about $29 billion early in 1994, to protect the upper limit (the most depreciated level) of the band in which the peso was permitted to fluctuate. Reserves were lost, but were not exhausted until the end of 1994, when they were headed toward zero. Mexican nationals were the first to jump ship, but foreigners were not far behind. Finally, on December 20, Mexico devalued the peso by raising the upper limit of the band by 15 percent. Rather than contain the hemorrhaging of capital, this action set off further capital flight. The cost to rectify the situation was staggering, involving a drastic fall in gross domestic product, growing unemployment, declining wages, large-scale bankruptcies, and untold personal hardship.

This was the backdrop that stimulated the worldwide interest in Mexico. The darling of the money markets became the pariah. Governments and private interests outside the country became keenly interested in the backlash affecting them, the so-called tequila effect. The United States, together with the IMF and many central banks across the globe, mounted a rescue effort that was unprecedented in size – potentially more than $50 billion.

As the reality of the Mexican collapse sank in and concern mounted about the effect of the Mexican situation on the international financial system and the banking and investor situations in other countries, the peso crisis – really, the Mexican financial – economic débâcle and its potential repercussions – became the subject of widespread analysis throughout the world. What happened? What turned around the earlier favorable perceptions about Mexico's economic management? How can comparable future crises be avoided? How can they be contained?

It is fair to say that international financial thinking crossed a divide – from a sense of relative relaxation about the effects of large-scale capital movements before the Mexico crash to concern about the potential crushing effects of such movements on countries with modestly sized economies after the crash. For a few years, the Mexican crisis, dubbed the first of the twenty-first century because of the role of technology speeding the flow of capital and the repercussions around the globe, remained unique. Then, in 1997, a chain of crises arose in Northeast and Southeast Asia. Countries whose economies were admired – Japan, South Korea, Thailand, Malaysia, and Indonesia – suddenly changed from models to emulate to examples to avoid. The circumstances in those countries differed from each other, and they differed from Mexico, but there were common threads in capital movements, bank weaknesses, overvalued exchange rates, and, in some cases, corrupt and undemocratic governments.

I undertook this examination of the Mexican case because it involves so many aspects of domestic policies and fallouts around the world. I could have called the study "From Admiration to Contempt to Partial Recovery of Respect." My interest was not just in the economic policies that led to the collapse, which many have examined and whose analyses I have studied. My deeper interest was to understand the nature of Mexican society that influenced the decisions that were made. Did the formation of the Mexican policy-makers play a role in their decisions? If so, what were the conditioning factors?

This book is a study of decision-making on fundamental economic matters. These decisions affected 90 million Mexicans and were the catalyst for a seemingly infinite number of studies throughout the world about what to avoid and what positively should be done to prevent or deal with later crises. Such crises surely will come, beyond East Asia. One took place in Russia in 1998. Brazil only barely avoided a Mexican-type collapse in 1999. My goal was to combine economic analysis with political thinking, historic formation, and sociological influences, all of which were involved in the drama that was played out in the Mexican case. It is necessary, I am convinced, to combine all these influences in the examination of a breakdown of the magnitude that took place in Mexico.

Many of the habits of Mexican decision-makers discussed throughout the book, particularly in Chapter 1, are not unique to that country. A penchant for secrecy among senior policy-makers is widespread. An unwillingness to alter a policy course that is not achieving its objective is a phenomenon that has beset many countries. All countries have policy failures, in matters big and small. However, there are differences of degree between countries and each country's decision-makers have their own idiosyncratic formations. This book is a study of Mexican decision-making. A broader comparative study will be possible when similar analyses are completed for countries in East Asia, Russia, and elsewhere.

Washington, DC   SIDNEY WEINTRAUB

Acknowledgments

This book was made possible by the graciousness of scores of people who met and talked with me about how economic decision-making took place, as viewed from inside their respective systems. Most of the interlocutors were Mexican, but there were Americans who provided insights into thinking inside the US government and in the private investment community about events in Mexico as they unfolded during 1994. Policy officials in the World Bank and the International Monetary Fund (IMF) did the same.

The heart of the analysis in this book is to understand the contemporaneous thinking inside the Mexican government and central bank and most of the interviews were with people involved in this process. Respondents varied in their degree of candor. Some were voluble and open, others more guarded. Many of the respondents who were prepared to discuss the thinking and analysis that took place within the government preferred not to be cited by name, and I have respected this preference. I discovered, after speaking with many people about the same events and issues, that gaps in information tended to be filled in. Opinions of interviewees based on their friendship with one or more of the key actors were not normally included in the text of the book, unless independently verified. Much greater reliance was placed on judgments repeated by several respondents.

The interviews were not conducted in a vacuum. The written record was reasonably extensive about Mexican economic policy and about thinking in the US government. Many competent experts have dissected the decisions made by the Mexican authorities and these technical assessments were available and are acknowledged in the text. There is considerable published material on what was done incorrectly in Mexico that led to the crisis at the end of December 1994 and the lessons that emerged from the experience. My interest, as explained in the Preface, is to use the economic backdrop as the basis for assessing the nature of decision-making in Mexico and to bring into the analysis the elements that led the small group of senior decision-makers to act as they did. My conviction is that this type of analysis on an issue as important as that discussed in this book can provide more insights about how Mexico operates than can disembodied economic analysis or abstract philosophizing.

I spoke to about 100 individuals and many of them are identified by name in the text and the citations at the end of the book. Carlos Salinas de Gortari, the Mexican president for the six years ending December 1,1994 when Ernesto Zedillo Ponce de León was sworn in as president, was in Dublin when I was doing research for the book but, on several occasions, I contacted him by mail. He did not respond.

I could not have written this book without the financial support I received from a number of sources. These were the following: The US–Mexico Policy Studies Program of the Lyndon B. Johnson School of Public Affairs, The University of Texas at Austin, which in turn had been funded by the William and Flora Hewlett Foundation of Menlo Park, California; The Tinker Foundation of New York; the North–South Center of the University of Miami; and a number of private companies from Monterrey, Nuevo León, México. These were Grupo IMSA, Cementos Mexicanos, Grupo Protexa, Grupo Alfa, Grupo Cydsa, and Fomento Económico Mexicano.

I could not have done my research in Mexico without the kind assistance of the rector of the Instituto Tecnológico Autónomo de México (ITAM), Arturo Fernández, who not only granted me several interviews, but was kind enough to provide me with an office at ITAM, complete with a computer and the ability to make calls and receive messages. Rafael Fernández de Castro, who directs the program in international relations at ITAM, provided guidance and assistance at every stage of the research about Mexican institutions and personalities. Rafael helped me set up the first appointment with the senior businessmen from Monterrey.

Enrique Pani, then completing his undergraduate studies at ITAM, worked as my administrative assistant while I was in Mexico. He was efficient, thoughtful, and well informed on banking and financial matters (he now works professionally for an investment bank), and he set up appointments and accompanied me on many visits. Anyone who has tried to fix precise times for appointments with Mexican officials or senior private sector personalities knows that this is a time-consuming job that requires patience and flexibility, and Enrique had these qualities.

My administrative support came from two institutions with which I am affiliated, the Lyndon B. Johnson School of Public Affairs and the Center for Strategic and International Studies in Washington, DC.

I wish to thank the following individuals who made suggestions on the entire manuscript or parts of it: Norman Bailey, Kristopher Bengtson, Rafael Fernández de Castro, Peter Hakim, Frank Lysy, Joanna Meronk, Armand Peschard-Sverdrup, Erik Peterson, Jacques Rogozinski, Chandler Stolp, Larry Storrs, and Carol Wise.

Permission has been granted by the North–South Center Press at the University of Miami to include a revised and updated version of the following paper as Chapter 7 in this book, *As Mexico Imploded: Action and Inaction in the United States*, North–South Agenda Paper Twenty-Eight. Coral Gables, Fla.: North–South Center Press at the University of Miami (July 1997).

List of Abbreviations and Acronyms

AFL–CIO	American Federation of Labor–Congress of Industrial Organizations
Bancomext	Banco Nacional de Comercio Exterior (National Bank for Foreign Trade)
Banobras	(Banco Nacional de Obras y Servicios Públicos (National Bank for Public Services and Works)
Banrural	Banco Nacional de Crédito Rural (National Bank for Rural Credit)
BIS	Bank for International Settlements
Bolsa de Valores	Mexican Stock Market
CEMLA	Center for Monetary Studies of Latin America
Cetes	Certificados de la Tesorería de la Federación (Treasury Certificates)
CIDE	Center for Economic Investigation and Instruction
CNBV	Comisíon Nacional Bancaria y de Valores (National Banking Commission)
CONASUPO	Compañía Nacional de Subsistencias Populares (National Company of Popular Subsistence)
CPI	Consumer price index
DF	Federal District
EMS	European Monetary System
ESF	Exchange Stabilization Fund
EZLN	*Ejército Zapatista de Liberación Nacional* (Zapatista Army of National Liberation)
FDI	foreign direct investment
Fed	Federal Reserve Board (or Bank, when so specified)
Fobaproa	Fondo Bancario de Protección al Ahorro (Bank Fund for the Protection of Savings)
G-7	Group of Seven (industrial countries)
GAAP	Generally Accepted Accounting Principles
GAO	General Accounting Office
GATT	General Agreement on Tariffs and Trade
GDP	gross domestic product
IEPES	Institute of Economic, Political, and Social Science

	(now Fundación Nacional Colosio)
IFE	Federal Electoral Institute
IMF	International Monetary Fund
IMSS	Mexican Social Security Institute
INEGI	National Institute for Statistics, Geography, and Information
ITAM	Instituto Tecnólogico Autónomo de México (Autonomous Technical Institute of Mexico)
Libor	London interbank offer rate
NAFA	North American Framework Agreement
Nafin	Nacional Financiera (a Mexican Development Bank)
NAFTA	North American Free Trade Agreement
OECD	Organization for Economic Cooperation and Development
PAN	Partido de Acción Nacional (National Action Party)
Pemex	Petroleos Mexicanos (Mexico's oil monopoly)
PNR	Partido Nacional Revolucionario (National Revolutionary Party)
PRD	Partido de la Revolución Democrática (Party of the Democratic Revolution)
PRI	Partido Revolucionario Institucional (Institutional Revolutionary Party)
PRM	Mexican Revolutionary Party
Procapte	Programa de Capitación Temporal
Pronasol	National Solidarity Program
PSBR	public-sector budgetary requirement
Secofi	Secretariat for International Commerce and Industrial Development
SME	small and medium-sized firm
SOE	state-owned enterprise
SRE	Secretaría de Relaciones Exteriores (Secretariat for External Relations)
Telmex	Teléfonos de México
Tesobonos	Bonos de la Tesorería de la Federación (Treasury Bonds)
TIIP	Tasa de interes interbancaria promedio (Average Interbank Interest Rate)
UNAM	National Autonomous University of Mexico
WTO	World Trade Organization

Chronology of Key Events

1994

January 1.	NAFTA goes into effect and on the same day there is an uprising in the state of Chiapas by a group calling itself the Zapatista Army of National Liberation (EZLN).
February 4.	The US Federal Reserve raises the federal funds rate by one-quarter of a percentage point, the first such increase since 1992.
February 21.	The Mexican government opens peace talks with the EZLN.
March 14.	The president of the largest bank and brokerage firm in Mexico is kidnapped for ransom.
March 22.	The Federal Reserve raises the short-term interest rate by another one-quarter point.
March 23.	PRI presidential candidate Luis Donaldo Colosio is assassinated.
March 24.	The Federal Reserve and the Bank of Mexico open a swap facility of $6 billion. The agreement had been negotiated but not signed in the runup to NAFTA ratification. As a further measure to reassure market players, the government renews its *pacto* with labor and business.
April 8.	A number of US investment bankers, under a grouping known as the Weston Forum, suggests, among other steps, that the government issue more *tesobonos* as a confidence-building measure.
April 14.	Mexico is formally accepted as a member of the Organization for Economic Cooperation and Development (OECD).
April 18.	The Federal Reserve again raises the federal funds rate by one-quarter point.
April 25.	The son of the owner of an important supermarket chain is kidnapped.
April 26.	The North American Framework Agreement (NAFA) is signed, setting up a North American Financial Group. The agreement also makes permanent the

	$6 billion US–Mexico swap facility and expands a pre-existing Canada–Mexico swap line to C$1 billion.
May 17.	The Fed raises the federal funds rate by one-half of a percentage point.
August 16.	The Fed again raises short-term interest by one half-of-a percentage point.
August 21.	Ernesto Zedillo wins the presidential election.
September 24.	A new wage–price pacto is signed.
September 28.	José Francisco Ruiz Massieu, the secretary general of the PRI, is assassinated.
November 1.	President Salinas delivers his final *Informe*, or state-of-the-union address. It gives no hint of coming trouble.
November 15.	The Fed raises the federal funds rate by three-quarters of a percentage point. This is the sixth increase during 1994. The cumulative total increase is now 2.50 percentage points.
November 23.	Mario Ruiz Massieu, the deputy attorney general, resigns and charges that the government is obstructing his investigation of his brother's murder.
November 20.	What later becomes a highly publicized meeting between key officials of the incoming and outgoing governments, including the two presidents and finance secretaries, is held at President Salinas' house and the suggestion of a peso devaluation is rejected.
December 1.	Ernesto Zedillo is inaugurated as president of Mexico.
December 19.	Subcomandante Marcos announces that the Zapatistas have occupied 38 localities in the state of Chiapas and, even though this proves to be exaggerated, the report leads to a sharp fall of the peso.
December 20.	Following a meeting of the pacto, the new finance secretary, Jaime Serra Puche, announces that the ceiling of the peso band will be raised by 15 percent. International reserves at that point are $10.5 billion.
December 22.	Following a fall in reserves to less than $6 billion and a sharp run on the peso, the trading band is dropped and the peso is permitted to float.
December 28.	A delegation from the IMF arrives in Mexico City.
December 29.	The president announces that Guillermo Ortiz Martínez will replace Jaime Serra as finance secretary.

1995

January 2. The Mexican government announces a new financial support package of $18 billion – $9 billion from the United States (an increase over the earlier swap line of $6 billion), C$1.5 billion from Canada, and $5 billion from other central banks operating through the Bank for International Settlements (BIS).

January 6. The IMF and Mexico announce their intention to enter into negotiations for a standby credit.

January 9. Mexico announces it has made its first drawing from the financial support package, $500 million from the United States and C$83 million from Canada.

January 12. President Clinton proposes legislation for a $40 billion loan-guarantee package for Mexico.

January 31. Because of congressional opposition, President Clinton withdraws his proposed legislation for a $40 billion loan guarantee to Mexico and states that the government will use its executive authority to provide a $20 billion loan package to Mexico using the Exchange Stabilization Fund (ESF). The total loan package from all sources comes to $52.5 billion – $20 billion from the United States, $17.8 billion from the IMF, $10 billion from other countries through the BIS, C$708 million from Canada, $1 billion from Argentina, Brazil, Chile, and Colombia, and $3 billion from international banks.

February 1. The Fed raises the federal funds rate by another one-half of a percentage point.

Source: Patricia A. Wertman, "Mexico: Chronology of a Financial Crisis," Congressional Research Service, Library of Congress (September 27, 1995).

1
The Cultural Setting

The central argument of this book is that Mexico got into trouble in its economic decision-making in 1994 as a result of a combination of secrecy, exclusivity, arrogance on the part of decision-makers, and unwillingness to entertain contrary views from outside a small inner circle. In order to sustain this thesis, it is necessary to ask what engendered these characteristics. Then, in reviewing the economic decisions that were made, the influence of these characteristics must be demonstrated.

The persons making the major economic policy decisions were talented and highly trained professionally. Almost all the senior officials had received doctoral degrees from outstanding US universities and came to their tasks in the Salinas administration with impressive backgrounds that included previous high-level government experience.[1] There is no evidence of corruption on the part of officials just below the president in the decision-making hierarchy. The failure of policy, consequently, cannot be ascribed to lack of preparation or a desire for personal financial aggrandizement by these officials, although the facts with respect to Salinas himself are ambiguous.

The Bank of Mexico, the central bank, is adamant that the problems that arose at the end of 1994 were not the result of faulty decisions, but rather of a series of shocks that could not be foreseen.[2] There is no doubt there were shocks. They started on January 1, 1994, when the *Ejército Zapatista de Liberación Nacional* (EZLN or Zapatista Army of National Liberation) rose up in rebellion in the state of Chiapas. The internal shocks continued unrelentingly during the year and included the assassination of the presidential candidate of the Partido Revolucionario Institucional (PRI or Institutional

Revolutionary Party) on March 23, another murder of the number two official of the PRI, José Francisco Ruiz Massieu, on September 28, and then the announcement on December 19, the day before the devaluation of the peso, of further and reportedly (which turned out not to be true) successful rebellious action by the Zapatistas. The US Federal Reserve Board raised short-term interest rates six times in 1994 and this complicated the management of monetary policy by the Bank of Mexico. (A chronology of events is shown on p. xviii.)

Yet, the function of the central bank and of senior officials of the central government is to base policy on the realities facing the country, and these surely include internal and external shocks. It can be argued that there was no call for altering monetary policy after the first severe shock, the Chiapas uprising; and, indeed, Mexico's foreign-exchange reserves actually rose in the two months following this incident. It also was rational not to make an abrupt monetary policy change immediately after the assassination of Colosio, despite the sharp drop of foreign reserves of more than $10 billion in the following month, on the grounds that it would be unwise to add even more economic turmoil to the political shock of the assassination. The capital hemorrhage after the Colosio assassination ceased after about a month and foreign reserves then remained reasonably stable until November 1994.

But the accumulation of evidence during the year that the exchange rate was considered overvalued by market players both inside and outside Mexico, the failure of a buildup of foreign reserves during the year as portfolio investors remained wary, plus the growing level of short-term, dollar-indexed government debt (the *tesobonos*), should have triggered much more internal soul-searching about the correctness of the monetary–financial course being followed than it did.

These are issues that will be taken up in detail later, but for now the task is to ask why a policy that seemed to be on a collision course with the underlying reality of the country – although no one, not even the severest critics of the policy, foresaw the extent of the catastrophe that did occur – was defended until there was no longer any option other than its abandonment. Were there features in Mexican sociological culture and habits of operation at the top levels of government that influenced decision-making?

The impact of history

Enrique Krauze, in a blockbuster book on Mexican history, makes the point early in his Preface that "The weight of the past has sometimes been more present than the present itself."[3] This theme of the influence of history on contemporary Mexico permeates the work not only of Krauze, but of his distinguished mentor, the late Octavio Paz. Krauze states several times in his book that the most distinguished analysis of the Mexican character is Paz's own book written four decades earlier, *The Labyrinth of Solitude*.[4] One of the many ways in which Paz expresses his view about the importance of the past in modern Mexican thought is that "The history of Mexico is the history of a man seeking his parentage, his origins."[5]

It is not remarkable that a country's history has great influence on its current character. What is germane is to explore what in Mexican history is relevant to the current outlook and to shaping the way its leaders behaved in 1994. Three such features, each with its own offshoots, deserve stress:

1 There is a constant emphasis in official Mexican statements, a stress which is reflected in official actions, on a *defensive variety of nationalism* – a form of solitude, to use Octavio Paz's term – that developed as a result of historical experience. One of the most influential authors of the Mexican character antedating Paz, Samuel Ramos, referred to a national inferiority complex developing as a consequence of history.[6] One form this brand of nationalism took was to repeatedly admonish other nations – really the United States – to stay out of internal Mexican affairs just as Mexico promised to stay out of the internal affairs of others. We'll mind our business and you mind yours! Fair enough, but it was evident to most analysts of the Mexico–US relationship that the United States would not stay out of internal Mexican affairs because these were seen to be part and parcel of US internal matters as well.

2 The preference of Mexicans for *strong national leaders*, a trait that developed from the need to unify the country after the Revolution and the divisive civil wars of the 1920s. Krauze asserts, for example, that Salinas' influence and popularity grew during his *sexenio* (six-year term), at least until the final year (1994), because he was seen as a leader who had *huevos* (balls).[7]

3 The long period of *one-party rule* from 1929 until the present day shaped the way Mexican leaders conducted the daily business

of governance. The dominance of the PRI has been attenuated in recent years, but the party still controls the presidency. This single-party authoritarianism instilled habits of leadership that quite consciously limited popular participation in national decision-making. It led to ancillary practices – such as minimal press freedom, a pro-PRI near-monopoly of television news under Televisa, a non-inquiring congress, a weak judiciary, and a highly centralized government – that made secrecy a routine way of doing things and arrogance a constant attribute of leadership. Just as its nationalism told other countries to stay out of Mexico's internal affairs, one-party rule implicitly told the general population to stay out of the affairs of government. The combination was powerful in forming habits of conduct in the senior ranks of government.

The extent of the influence of these features in conditioning actions by senior government officials is arguable, but not really their existence. It can and has been debated whether a national inferiority complex exists, or existed, which contributed to the kind of nationalism that has been called *estadolatria* (idolatry of the state), but the nature of this nationalism is surely a reality.[8] The author who used this term, Rolando Cordera, draws on Gramsci for his commentary, a source used frequently by Mexican political analysts. It is understandable that Mexican intellectuals are drawn to Gramsci's insights on hegemony, particularly as this refers to the power of the ruling class over the whole of society.[9]

Nationalism *à la* mexicana

Nationalism is not a theme on which I wish to dwell excessively because it has long been a subject of analysis by Mexican scholars. Perhaps more relevant to the purpose here is that nationalism as it manifested itself in Mexico is an explanatory variable in shaping decision-making habits – mostly, however, when viewed in connection with the other two variables. National pride can be a source of strength as well as shortsightedness in its influence on behavior. Even more basically, Mexicans have much to be proud of in their antecedents. The cultural accomplishments of the peoples of the land that is now Mexico are more profound than those of the United States and the cultural heritage has roots even deeper than those of Europe. In addition, as Krauze states repeatedly, Mexico was able early in its history to achieve an ethnic amalgam, a *mestizaje* (joining of the national races), that was more tolerant and all-inclusive than in practically any other country in the Western Hemisphere.[10]

Yet, as one traces Mexico's past from independence until today, this history instilled a form of nationalism that had as many elements of defensiveness as it did the positive projection of national pride. Mexico's nationalism developed largely from setbacks and conflicts, rather than from solid political or economic accomplishments. Examples of these problems are known to students of Mexican history, but are largely a jumble of disconnected events to most non-Mexicans. This is not the place to give a detailed review of Mexican history; in addition to Krauze's work, there are many insightful histories of Mexico written by distinguished Mexicans and well informed foreigners. But a few examples of the problems that Mexico had to face and the setbacks it had to overcome can be cited to frame the discussion of why nationalism there has been defensive rather than triumphant, as in the United States.

One place to start is the troubled situation that followed the rebellion of 1810 that led to independence from Spain in 1821; independence was achieved with considerable travail and then was followed by a stormy history. Some of the events of the nineteenth century that merit mention are the coronation as emperor of Agustín de Iturbide in 1822, his abdication less than a year later and his subsequent execution, and the long period of uncertainty during the following decades from the actions – antics may be a better word – of Antonio López de Santa Anna. As Krauze puts it: "If Iturbide's empire had been the dramatic enactment of a tragedy, Santa Anna's eleven presidencies might be compared to the less distinguished genre of operetta."[11] It was not operetta filled with moments of great splendor or successful climaxes.

The most searing experience shaping modern Mexican nationalism was the loss of territory to the United States. Texas declared its independence from Mexico in 1836 and became part of the United States in 1845. The subsequent war with the United States, ending with the Treaty of Guadalupe–Hidalgo in 1848, confirmed US title to Texas and Mexico was also forced to cede the large California and New Mexico territories. Mexico's territory was reduced by half; it was Mexico's misfortune to have lacked internal strength and resolve at the height of the US period of manifest destiny.

To this day, it is hard for an American to have a discussion with a Mexican on relations with the United States without being reminded of this US territorial aggrandizement. This history is a basic lesson in all elementary and secondary school history textbooks in

Mexico, whereas for Americans it is largely part of the background noise of US history.

There were other humiliations which the Mexicans had to endure. Guadalupe–Hidalgo was not the last cession of territory. The later Gadsden Purchase of 30 000 square miles of territory (in what is today southern New Mexico and Arizona) was one of the precipitating factors in ending Santa Annas's eleventh and last presidency. Mexico then had to endure its second empire, the bizarre period between 1864, when Maximilian von Hapsburg was crowned with the support of the French army and conservative groups in Mexico, and 1867, when Maximilian was executed and Benito Juárez was able to re-establish the republic.

This was not the end of turmoil. The *porfiriato*, the period between 1876, when Porfirio Díaz became president, and 1910, when the Revolution erupted, was a defining period of Mexican nationalism. Díaz welcomed foreign participation in the Mexican economy, and this was accompanied by a powerful authoritarianism that has not dissipated to the current day. Mexico's Revolution (upper-case "R") and subsequent civil wars did not come to an end until the mid- to the later 1920s. The Revolution was bloody; one estimate is that 1.5 million of a total population of about 15 million – 10 percent – died in the decade after 1910.[12] Many more died in the civil wars that raged in various regions of the country until order was restored in the 1920s.

Two final conditioning considerations for modern-day nationalism should be mentioned. The first is the murders of Francisco Madero, the leader who sparked the Revolution and the first president after the overthrow of Díaz, and José María Pino Suárez, his vice president, in February 1913. While it cannot be stated with certainty who ordered the murders, there is no doubt that the US ambassador at the time, Henry Lane Wilson, plotted with the Mexican instigators of the overthrow of Madero and then did nothing subsequently to save his life.[13] The agreement that led to Madero's overthrow is referred to in Mexico as the *Pacto de la Embajada* (the embassy agreement – the US embassy) and the period between the coup against Madero and his death is known as *La Decena Tragica* (the 10 tragic days).

The second conditioning consideration is more positive, namely, the nationalization of foreign oil properties by President Lázaro Cárdenas in 1938.[14] Cárdenas acted only after the oil company executives defied decisions of both the executive and the Mexican judiciary, and the action had particular resonance among the population because it came after a century or more of humiliation by the United States, including what can only be described as imperious behavior by the oil companies themselves over many decades. The oil nationalization was at once a defensive action and a declaration of national sovereignty. Many arguments can be made today about undoing some effects of the nationalization in the interest of attracting more foreign investment for oil and gas exploration and exploitation, and some steps to ease restrictions on private investment have been taken, but any politician would have to be foolhardy – or courageous, to use a more positive word – to take sweeping measures affecting government control of national hydrocarbons. So much history and considerable national pride is involved in the oil industry in Mexico.

Krauze is not the only authority to extol and take pride in the *mestizo* culture of Mexico. Indeed, this pride, that Mexico does not have a racist or intolerant society, has long been official doctrine. While there is much truth to this contention, the reality is complex. *Mestizaje* is more extensive in Mexico than in, say, the countries of the southern cone of South America (Argentina, Chile, and Uruguay), but this is more the consequence of the fact that the native groups in those places were not large to begin with and those that existed were largely wiped out. Mexico, by contrast, had a large indigenous population when Cortés and the *conquistadores* arrived without women. Mexico's business, intellectual, and government leadership is predominantly European. The poverty that is so widespread in Mexico largely affects the various Indian populations and those mixed groups that are predominantly Indian. The weakest educational opportunities are in areas where native and mixed populations are the large majority.

There is no state-sponsored racial intolerance in Mexico but distinctions among people based on color and ethnic origin exist in everyday life. One need only walk through the different neighborhoods in the country's large cities to note not only the income disparities, but also the overwhelmingly Indian hue and features of the people in the poor *barrios* and the white, European cast in the more affluent. The most impoverished rural areas are native in makeup.[15] The rebellions that have erupted from time to time in various states of Mexico, in Chiapas in January 1994, in Guerrero both before and after that, and in a number of locations in Oaxaca, involve mainly brown-skinned and not white persons.

Mexico's nationalism has been described by one of its leading social analysts as the legitimating source of a dominant, exploitative system.[16] Jonathan Heath, an economist, has made much the same point, arguing that Mexican insistence on sovereignty has been based on the struggle for domination by the small ruling class. Some of these struggles, he said, are with forces abroad (and the word "sovereignty" is used), but others take place within the ruling class inside the country.[17]

One of the consequences of the use of nationalism (or sovereignty) as an instrument in the power struggle among elites or between dominant groups and the general public is that it substituted myth for the development of modern democracy.[18] Paz made a related point in *The Labyrinth of Solitude* when he noted that unlike criticism in the United States which generally respects existing systems without touching their roots, such criticism has been rare in Mexico.

Nationalism was used to justify the highly restrictive import structure and the limits placed on foreign direct investment (FDI) that existed in Mexico until the 1980s. A theoretical economic rationale was put forward, that this infant-industry protection was needed to develop an industrial base controlled by Mexicans, but the policy served as well to entrench privilege in Mexico.

Just as the closed and secretive nature of decision-making by Mexican political leaders and the senior bureaucracy was part and parcel of the hegemonic exercise of domestic power, so, too, is defensive nationalism used to deflect outside counsel. This took place repeatedly in 1994 when Mexico rejected outside advice that its economic policies were on a collision course with failure. In the course of interviews for this study, several senior officials of the US government and international agencies told me that it was a trying experience to negotiate with Mexicans, more so than dealing with officials of most other countries. Many of the Mexicans with whom I spoke made clear that they found negotiators from the IMF overbearing in expressing their opinions, but the reverse also was true. The impression left with me in discussions with Mexican officials was that they felt they knew the true situation in their own country much better than officials from international financial institutions parachuted into Mexico for negotiations. They undoubtedly did, at least from their vantage point. Yet, the reality is that the outside experts came because the Mexican authorities requested them – Mexico needed either the credits from the multilateral development banks or the financing and seal of approval from the IMF.

Yet, here too, there is ambivalence. Mexican media generally search out foreign experts to cite their analyses of Mexican events. This is sometimes embarrassing to the foreign experts quoted in that their judgments are given too much weight within Mexico.[19] The US–Mexican relationship is full of asymmetries and this is another: the opinions of US experts on Mexican affairs can be highly influential, but it is rare that statements of Mexican experts carry much weight in the United States. The Mexican press is prone to reprint articles that appear in leading US newspapers dealing with developments in Mexico because these have more credibility than do home-grown articles. This practice supports Samuel Ramos' inferiority complex thesis.

The defensiveness that used to prevail in relations with the United States, and to a great extent still does, sometimes spills over into bitterness. One dramatic example of this occurred during the visit to Mexico by US President Jimmy Carter in 1979. The US government shortly before had rejected what appeared to be an agreement on the pricing of Mexican natural gas to be sold in the United States. In the toast delivered during a state dinner, President José López Portillo referred to "sudden deceit" by the United States. This was not a private, one-on-one statement, but a declaration deliberately publicized by the Mexican authorities, presumably for domestic political purposes.

Defensive nationalism, while less pronounced than earlier, was still evident in 1997 and 1998 when Mexico expelled a reported 200 foreigners from the country for allegedly meddling in political affairs in Chiapas. A French priest who was ordered to leave had lived in Chiapas for 32 years. The foreign secretary, Rosario Green, was quoted as saying that "To reproach and reject foreign meddling in our affairs is not xenophobia."[20]

Carlos Salinas, when he became president, deliberately set out to change the tenor of the relationship with the United States, really to alter many of the less attractive outward manifestations of Mexican nationalism, while carefully husbanding the internal hegemonic aspects. The entry into NAFTA was the prime example of this outward effort. As economic relations were made more cooperative and less confrontational, this was also reflected in the political relationship. It is hard to imagine the current Mexican president making the sort of statement that López Portillo did, any more than the current US president would deliberately insult his Mexican counterpart in an open forum. These insults are left to US legislators, who seem to feel no responsibility for inflammatory words.

The looking within that long typified Mexican political and economic policy, and which was justified in large measure by appeals to nationalism, began to give way as Mexico's involvement in global affairs grew in importance. The debt crisis of 1982, which made evident that the long-standing policy of "development from within" was bankrupt, was the starting point of national introspection about the value of nationalism as practiced until then. Mexico was forced to come hat-in-hand to the United States and the IMF for a bailout. It turned out that López Portillo's senseless and deeply damaging nationalization of private banks at the end of 1982 was the last blatant hurrah of the old mentality. He blamed the *sacadolares* (those who unpatriotically sent dollars out of the country) for the crisis, rather than look at his own policies. The rubber-stamp legislature accepted his action. After he left office in December 1982, his successor, Miguel de la Madrid, methodically went about changing the model from depending almost entirely on domestic demand for economic stimulus to looking outward as well. He did this, he said, because he concluded he had no other choice.[21] Looking outward, what was called "export-led growth," was accelerated under Carlos Salinas and continued in the administration of Ernesto Zedillo.

When it became evident that shunning foreign direct investment to the maximum extent possible and instead relying on foreign debt to finance infrastructure and productive activities could be catastrophic, this policy was also changed. Those entrepreneurs who sought capital and alliances with foreign investors had earlier been labeled as *vendepatrias* (those who sold their patriotism); this nationalistic terminology had to change as Mexico consciously sought out foreign capital. Mexico today brags about how much foreign investment it is able to attract, now second or third among developing countries on an annual basis after only China and sometimes Brazil.

Mexico had to be bailed out again from its own debt folly in 1995 after the inept devaluation of December 20, 1994 turned into catastrophe. The economic policy that followed was highly orthodox, made necessary by conditions imposed by the external lenders, especially the IMF and the US Treasury, but also based on the philosophic conviction of those making economic policy for Mexico. Mexico had become part of the global economy – even if the globe was largely the United States. The old nationalism had to take on new trappings. Self-sufficient Mexico, so far from the world, had to become interdependent Mexico deeply involved in the process of globalization.

Nationalism still plays its role but, except for hard liners of both the left and the right who cling to old myths, it is becoming less strident. Mexican leaders must be cautious not to overly offend either the United States or the international financial institutions because this could prejudice the country's vital economic interests. Mexico did not try to correct its balance-of-payments crisis in 1995 by imposing import controls, as it had done in 1982 under López Portillo, because this would have destroyed NAFTA. Instead, macroeconomic belt-tightening was used and buoyant exports to the United States were a key element of the rapid recovery. Even less could Mexico contemplate capital controls, which also were tried briefly in 1982 to slow down dollar flight, because what Mexico needed was revitalized dollar inflow. This, too, after a modest lapse, took place.

The framers of economic policy in 1994 thus came from a cultural milieu of ambivalence about nationalism. Their formation was defensive nationalism, but the reality of the world they faced no longer permitted this to the extent that had been possible earlier. Twenty years earlier, politicians could be overtly anti-American and garner popularity at home and not be overly concerned about the reaction abroad. This is no longer the case. Indeed, the politicians of all parties, from the PRI, the left (Partido de la Revolución Democrática, or PRD) and the right (Partido de Acción Nacional, or PAN) found it convenient to visit and meet opinion-makers in the United States and elsewhere to make clear that they understood the new rules of the game. They also learned to be careful in their internal statements as they realized these were read immediately outside Mexico as well.

Most policy-makers understood this new world and moderated the ultra-nationalistic aspects of their actions. A few did not, mostly in the legislature rather than the executive branch. Those who altered the manner in which nationalism was used abroad did not always simultaneously alter their hegemonic practices at home. It was an article of faith on the part of Carlos Salinas that political opening in the country had to be put on a slow track until the economic transformation was locked into place. This was the pattern in Southeast Asia, where authoritarian regimes also existed. It will be argued later in this chapter that this decision to slow down political opening – which was part of the cultural formation of Salinas and many of his closest advisors – contributed to the débâcle that occurred.

The preference for strong leaders

Krauze states in his book that "[Porfirio] Díaz believed that the only possible relationship between a government and its people was that of authority."[22] Krauze later notes that another Díaz, this time Gustavo Díaz Ordaz, who was the president during the 1968 student uprising, "believed religiously that the system could not yield a particle of power without losing its very existence, its *being*."[23] Alduncin, who over many years directed a series of studies on the values that Mexicans hold, found in a 1987 survey that 77 percent of those questioned believed that the country required a firm hand to prosper.[24] In that same survey, Alduncin found that only 50 percent felt that Mexico needed more democracy, while the other half felt that it did not (20 percent) or had no opinion (30 percent).[25]

These values change with the times. Krauze himself attracted much attention from a book published in 1986 under the title *For a Democracy without Adjectives*, reprinting a series of columns and essays he had written earlier.[26] The attention was based as much or more on the title than on the essays themselves. In a more recent analysis of what three authors believe is a convergence of values taking place among the three North American countries, Canada, Mexico, and the United States, data are presented on the growing desire in Mexico for more democratic political institutions.[27] The congressional elections that took place in Mexico on July 6, 1997, which led to an opposition majority in the lower house of the Mexican legislature, the Chamber of Deputies, for the first time in modern Mexican history, is a manifestation of the growing power of democracy.

In the post-revolutionary turmoil and especially after the influence of regional *caudillos* was brought under the control of the Partido Nacional Revolucionario (PNR, or National Revolutionary Party, the original predecessor to today's PRI) at the national level in 1929, Mexico needed strong, decisive leaders to counteract the centrifugal forces to national unity. This authoritarian imperative endured longer than was necessary for the well-being of Mexican society.

Mexican democracy is new and still evolving. Mexican authoritarianism, by contrast, is long-standing and has much deeper roots. In a survey conducted in many Latin American countries in 1997, MORI de México found that only 52 percent of Mexicans believed that democracy was preferable to other forms of government. This compared with 86 percent preference for democracy in Uruguay, 83 percent in Costa Rica, 75 percent in Argentina, and percentages higher than in Mexico in the 12 countries surveyed other than Brazil, Ecuador, and Paraguay.[28] The yearning for democracy and a latent preference for authoritarianism obviously can coexist. The question that interests us here is whether the decision-makers in the Salinas administration, including Salinas himself, were more attuned to democracy or to authoritarianism and firm leadership. The answer surely is the latter, the exercise of hegemonic power. The power of tradition was greater than the pressure for a change in the habits of governance.

Salinas made it evident that for him it was economic reform first and political opening later – as late as possible. Krauze states repeatedly in various ways that Salinas' priorities had little to do with political reform and that he wished to retain personal domination until he had the economic reforms locked in. "The economy first, the Political Reform second, and in its own good time."[29] When discussing Salinas' *sexenio*, Krauze asserts that this was the "heyday" of the economists and that "They were an imperious and impatient group."[30]

Krauze's discussion is quite harsh toward the economists, but the failure to open the political system more rapidly was less of their making than it was of Salinas himself and his closest political advisors. It was the professionals in the PRI who were most devoted to the closed political system. When the PRI, in its national assembly in 1996, ruled that future presidential and other senior nominees had to have been *militantes* of the party – that they had to have held elective office to be eligible as nominees for president, what in Mexico is referred to as the *candado*, or lock, on the nomination – they were making a statement that they did not want more economists, more *técnicos*, to run the country, but the motivation was to save their own political skins. The most scathing criticisms of Ernesto Zedillo were based on his lack of forceful leadership and they came primarily from within the PRI. The legacy of Salinas, as was evident by the devaluation that came only three weeks after he left office, was a depreciated party and economic shambles. Economic growth in Mexico, once the economy was put back on track after the 1995 débâcle, has been substantially greater during the

Zedillo years than they were under Salinas. It may in the end turn out that the savior of the PRI will be the non-charismatic President Zedillo because of his economic accomplishments.

Krauze's history is a recounting of what individual leaders did. It is less an analysis of the great national and worldwide movements that shaped Mexico's destiny, but of actions and errors of individual leaders. He says as much when he refers to personalized *ismos* attached to different periods of Mexican history: *juarismo, porfirismo, zapatismo, cardenismo, salinismo*.[31] The chapters of his book reflect this conception of Mexican history; they are named after leaders and discuss events that took place during their periods of dominance. My view is that Krauze's book is weakest in dealing with recent periods. The leaders since the late 1920s served single presidential terms and while *personalismo* has its place, history does not occur in six-year bites.

One of Mexico's most illustrious historians, the late Daniel Cosío Villegas, brought out this *personalismo* in governing in a most unflattering way in his book about Luis Echeverría, a president he did not admire, entitled *El estilo personal de gobernar* (The Personal Style of Governing),[32] Echeverría's successor as president, José López Portillo, was perhaps even more dictatorial in his actions and his administration ended with the debt crisis. Krauze calls his chapter on Salinas "The Man Who Would be King."

Mexico's history is one of authoritarian leaders who, all too often, led the country to catastrophe during their periods of power. This was true of Santa Anna, Porfirio Díaz, and more recently Echeverría, López Portillo, and, in the end, Salinas. Polling evidence indicates that there has long been a popular preference for strong, authoritarian leaders. The pace at which this is changing is unclear. Zedillo is not authoritarian and is more popular with the general public, at least as this is written, than he is with the professional politicians of his own party. A disconnect may be developing between the political insiders and popular sentiment, but it will take more time to verify or discard this hypothesis. The growth of democracy and popular participation, if it continues to flourish, may put an end to the preference for authoritarian leaders, but it is rash to predict when habits that have been ingrained for almost two centuries of Mexico's modern era will dissipate. In any event, the decision-making in 1994, and in the years prior to that which contributed to the economic débâcle that ensued, took place under an authoritarian structure.

Secrecy and arrogance

There have been examples in other countries of political parties and organizational structures that have maintained national power over decades, but few if any of these did so with the sophistication demonstrated by the PRI. The Communist Party held sway in the Soviet Union for more than 70 years, but this was done with mass murder, overt repression, and the use of an iron hand. Authoritarian regimes in East Asia lasted for decades, but usually under the aegis of military leaders. The Liberal–Democratic Party and its predecessors dominated post-Second World War Japan, but this was in a society used to tight discipline. The PRI discarded the practice of choosing former generals as president with the selection of Miguel Alemán in 1946, and he was at least as authoritarian as his military predecessors.

The PRI used a combination of concessions to its opponents and coopting of promising young leaders alongside outright repression, especially in rural areas, and made a show of all the trappings of elections whose outcomes were known in advance. The press was nominally free, but for decades the supply of newsprint was controlled by a government-owned monopoly, advertising revenue came predominantly from the government, and reporters were placed on government payrolls for reasons of control and not selfless charity. Televisa, the country's largest television network, was unashamedly pro-PRI and this had great social influence because most people received their news from that medium.[33] Violence against reporters who uncovered unpleasant political realities was quite common and, unfortunately, the habit persists to the present day, although practiced now also by narcotics dealers.[34]

This extensive period of domination, with its combination of favors and punishment, lasted as long as it did because the PRI-led government delivered steady economic growth in the 6–7 percent range a year from the late 1930s to the early 1980s. The growth was not equitably distributed, but even the poor participated in Mexico's economic advances. The powerful benefitted most from this structure, but a middle class also was created, and these influential groups were the backbone of the system. Obscene inequalities in income and opportunity were tolerated because the poor were not left completely by the wayside, and the poor were mostly powerless.

This combination of growth with inequity broke down when the growth ceased and the inequity increased. The debt crisis of 1982 led to four years of economic decline and stagnation during which the wages at the bottom of the income scale – those working at the minimum wage – fell by as much as 50 percent. The real income of the newly created middle class also fell after 1982 and this undoubtedly was more unsettling to the structure because these were people who knew how to use the political system for their benefit.

The PRI monopoly thus became less solid during the 1980s and the opposition – the PAN, the conservative party which did not represent the impoverished majority – was permitted to win a number of state gubernatorial elections, capture some seats in the federal senate, and take over the management of many key cities. There were political reforms in this period which granted opposition parties more power in the federal legislature through a combination of proportional representation alongside first-past-the-post elections, but always carefully rigged to maintain PRI control.

The PRI monopoly was finally ended by the economic débâcle of 1994–5, which made it evident that one-party dominance could no longer guarantee steady economic growth. The economic opening that began in 1982 and then accelerated under Salinas when he assumed the presidency in 1988 surely contributed to more private participation by removing many key economic decisions from government officials and placing them in the hands of players in the market.[35] The PRI, in the July 1997 congressional elections, lost control of the Chamber of Deputies, the lower house of the congress, for the first time in the party's history. The position of Mayor (*regente*) of Mexico City, which had been changed from a presidential appointee to an elected office, was decided overwhelmingly in favor of an opposition party. In both cases, the big winner was the PRD, the party to the left of the PRI and one dominated by ex-*priístas* who had little sympathy with the policy of economic opening initiated in 1982.[36]

The authoritarian, PRI-controlled, structure led inevitably to corruption. PRI politicians took it for granted that the party was the only one fit to rule Mexico. They took care of themselves in a variety of ways, enrichment while in office and sinecures after leaving office in the many state-owned enterprises that were established. The corporatist structure of governance gave privileges to the many elements of the party, such as public-sector labor unions and party-controlled *campesino* organizations. Gabriel Zaid, who has commented extensively on the nature of Mexico's political structure, has written: "Official lies are not a consequence of corruption (to hide it): it is the basic condition."[37] Or: "Corruption is not a disagreeable characteristic of the Mexican political system: it is the system."[38]

The Mexican economy was highly statist in nature. It is hard to say with precision what percentage of Mexico's economy was controlled by the government because the exact figure depends on what is being measured, whether the denominator is the entire GDP, investment expenditures, wholesale or retail sales, or some other variable. The percentage, in any event was high by any standard, higher than in most non-communist countries.[39]

The underlying philosophy of this statism was for the government to be the *rector* (the director) of the economy and to control its commanding heights; this philosophy was enshrined in the 1917 constitution. The commanding heights consisted of minerals in the ground, especially oil, electricity generation, and railroads. State ownership in these activities all had historical roots. The philosophical rationale also justified control of related activities, such as delivery of energy and movement of goods. Retail sales of gasoline were part of the Pemex monopoly. The government owned steel mills, so as to control the raw material delivered to steel-using industries, copper smelting, and the use of newsprint. Airlines and ports naturally came under government sway. Basic petrochemicals, the inputs into the fertilizer and plastic industries, were controlled by the government. So was CONASUPO (Compañía Nacional de Subsistencias Populares), the agency which controlled much food distribution. The brother of President Carlos Salinas, Raúl Salinas, who has been charged with illegal enrichment, was a senior official in CONASUPO. Political authoritarianism is facilitated when the government also runs large segments of national economic activity.

Beyond these activities, which fit the "commanding-heights" model, the government also owned unrelated businesses, such as hotels, textile plants, and sugar mills, which were less easily justified by the philosophic need to control the key levers of the economy. Both types of government ownership, the philosophically correct and the ideologically ambivalent, provided opportunities for rewarding the faithful. The total of all types of public enterprises – decentralized agencies, those with majority and minority government ownership, and trust funds – was 1155 in 1982, when the old economic model collapsed and a process of privatization began.[40] By

1994, the number was down to 219.[41] James Q. Wilson, in his study of bureaucracy, refers to cultural differences that make for variations in patterns of government activities in different countries. He makes particular mention of the statist model that existed in Mexico.[42]

The purpose here is not to charge, or even imply, that the key officials making macroeconomic policy decisions in Mexico during the Salinas administration acted out of motives for self-enrichment. President Salinas may have amassed (or may have permitted his family to amass) wealth based on his political position, but the premise from which this study starts is that other senior officials in the Mexican Treasury (*Hacienda*) and the central bank (the Bank of Mexico) were honest, hard-working, sincere public servants. But they were formed and worked in a cultural milieu in which the power of the PRI was accepted and in which state control of many activities was the norm. To their credit, the process of economic reform – opening the economy to import competition, selling many of the state-owned enterprises, and, for the most part, practicing fiscal austerity – was significant during their tenure.

When the government controls as much economic activity as it did in Mexico, transparency in the conduct of public affairs is generally lacking. Discussions took place in small, insider groups from which the public was excluded. Civil society, the role of watchdog groups, was given little chance to flourish. When things went wrong, the government provided its own explanations to a public that had not been informed fully of many of the decisions made earlier. As a consequence, governments in Mexico had little credibility. When things were going well, when incomes were rising, this was accepted without too much objection from the general public. When things went badly, as they did repeatedly starting in the 1970s, official explanations were met with skepticism.

Lorenzo Meyer, a respected academic historian and frequent commentator in the media, stated the following in one of his essays: "It is possible that the most important deficiency that the Mexican government has had is not with the exterior, but internally. And among these, credibility stands out."[43] If one were to rate countries by the degree of disbelief with which their public received official pronouncements on a scale of 0 (low credibility) to 1 (high credibility), Mexico would be close to 0. This disbelief was nurtured over a long period and may have reached its zenith in 1994–5.

The statist model, with its penchant for secrecy, required that the decision-making process be highly centralized. Control would be dissipated if there were too many centers of power. Information would get out much more readily if it was widely shared throughout the country. Each element of the structure was built on the others. The perpetuation of PRI hegemony, the granting of rewards to insiders, state domination not just of political power but of the levers of economic activity, the need for secrecy, the excessive centralization of decision-making and fund-raising in Mexico City – each has its logic in combination with other aspects of the system. It is no accident, now that the opposition controls the federal Chamber of Deputies, that the PAN – which also controls the governorships in many states and the leadership in many of Mexico's key cities – seeks much more federal funding of states and municipalities.[44] As the old system begins to break down, so, too, is the centralization of power in Mexico City under attack.

The corporatist nature of governance that existed for many decades was designed to control popular participation. This was a structure that was brought into being under President Lázaro Cárdenas (1934–40), based on incorporating large, interest group sectors – labor, *campesinos*, bureaucrats, and, for a time, the military – into the governing party. In order to emphasize that national political organization had been altered, the name of the party also was changed in 1938 from the PNR to the Partido Revolucionario Mexicano (PRM, or the Mexican Revolutionary Party). The motive of the structure, according to one leading analyst, was to organize politics around these groups and, through their leaders, control the masses.[45]

Mexican presidents after Cárdenas were all from the PRM, or the PRI after the party name was changed again in 1946 to signify a wider sectoral composition. The presidents after Cárdenas tended to alternate between left of center and right of center, but the corporatist structure of control remained in existence. Even in the era of *técnico* presidents – such as De la Madrid and Salinas, who came from economic rather than political cabinet positions – the corporatist structure persisted. It is only now, since the 1994–5 collapse, that this organizational model is breaking down.[46]

The anti-inflation pactos that began in 1987 were built around a corporatist structure.[47] This was an arrangement familiar to Mexican leaders and the general population. The pactos were commitments toward price, wage, and fiscal responsibility entered into among government, business, and labor to bring down inflation. The meeting on December 19–20, 1994, where the decision was taken to raise the ceiling of the peso band by 15 percent, in effect to devalue the peso by this percentage, was a pacto meeting. The public was not brought into the debate until after the decision was made by elites – but this time, when the day of reckoning came, the public did not accept the decision.

Conclusions

In the end, the habits of secrecy turned out to be costly. Priority was given to combating inflation during the Salinas sexenio and this, in turn, involved decisions leading to an overvalued peso. There were dissenting voices, both inside and outside the government and inside and outside Mexico, but they were not heeded. The unwillingness to devalue the peso before the decision became inevitable in December 1994 led, in turn, to the excessive use of tesobonos to finance the growing deficit in the current account of the balance of payments. Discussion on these technical matters is contained in subsequent chapters, but for now the key point is that there was precious little public debate on these decisions. This was standard operating procedure in Mexico: the elites knew best and transparency in decision-making be damned. This was the cultural milieu in which the senior public servants operated. There was a joke in the Bank of Mexico that when the daily newspaper *Excelsior* was brought in each morning, it was stamped "secret." *Excelsior*, for many years, was considered the newspaper of record, much like the *New York Times* in the United States.

The 1994–5 economic débâcle has induced many changes. Mexico, prior to the crash, published its foreign reserve figures only with a lag; they are now published more regularly. It was like pulling teeth to get much information normally released in other countries from the Bank of Mexico; most data are now available on a reasonably current basis on the Bank's web pages. The views of the legislature in setting economic policy were not germane earlier; now the opposition parties control the lower house of the congress and insist not only on open discussion of public policy, but a voice in setting that policy.

The events of 1994 were a watershed in Mexican decision-making. What was largely closed before is now much more open. The government now seeks to get out economic information as rapidly as possible, whereas before data were available only to insider groups. Public officials are called to account by the legislature, whereas before the law-makers were treated with veiled contempt. Mexico has not moved from complete secrecy to complete openness in its decision-making; secrecy was not complete before and openness is not thoroughgoing today.[48] But the changes are profound.

Perhaps, the most important change stemming from the events of 1994 is that the accepted mode of behavior of public officials is changing. This cultural change means that the old ways of decision-making are dead, just as the old way of political domination by a single party has been shunted aside.

2
Antecedents to the Decisions of 1994

The purveyors of nostalgia look back to Mexico's glory years, starting roughly from the late 1930s until the debt crisis of 1982, in order to contrast the good times of the past with the crises of the past two decades. There is some substance to this sentiment, but it should not be pushed too far. The débâcle of 1982 came in the wake of decades during which the old import-substitution model was in effect. The "good" times of the past benefitted many, but a large segment of Mexican society reaped only modest benefits. The old era was also dominated by an authoritarian political structure that suppressed democratic aspirations.

The breakdown of the import-substitution model

There were considerable achievements during Mexico's import-substitution years. The country's gross domestic product (GDP) grew by an annual average rate of more than 7 percent from the 1950s through the 1970s.[1] These were the years of the Mexican "miracle." The peso was devalued in 1954 and remained stable after that at 12.5 to the dollar for 22 years. There is a school of thought that fixed exchange rates, sooner or later, lead to disaster. They did eventually in Mexico, but the accomplishments in the interim did much to transform the country. It was in these years that the middle class grew and solidified in Mexico, and this not only altered the social structure, but also made possible the significant political changes that have taken place more recently.[2] The years of the "miracle" fostered an articulate group of people able to use the levers of the political system and achieve reform when the circumstances later became propitious. The PRI's success in the glory years actually sowed the seeds of the party's loss of political monopoly when the good times stopped.

Mexico avoided the Latin American "disease" of high inflation until the 1970s. The consumer price index (CPI) rose by more than 16 percent in 1954 (December-over-December), which was one of the triggers for the devaluation that year, but quickly settled down to a modest rate averaging 3.5 percent a year for the years 1955 through 1970.[3] The development model during this period, before the changes instituted by President Luis Echeverría, went under the apt label of "stabilizing development." The country's economy grew rapidly year after year, real incomes rose, many new stakeholders (the middle class) were created, and, even for the poor, many social benefits were in place, particularly for health care.

These facts are the basis for the yearning by many to return to the past. The state played a large role in the economy, acting as the *rector*, or the quite visible guiding hand of policy. An industrial structure was created behind high import restrictions, particularly a system of import licenses. In concept, the technique was simple: no license, no legal import. Mexico's model of import-substituting industrialization was described as *desarrollo hacia adentro* (development from within). The fact that the industries established were mostly non-competitive in world markets was not considered to be of great consequence because imports were restricted and no great effort was made to export manufactured goods.

Two sexenios of failure

The most glaring economic shortcoming of this rosy picture was the great inequality that accompanied the high rate of growth. In 1970, the year Echeverría became president, the bottom 50 percent of families received 17 percent of national income while the top 10 percent captured 50 percent.[4] The rationale used to explain this at the time was based on the work of the economist Simon Kuznets, who had demonstrated that the developed countries had first gone through a period of increased income inequality in the early phase of economic development, but that this became self-correcting as development progressed and incomes rose further. While the work of Kuznets provided an excuse for what was taking place, the more fundamental reason for the tolerance of this inequality – in addition to the fact that the rising tide was lifting most boats – was a greedy oligarchy buttressed by an authoritarian government.

Echeverría made clear that he intended to make Mexico's income distribution more equitable. Even the name of the economic model was changed from "stabilizing" to "shared" development (*desarrollo compartido*). The motive may have been splendid, but the economic results were destructive. In the last year of Echeverría's sexenio, 1976, consumer prices rose by 27 percent and the peso was devalued just before he left office.[5] The main reason for the substantial increase in inflation was the sharp rise in government expenditures without compensating revenue, plus an expansion of the public sector generally. The success of a fixed exchange rate requires macroeconomic discipline, which existed during the "golden" years before the 1970s, but was discarded in the 1970s. At the end of the day, when Echeverría left office in 1976, income distribution had not improved – the development was not shared.

Echeverría's successor, José López Portillo, became president when large, new oil output came on line, providing the country with ample dollars both from oil exports and from foreign borrowing based on the assurance that the loans were backed by oil reserves. These were years when US banks and those in other industrial countries were flush with petrodollars and recklessly loaned these out under the assumption that sovereigns don't default. The evidence for this belief is shaky; and, in addition, sovereigns do demand debt rescheduling. It was Mexico, during the López Portillo presidency, that set off the debt crisis in August 1982, just a few months before he left office.

López Portillo had been profligate. Mexico, he said, had to learn to "administer abundance."[6] He mortgaged his country on the assumption that oil prices would go up forever. He compounded this by altering the constitution – with the consent of a compliant Congress – by nationalizing all Mexican-owned banks (the US-owned Citibank was spared) under the spurious argument that they were abetting capital flight. He excoriated what he called the *sacadolares* (those persons removing dollars from the country) who, in truth, were people acting rationally to protect their assets from their diminution that his policies helped set in motion.

When Echeverría assumed office in 1970, there were 12.5 pesos to the dollar, a rate that had remained stable from 1954. When he left office in 1976, the rate was around 20 pesos to the dollar. When López Portillo left office in 1982, the rate was 148.5 pesos per dollar.

The crash of its economy in 1982 was made mostly in Mexico, but with some assist from external developments.[7] Mexico became a big borrower from external sources during the late 1970s and early 1980s, and did not always use the funds wisely. It was as though the export earnings from high oil prices burned a hole in the pockets of the Mexican authorities. Yet, there was a logic to the borrowing in that interest rates were relatively low, inflation in the United States quite high, and this combination made the real cost of borrowing modest. What happened, however, was that world oil prices declined and the United States, at roughly the same time, effectively addressed its inflation problem, largely through restrictive monetary policy. The rising US interest rates changed the effective cost of Mexican borrowing at the very moment that Mexican foreign-exchange resources were declining owing to a shift in the oil market. Contrary to the assumption made by López Portillo, oil prices could move in both directions, down as well as up. Paul Volcker, the Chairman of the US Federal Reserve Board at that time, has asserted that easing US interest rates would have made little difference, that "The debt crisis was on an express train of its own."[8]

My view is that it was not the debt crisis as such that was on an express train, but rather that some kind of convulsion of the Mexican economy was coming from the exhaustion of the import-substitution model. The internal Mexican market was capable of sustaining steady growth for many years because it was starting from scratch. As the initial phase of the import-substitution model ran its course, the operations necessarily became increasingly complex. Mexico was able to first substitute domestically produced for imported consumer goods. By itself, this was not a remarkable achievement because the inputs, the semi-finished products and raw materials, going into this production could still be imported and be financed by foreign exchange earned from oil exports. Import-substitution does not necessarily mean fewer imports, but rather a different composition of imports.

After that, the Mexican authorities, in order to deepen the import-substitution, required domestic producers of consumer goods to use nationally produced intermediate goods by imposing required levels of domestic value added, even though the national products generally were more expensive and of lower quality than imported products. These rules on domestic content became increasingly complex, especially in the automotive industry. The Mexican consumer was forced to tolerate shoddy goods and pay high prices. Mexico's small and medium-sized industries providing both the final and intermediate products were generally non-competitive and it was quite natural for them to oppose market opening and then the entry of Mexico into NAFTA. To this day, Mexico imports a large proportion of its industrial inputs, rather than produce them competitively domestically.[9] Mexico's intermediate product imports are generally in the neighborhood of 70 percent of total imports for non-maquiladora production, and more than 95 percent for the maquiladoras.

What kept the model going as long as it did was the ability during the 1970s to obtain foreign exchange from the oil bonanza, coupled with the mortgaging of the country by contracting a high level of external debt. Had a policy shift taken place earlier, had Mexico started to open its economy gradually a decade before it did so, as many national economists advocated, the hardship faced by the country after 1982 might have been avoided.

The purpose here is not to dwell on Mexico's past economic policies but rather to bring out the legacy that was inherited after two failed sexenios, those of Echeverría and López Portillo. A country with a stable currency and low inflation was transformed into one with an unstable currency and high inflation. The decision to rely almost exclusively on oil for merchandise export earnings led unerringly to catastrophe when oil prices fell. (In 1982, the year the debt crisis became manifest, petroleum exports accounted for 78 percent of total merchandise export earnings.) Subsequent Mexican administrations have had to contend with this inheritance.

The two presidents also established a pattern that has haunted Mexico ever since. This is that collapse came in the last year of a six-year administration. In each case, there was a devaluation in the final year. López Portillo aggravated this by nationalizing the commercial banks as he was leaving office and the conditions of the reprivatization later became the source of much of the financial difficulty in 1994 and since. When the peso was again devalued at the end of 1994, this time not by the outgoing president, Carlos Salinas de Gortari, but at the start of the administration of his successor, the players in the world's money markets could not help but think "Here we go again." It is hard not to speculate that one of Salinas' motives for not devaluing the peso during his administration was to avoid the opprobrium that has attached to the reputations of Echeverría and López Portillo for what happened to the purchasing power of the peso during their tenures. The loathing of Salinas came almost immediately after he left office; Mexico escaped nothing.

And one sexenio of adjustment

Miguel de la Madrid Hurtado, who succeeded to the presidency at the end of 1982, inherited a mess. He acted responsibly for the most part, but there were serious lapses, particularly letting inflation get out of hand. This had substantial repercussions in the succeeding regime of Carlos Salinas, who made inflation control the single most important policy objective when he became president six years later.

The growth rates during the fourth and fifth years of López Portillo's administration, 1980 and 1981, were quite high. Real GDP, based on figures from the Bank of Mexico, rose by 9.1 percent in 1980 and 8.8 percent in 1981. These were rates well above the norm, which itself had been quite high before the crisis of 1982. These high rates can be explained by the expenditures made possible by high oil revenues and large-scale public borrowing. They were sustainable, in other words, only if high oil prices and inflows of capital continued even as the country's external debt level grew. This, in itself, should have been a warning, both inside and outside Mexico, of potential danger ahead.

Inflation during the López Portillo sexenio did not decline from the Echeverría years, but instead remained in the high 20s, and then soared to close to 100 percent in 1982. Mexico had contracted the Latin American disease. The high point of inflation came in 1987, the penultimate year of the De la Madrid administration, when consumer prices rose by 160 percent.[10] It was this high rate, extraordinary by previous Mexican standards, that prompted the pactos, which became a feature of Mexican economic policy from that year right through the Salinas years. The use of these pactos, a form of incomes policy, became an important part of Mexico's decision-making, but more on this later. The pactos, put simply, were a form of agreement among business, labor, and the government, under which each group agreed to impose discipline on itself – price discipline by business, wage discipline by labor, fiscal discipline by the government – which in their way were a prototypical form of corporatism as practiced in Mexico.[11] Recorded levels of inflation did decline after 1987, reaching a low of 7 percent in 1994, before the rate shot up again with the new crisis.

The high economic growth rates of 1980 and 1981 did not last. Instead, there were declines in GDP in three of the next five years and then low to modest positive growth for the rest of the De la Madrid and for all of the Salinas administrations. It is fair to say that Mexico never recovered fully from the crisis of 1982. Years of modest growth were interspersed with years of modest economic decline – modest, that is, until 1995, when the decline was precipitous. Inflation waxed and then it waned under the pactos, only to explode again in 1995. The inflation inheritance of the economic model change in the 1970s has lasted for several decades, although new elements were added over time. One test of whether this legacy is now over will come in the year 2000, when the current administration terminates; and whether market players believe that the curse of the last year of an administration has been conquered.

Perhaps the most important decision of the De la Madrid administration was to put in place a basic change in the economic development model, from a stress on import-substitution to one favoring export promotion. De la Madrid did this, he said, because he felt there was no other feasible option.[12] This was a more profound paradigm shift than under Echeverría because it entailed a number of corollary alterations. Tariffs and other import barriers, particularly the use of import licenses, had to come down – and they did, modestly at first. The failure to enter into the General Agreement on Tariffs and Trade (GATT), which was an explicit decision under López Portillo, was discarded and Mexico became a contracting party in 1986. A policy based on promoting exports, particularly of manufactured goods, required these two features: unburdening domestic producers from the high cost of intermediate products, which naturally followed import protection; and obtaining more secure access to foreign markets, which GATT negotiations made possible.

Yet, there were profound shortcomings in other aspects of De la Madrid's program. The public-sector deficit, as measured by the public-sector borrowing requirement (PSBR), which had risen to almost 17 percent of GDP in 1982, declined gradually in the De la Madrid years, but never fell below 8.5 percent – which, by any reckoning, is still high. It soared back up to 16 percent in 1987. De la Madrid, in other words, never did achieve fiscal discipline, and this was the main reason for the high inflation of his sexenio.

Mexico, in these years, was not really creditworthy in international financial markets. The unsatisfactory fiscal and inflation performance, coupled with the poor overall economic outcome – there was essentially no real growth in GDP during the De la Madrid administration – are sufficient explanation for this reticence by international lenders. There were other reasons as well, however, such as the legacy of the López Portillo years – his bank nationalization, seizure of the so-called Mex-dollar accounts which Mexico had solicited but then paid the holders in depreciated pesos,[13] and the use of some short-lived but not easily forgotten capital controls. These all came on top of the crushing international debt burden that Mexico faced and which was not resolved until the Brady Plan debt agreement and the financial workout with creditor banks were completed in 1990. Mexico did not really regain entry into international capital markets until 1989, seven years after the 1982 debt crisis.

Real wages in Mexico declined sharply during the De la Madrid years. Using an index with 1994 at 100, the real minimum wage was at 254 in 1982 and 129 in 1988, a drop of 50 percent during the years De la Madrid was in office.[14] The minimum wage is not always the best measure for actual wages paid in Mexico because it affects around 20 percent of wage earners. However, the US Bureau of Labor Statistics, in its comparison of compensation (wages and benefits) for production workers in manufacturing, concluded that placing the US wage at 100, the Mexican wage was 22 in 1980 and fell to 11 by 1990:[15] again, a 50 percent fall. Workers in Mexico took a big hit from the failures of economic policy. The onus for this outcome should not be placed solely on the De la Madrid administration, but on the problems he inherited. The De la Madrid administration also sought to minimize open unemployment during these difficult years of adjustment, and this involved taking the hit in lower wages.

These years of failures of economic policy and the hardships they inflicted on the general population obviously had their effect on the political situation in Mexico. Echeverría, when he came to power, brought with him a group of collaborators who sought change in political alignments. Echeverría entered office under a cloud of mistrust because he had been the Secretary of *Gobernación* (Interior) when students were killed in an area of Mexico City known as Tlatelolco during the 1968 protests. It is unclear to this day who gave the order to fire on the protestors, Echeverría or his chief, President Gustavo Díaz Ordaz.[16] When he assumed office, Echeverría, in effect, coopted many of the activists in the 1968 protests and this gave his administration a decided nationalist and politically reformist coloration. It was during these years, for example, that the nationalist legislation restricting foreign investment was enacted. The PRI, in these years, moved to the left and the divisions within the party remain to this day.

López Portillo left office as a pariah who could not appear in public without being subjected to rude criticism. Not long before the peso was devalued at the close of his administration, he had promised publicly to "defend the peso like a dog," and he was greeted in public with imitations of dogs barking. The hill in Mexico City where he built of a complex of homes for himself and his family became known as the "hill of the dogs." For the most part, he was forced to remain secluded.

De la Madrid suffered none of these indignities and he was not believed to have engaged in unreasonable self-enrichment. He left office with his moral reputation intact. However, he did preside over years of adjustment and hardship. Once his successor, Carlos Salinas, entered office, De la Madrid became something of a nonentity, a transitional figure who did his job honorably, effectively in many respects, and poorly in others.

In the 1988 presidential elections, the main opposition candidate to Salinas, the PRI candidate, was Cuauhtémoc Cárdenas, an ex-*priísta*. If Echeverría had to overcome mistrust over his role in the 1968 Tlatelolco killings as he began his presidency, Salinas had to overcome the obstacle of suspicion that he stole the 1988 election. In that election, the vote count was halted in midstream at a moment when preliminary reports indicated that Cárdenas was ahead. The reason given was a computer breakdown. When the "problem" was fixed, the momentum in the count moved in favor of Salinas. The final vote count showed Salinas winning with 50.47 percent of the votes cast, and Cárdenas with 30.90 percent. That was the lowest percentage for a winning presidential candidate since the PRI (and its predecessor parties) was formed in 1929. Was the vote count rigged? If so, only those who rigged it know for certain.

In any event, the outcome of the presidential contest made it clear that the PRI was falling out of favor. It could hardly have been otherwise in the hodgepodge of paradigm shifts, economic disasters, and the general view that the whole authoritarian system was thoroughly corrupt.

Salinas' first five years

The political analyst Rafael Segovia, of El Colegio de México, has commented that one should not talk about the Salinas sexenio, but rather separately of the first five years and the final year because it is impossible to add unlike objects. Salinas was widely admired, both inside Mexico and abroad, for his political and economic mastery during his initial five years, and this turned to contempt as his final year progressed. This deepened into outright hatred when the peso was devalued barely three weeks after his successor, Ernesto Zedillo, was inaugurated as president. Enrique Krauze, in his book on the history of Mexico, entitled his chapter on Salinas "The Man Who Would Be King."[17] The king was transformed into the country's "favorite villain," to use Salinas' own words.

The start made in the De la Madrid administration to change the underlying economic development model was accelerated and deepened under Salinas. Tariffs were simplified to five different levels and averaged around 10 percent by 1989; and by 1992, less than 11 percent of the value of imports was subject to prior license requirements. The emphasis on export promotion, particularly of manufactured products, was thoroughly built into the country's trade policy. Much of this *apertura* (opening) was done unilaterally, although Mexico also entered fully into the Uruguay Round of trade negotiations in the GATT, where the practice was one of reciprocity or an exchange of tariff and other trade concessions.

The original intention of Salinas was not to enter into a free-trade agreement with the United States, but rather to diversify Mexican export markets and obtain increased direct investment from Europe. Salinas learned from discussions with European leaders that their preoccupations were centered more on Europe itself and on relations with Eastern Europe and countries of the former Soviet Union as the old East–West divisions were breaking down. He then focused on the large potential market next door, the United States, which Mexico was hardly exploiting. He first proposed a series of sectoral agreements and, when these did not flourish, he floated the idea in 1991 of a free-trade area between Mexico and the United States. The North American Free Trade Agreement (NAFTA) was born out of this initiative, after Canada decided to join the negotiations.

NAFTA would not have been possible had Mexico not already set the stage by the unilateral reduction of its import barriers and the abandonment of the highly restrictive foreign investment legislation and regulations enacted in the Echeverría administration. Similarly, NAFTA was made possible by other changes of economic policy under Salinas. The increased role of the state as the *rector* of the economy, which was part and parcel of the Echeverría years, was reversed. In its place, Salinas embarked on an ambitious privatization program. Budgetary discipline, which was lacking during the De la Madrid years, was enforced. The public sector deficit (the difference between revenues and expenditures of the non-financial public sector) was 14.4 percent of GDP in 1987 and 9.3 percent in 1988, the last years of the De la Madrid sexenio, and fell sharply after that, actually reaching surplus in 1992 and 1993 – excluding revenues from privatizations. The regulatory framework that placed much policy responsibility on federal officials was altered, although this reform was far from thoroughgoing. The financial system was opened moderately in the NAFTA negotiations and then more completely after the economic crisis erupted in late 1994 and early 1995. The banks, which had been nationalized under López Portillo, were reprivatized.

Perhaps the most significant policy measure was the use of the pactos, begun before Salinas took office, to bring down inflation. More stress was put on this objective – reduction of inflation – than any other during the Salinas years. This was done by using the exchange rate as the anchor for the anti-inflation policy, and this turned out at the end of the day to be a significant element in the financial collapse that occurred at the end of 1994. When the pactos began in 1987, the nominal value of the peso was depreciated sharply from what had been a market rate of 915 pesos to the dollar at the end of 1986 to 2227.5 at the end of 1987 – a depreciation of 143 percent. The intent was to undervalue the peso so that it could be allowed to gradually appreciate subsequently without becoming too overvalued. Thereafter, the peso was controlled, using a variety of techniques over the years to do this, limiting its depreciation in order to reduce the inflationary impact on the economy from imported goods and services and the transference of this imported inflation to domestic prices. The market rate of the peso from the end of 1987 (2227.5 pesos per dollar) to the end of November 1994, the month before the December devaluation (3449.8 – or more precisely, 3.4498 pesos per dollar because three zeros were eliminated from the stated value of the peso) depreciated by 55 percent, far less than the one-shot devaluation at the end of 1987 alone.

Using a base of 1980 as 100, the real value of the peso, based on changes in consumer prices, was 63.64 in 1987 and increased in value to 96.06 at the end of the third quarter of 1994, a substantial appreciation.[18] Put differently, the peso was depreciated each year by less than the increase in consumer prices. The rise in consumer prices did, in fact, decelerate steadily under the pactos, from

159 percent in 1987 to a low of 7.1 percent in 1994. One can argue, therefore, that the primary economic objective of the Salinas administration – reducing inflation – was achieved. In 1995, however, the first year of the Zedillo administration, consumer prices shot up again to 52 percent (on a December-to-December basis). The earlier anti-inflation success turned out to be not meaningful. The effort to limit the depreciation of the peso, similarly, was all in vain. Its market rate at the end of November 1994, before the December devaluation, was 3.4498 to the dollar; by the end of 1995, the market rate was 7.6420 to the dollar, a depreciation of more than 121 percent.

These double failures – holding the exchange rate only to see the peso to collapse, and the use of incomes policy to hold down inflation only to see this explode – were devastating. They signified that all the travail through which the country was put was for naught. Growth in real GDP was held down under the policy based on the premise that price stability was necessary first; and the exchange rate was allowed to become overvalued using the rationale that this was necessary to achieve price stability.

Salinas was proud of his achievements, certainly during his first five years – and, indeed, much was accomplished. These achievements were the stuff of his annual *Informes* (state-of-the-union addresses) to the Congress each year and they were the essential elements of the speeches of his key economic ministers in their respective fields. A series of books were published under the names of the key policy-makers that provided the details of what were seen at that point as successes. These dealt, among other issues, with bank deregulation, privatization generally, and commercial policy.[19] Pedro Aspe, the finance minister, had a book published in English in 1993 whose final chapter is best described as triumphalistic.[20]

Mexican elites supported the Salinas reforms. The general public was undoubtedly more skeptical because *per capita* economic growth was quite low – at most 2–2.5 percent a year, at worst, nil – for a country coming out of a long period of stagnation. While real wages were rising in manufacturing activities, they were not in construction and the minimum wage was declining in real terms.[21] The financial community outside the country was highly impressed with the Salinas accomplishments, as witness the billions of dollars of portfolio investment that were being sent to Mexico. Informed groups interested in trade policy admired what Salinas was doing to open the economy.²² The US government was so highly impressed with Salinas that it supported his candidacy to head the World Trade Organization (WTO).

Mexico under Salinas' first five years was seen as an economic trailblazer. The country was opened to world competition, transformed from an economy dependent on oil to one that was a major exporter of manufactured goods, entered into free trade with the United States, eliminated its earlier budgetary excesses, privatized many of its state-owned enterprises (SOEs), cut back on government regulation of private enterprise, reduced inflation, and moved the main management of the economy from the government to the private market. All this turned to ashes one year later. There may be an important lesson to be derived from this: it takes more time than a few years, or even a decade, to declare victory for any economic model. Just as the East Asian economies were hailed as finding a new way to economic growth only to find themselves in deep crisis at the end of 1997 and into 1998, so was Mexico transformed from a model to be emulated at the end of 1993 to a pariah at the end of 1994.

Based on its economic accomplishments, the Salinas administration also was riding high in the political arena within Mexico at the end of 1993. Salinas had succeeded, at least at that point, in erasing the misgivings about the legitimacy of his election in 1988. A series of political reforms were put in place, but they were controlled openings similar to the limited openings of previous administrations; they were openings designed to maintain effective PRI dominance. The opposition was given more representation in the legislature, but not enough to overcome its control by the PRI – and by the president. The stated policy of Salinas was economic reform first, and meaningful political opening only after that – and the hope, undoubtedly, was that the latter would never have to come.

Social inequalities remained deep and the level of poverty could not really be diminished in any meaningful way as long as GDP growth remained as modest as it was. While never stated explicitly but perhaps more significant, economic growth was put on the back burner until inflation was conquered; so, too, was social justice delayed until economic growth rates could be increased. Salinas talked a good deal about social policy (*política social*), going as far as to say in his final *Informe* that "The ethical nucleus of my government was social policy" ("*El núcleo ético de mi gobierno fue la política social.*").²³ The main program under which this was pursued was called Solidarity (*Programa Nacional de Solidaridad*, or Pronasol), under which funds were provided to poor communities and helped to foster much cooperation within these entities, usually in connection with a presidential trip to the area. While substantial sums were provided, it was a form of retail handouts, not comprehensive social policy. Solidarity also had strong political content – it was Salinas who was the benefactor, not the Mexican society as a whole operating through its executive and legislature.

There were important domestic critics of the overall thrust of policy. Many of these criticisms focused on exchange-rate issues, and these will be addressed in later chapters. Much of the complaints centered on the policy of economic opening and increasing the role of the private market, a point taken up earlier in the discussion of nostalgia for the old state-led model of economic development. There were also persistent complaints that failure to move faster to open the political system was a major shortcoming of the Salinas years.

David Ibarra, a finance minister in the López Portillo administration, argued that the concentration on reducing inflation – the program carried out under successive pactos from 1987 until the economic collapse in 1995 – and giving little or no emphasis to economic growth and employment, forced the country to live in a quasi-permanent recession. The thesis of his book is that without an emphatic effort to correct Mexico's historical problem of unequal income distribution, neither democracy nor a state based on laws would be possible.[24] Ibarra turned out to be correct in that the way the anti-inflation program that was carried out failed on almost all counts, but this does not demonstrate that control of inflation is not necessary for reducing inequality.

The commercial banks

One other important element of background to the economic decisions taken in 1994 was the situation of the commercial banks. They had been nationalized in the political frenzy at the end of 1982 when the economy was coming apart in the last days of the López Portillo administration. This action had a particularly deleterious effect on Mexico's standing internationally, and, as fate would have it, the damage was compounded after the banks were privatized during the Salinas administration. Guillermo Ortiz, then the senior Under Secretary of Finance, was the chairman of an interagency committee in charge of the reprivatization – or "disincorporation," as he called it in his book.[25] It is necessary to lay out the nature of the bank privatization in order to understand some of the crucial economic decisions taken in 1994.

The constitution had to be re-amended (to undo the amendments when the banks were nationalized) and then the laws and regulations had to be rewritten before the privatization could proceed. The principles under which the privatization was carried out were, on the whole, unremarkable: to set up an efficient, competitive structure; assure diversified participation in the banks; assure adequate capitalization; seek regional decentralization; obtain a just price; achieve a balanced financial structure; and stimulate sound banking practices.

One of the principles, however, reflected the nationalism, or national favoritism, that still existed – namely, to assure that the Mexican banking system was controlled by Mexicans. The necessary legal measures were completed in 1990, only a year before negotiations began on NAFTA and this insistence on national control of the banks was largely carried over into the provisions of this agreement. Foreign banks were allowed under NAFTA to gradually expand their aggregate share of the Mexican banking market from 8 percent in 1993 to 15 percent in 1999 and be limited throughout this period to 1.5 percent of total banking capitalization.[26] The limits were to be eliminated in January 2000, but there were a number of escapes until 2007, in addition to provisions effectively protecting Mexico's largest banks from foreign takeover. Miguel Mancera, the governor of the Bank of Mexico, was known to favor limited foreign ownership because he believed that the central bank would have more effective control over monetary policy if the owners and managers of the commercial banks were Mexican. Most of these limitations were eliminated in early 1995 in the face of the financial troubles the country was then experiencing.

As described by Ortiz, there were six packages of sales over 13 months during 1991 and 1992 to divest 18 banking institutions. Other figures provided by Ortiz were that the price/profit ratio, on average, was 14.75 and market/book value 3.068. The Mexican government at the time gave considerable publicity to the high sales prices in order to emphasize two points – the high degree of confidence in Mexico's economic future; and the hard bargaining by the government to enrich the treasury.

Unfortunately, it did not take very long for the sweetness of the deal from the government viewpoint to sour. The calculations about the growth of the Mexican economy, on which the bank bidding was predicated, proved to be overly optimistic. Some of the new owners turned out to be incompetent as bank managers and, in several cases, less than fully upright. The exclusion of serious bidding by non-Mexican banks served to limit competition, a phenomenon not unusual in the Mexican market for goods and other services in the years before the import market was opened. This is not to say that all banks were inefficient; in fact, many were quite efficiently run. But the Mexican authorities found themselves accepting in the financial field what they had already concluded was unwise in the industrial field – a largely closed market which permitted oligopolistic control.

The head of Mexico's National Banking Commission (Comisión Nacional Bancaria y de Valores, or CNBV), Eduardo Fernández, has since been quoted as follows: "Neither the administrators of the state banks, nor the authorities, nor the actual purchasers, were sufficiently penetrating in their analysis to realize that they would have problems."[27]

For a long period after the banks were privatized, interest rates were high. The new owners sought to recoup the high prices they had paid. Overdue loans increased by 56 percent in real terms from December 1992 to December 1993, and then by 44 percent over the same period of the next year.[28] The ratio of past due to total loans rose steadily from 5.3 percent in December 1992, to 7.1 percent in the same month in 1993, to 8.7 percent in 1994, and then ended 1994 at 15.7 percent. These figures, from the Bank of Mexico, understated the seriousness of the situation because of the way the Bank of Mexico then defined "past due loans" to include not the entire loan, but only that portion that was past due. Mexico has since adopted a more stringent international standard.[29] At the end of 1996, the past due ratio as given by the Bank of Mexico had risen to more than 21 percent.

Many actions were taken by the Mexican authorities to deal with the weak banking structure, including the purchase by Mexico's deposit insurance fund (Fondo Bancario de Protección al Ahorro, or Fobaproa) of almost half the loans of the banking system; the establishment under Fobaproa of a program to recapitalize the banks (called the Programa de Capacitación Temporal, or Procapte); and various other measures to protect banks and borrowers against the risks of inflation. The rescue effort is still not complete and its total cost, therefore, is unknown. It was estimated in mid-1998 to exceed 15 percent of GDP, but will be much higher. The savings and loan (S&L) rescue in the United States, to offer a comparison, cost about 3 percent of US GDP.

The weakness of the banks played an important role in economic decision-making in Mexico in 1994, as will be demonstrated subsequently. The total cost, therefore, is more than 15 percent of GDP, or whatever the direct rescue operations come to, because the fragile situation of the privatized banks limited the scope of monetary (interest-rate) policy of the Bank of Mexico throughout 1994.

Assessing the pre-1994 policy failures

The problems that erupted in Mexico in 1994 did not burst out full-blown, but had antecedents that date back many decades. The inflationary pressures that were at the core of economic policy during the Salinas years had their incubation in the 1970s. The import-substitution model that collapsed in 1982 dated back more than half a century and reached its full flowering in the years after World War II. The shortcoming was that this model of economic development lasted beyond its time, prolonged by oil and debt revenue that turned out to be less a bonanza than a curse. The commercial bank privatizations of 1991–2 were made necessary by the nationalizations carried out in 1982.

Governments owe their population a reasonable degree of predictability in their day-to-day economic activities. There will almost inevitably be good years and less good, but a regular pattern of booms and busts bespeaks bad governance. The reason that the 22-year period from 1954 to 1976 was considered golden in Mexico was the combination of consistent economic growth and steady value of the peso. Since that time, the peso has undergone persistent deterioration and no rational Mexican could consider his or her national currency to be a good store of value. Even currency depreciation might be tolerable if real per capita income showed a tendency to rise. This is not the case in Mexico, where real per capita GDP was actually lower in the mid-1990s than it was in the early 1970s, and considerably less than it was in 1980. All these shortcomings of economic policy went alongside a highly unequal pattern of income distribution and unequal opportunities for educational preparation.

Since the 1970s, the period on which this chapter has concentrated,

Mexican leaders have not delivered on the most elemental essentials of their responsibilities. The Mexican population as a whole is worse off today than it was two decades ago. During this period, the population has been subjected to two periods of economic bust. Political discourse in Mexico deals with this reality, although rarely directly. Mexico today has a far more democratic structure than it did just a few years ago. A credible opposition exists, one capable of winning the presidency, just as it already has captured the lower house of the federal legislature. Mexican democracy has a long way to go before it is as complete as those in more developed industrial countries, but authoritarianism is now a mere shadow of what it was in the past. This should make leaders more conscious of their obligations to the general population, but this is speculation.

Economic decision-making was defective in Mexico even before the errors of 1994. The reason that the 1994 shortcomings are so alluring to scholars is that they were played out on the world scene, whereas the earlier deficiencies were largely confined to Mexico and its population. There is also some hope that the lessons learned from the 1994 experience have been absorbed by Mexican policy-makers – and there is much evidence that this is so for now, but for how long is uncertain.

3
The First Quarter of 1994

This chapter will begin the examination of the contemporaneous situation in order to understand what motivated the economic decisions taken in 1994. Looking backward from the end of the process can tell a more complete story – and this will be done at the conclusion of the book – but cannot explain why policy-makers did what they did at the moment decisions were taken. What follows, therefore, in this and Chapters 4–6 is a chronological analysis of events and decisions in Mexico over three-month periods in 1994. The story being told comes from a mixture of public documents and private interviews with the key actors.

The mood of policy-makers as 1994 opened

The economic outcome in 1993 was mixed. The most favorable indicator was that consumer prices rose by only 8 percent (December-over-December). Consumer prices had risen by 159 percent in 1987, the year the pactos started, and the achievement of single-digit inflation was too important an accomplishment, and too juicy a symbol, not to be widely publicized by the government. On the other hand, real GDP growth was only 0.4 percent – which represented a decline of about 1.5 percent in per capita terms. If one uses the technical definition of a recession – a GDP decline in two successive quarters – Mexico had a recession in 1993. GDP declined in both the third and fourth quarters, by 0.8 and 0.1 percent, respectively.[1] The recession, one informant said, frightened President Salinas, particularly coming into an election year.[2]

This led, I was told by a senior Treasury (*Hacienda*) official, to a fierce debate on exchange-rate policy. A division that had existed for some time inside the Treasury re-emerged, with the Secretary, Pedro Aspe, favoring the existing exchange-rate policy of a generally fixed rate with small daily adjustments, and many in his professional staff favoring more flexibility. According to several informants, the designated presidential candidate of the PRI, Luis Donaldo Colosio, also favored more exchange-rate flexibility. Aspe's view prevailed.

An informant who was present at the pacto meeting in October 1993 – this was after the completion of the NAFTA negotiations, but at a time when approval of NAFTA by the US Congress was still in doubt – told me that the leaders of the senior business group at the meeting suggested a prudential devaluation of the peso by 10 percent. The reasoning was twofold, that the peso was overvalued by this amount and to provide a cushion for 1994, a presidential election year, when devaluation would be difficult. The second assumption proved to be correct. Bankers at the meeting were against a devaluation at that time, as was Miguel Mancera, the governor of the Bank of Mexico. Aspe, I was told, was silent and the devaluation did not take place. Had the peso been devalued then, just before the contentious issue of NAFTA approval was coming up for a final vote in the US Congress, that might have been enough to tilt the decision against the agreement. The year 1994, at least before the election in August, was not an easy period for a devaluation for domestic reasons, but acting just the month before a vote by the US Congress was even more problematic, in this case for external reasons.

According to one well placed official, however, the scare about low growth and the effect this would have on the presidential election in 1994 motivated the increased use of development banks – which, since the start of 1993, were no longer included in the balance of the financial budget of the public sector – to raise public expenditures without overtly breaking the commitment to fiscal stringency. There is an arguable technical justification for not counting the financial intermediation of most public development banks in budgetary expenditures, but the coincidence of their removal a year earlier and their increased use as conduits for public spending at this delicate moment is too much of a coincidence not to be suspicious of the motivation.[3]

There was no disagreement among senior policy officials on the importance of keeping inflation low. There also was general consensus on the use of the pactos – that is, of a cooperative or corporatist technique for carrying out an incomes policy to achieve this objective. The differences, instead, were ones of degree – whether lowering inflation and the symbolism of single-digit levels should be pursued regardless of the effect on economic growth. Aspe and Mancera were of one mind on this point, that inflation reduction took priority over other objectives and that economic growth would follow later and be more solid because of the non-inflationary environment. The political leadership – Salinas in particular, and Colosio, as the PRI presidential candidate – had to be concerned over low growth – indeed, recession – as Mexico was coming into an election year in which the PRI candidate faced unprecedented challenges.

The interplay between low economic growth and low inflation was the main theme of a speech in late September 1993 by Miguel Mancera.[4] He celebrated the single-digit inflation that was coming for the year as a whole and insisted that low inflation was necessary in order to raise the national savings rate, encourage investment, reduce interest rates, and raise wages in real terms. He explained the low growth in GDP in terms of the weakness in the world economy, the loss of sales of many domestic companies from the imports that came after the economic opening, or *apertura*, and the low domestic consumption stemming from high consumer debt.

As a general matter, one cannot argue with Mancera's logic about the importance of reducing inflation, but the complete omission of the effect of macroeconomic stringency and an ever-appreciating peso on GDP growth was ingenuous. The economic *apertura* had taken place many years before, starting in the 1980s, so that the argument that this helped explain the poor growth performance in 1993 is a weak one. Similarly, his contention that high consumer debt, which had existed for some time, led to low consumption has the ring of a well-known Yogi Berra joke, that "nobody goes there any more because it's too crowded."

The need to control inflation was a major point in all of Mancera's speeches over the period from the end of 1993 to early 1994.[5] A particularly explicit linkage between exchange-rate policy and inflation was made in an earlier speech in July 1993 when Mancera insisted that an accelerated crawl, which many in Mexico advocated to deal with what they were convinced was an overvalued peso, would merely trigger higher inflation.[6]

The content of Aspe's speeches was similar. He, too, extolled the accomplishment of controlling inflation and sought to assure his audience that this would lay the groundwork for higher economic growth. His language in a speech in September 1993 was precise on this point: "These elements [reduction of inflation and recovery in real wages] permit one to affirm that the Mexican economy will be in recuperation at the end of the year."[7] In a speech in January 1994, the theme was essentially the same – that inflation had been brought down from 160 percent in 1987 to 8 percent in 1993, laying the groundwork for reactivation of the economy in 1994.[8] The promise of economic recovery was again highlighted in a speech he made in February 1994.[9]

The unease that existed in Mexico about the interplay between the incomes policy as reflected in the pactos and the failure to devalue the peso to stimulate more growth was echoed outside the country as well. The most prominent non-Mexican critic of the policy was Rudiger Dornbusch, an economics professor at the Massachusetts Institute of Technology, where Pedro Aspe had received his doctorate in economics. In an article written about this time, Dornbusch and a colleague, Alejandro Werner, argued that a pegged exchange rate and incomes policy might be helpful at the start of a stabilization program, but that neither should be kept for too long. The pactos had started at the end of 1987. The key conclusion reached by these two authors was in the last sentence of their article: "In Mexico, that sad ending lies ahead unless the currency is devalued."[10]

The concern about the economy at the end of 1993 was aggravated by the uncertainty that existed as to whether the US Congress would approve NAFTA. Francisco Gil-Díaz, a vice governor of the Bank of Mexico, and Agustín Carstens, the general director of economic research at the bank, implicitly ascribed the fall in GDP in the third quarter of 1993 to the uncertainty about NAFTA approval. They noted in this same article that economic growth resumed in the first quarter of 1994, after NAFTA went into effect.[11] The data they provide to buttress their argument about the GDP decline in the second half of 1993 is not fully convincing; their chart shows that fixed gross real private investment began to decline about the third quarter of 1992, but resumed growth about mid-1993. Yet, there is no doubt that approval of NAFTA made a difference in the expectation of investors. Bank of Mexico data indicate that capital inflows averaged a little more than $2 billion a month for the first 11 months of 1993 and then jumped to more than $7 billion in December, after NAFTA was approved by the US Congress.[12]

Salinas had taken a leap of faith when he proposed that Mexico and the United States join in a free-trade agreement. This agreement is taken for granted today, but it was by no means routine when the decision was made. Mexico had devoted much energy in the period after the Second World War, and even before that, to keep as much distance from the United States as it could. The restriction of foreign investment – embodied most vividly in the 1973 law which carried the revealing title of the Law to *Promote* Mexican Investment and *Regulate* Foreign Investment – was one aspect of the nationalism designed to limit US economic influence in Mexico. The import-substitution model has an economic motive – that limiting imports was the best way for an emerging economy to develop an industrial base – but its rationale in Mexico also was to minimize imports from the United States, by far the country's dominant trading partner.

This way of looking at things – of playing on nationalism as foreign goods, services, and direct investment were constricted – was thoroughly indoctrinated into the Mexican psyche.[13] Habits of thought began to change in Mexico after the protracted economic downturn that erupted at the end of 1982. Nevertheless, neither President De la Madrid nor Carlos Salinas envisaged anything as radical as a free-trade agreement with the United States. Salinas first sought increased investment and better access to European markets, but found no solid response. He then suggested a series of sectoral trade agreements with the United States, an initiative that received no positive reaction largely because this approach had failed earlier when Canada made its first, timid, suggestions for free trade with the United States. When Salinas finally accepted the logic of a full-fledged free-trade agreement with the United States, this was an almost revolutionary step in the Mexican context. Salinas thereby staked his reputation on a change in this critical bilateral relationship. Once accepted, the idea of free trade began to take on mythic proportions, that it would resolve all of Mexico's problems. The domestic hyperbole took on this coloration. Most economists in Mexico with whom I spoke at that time knew better; they felt that free trade with the United States would stimulate Mexico's economic growth, but that it was not a vaccine against inadequate economic policy.

Despite initial opposition from the most senior US trade advisors, who wished to get on with the Uruguay Round in the GATT and not be distracted by negotiations with Mexico, President George Bush supported the Salinas proposal. He hardly could have done otherwise when the president of a populous neighboring country with which the relationship had been lukewarm suggested such an important political step of greater friendship. The opposition to NAFTA was fierce in the United States, more so than for any trade agreement in the postwar period. This is a well-known story. Ross Perot referred to the agreement as certain to lead to a "great sucking sound" as investment moved out of the United States into Mexico. Organized labor in the United States, the AFL–CIO, attacked the agreement because of the competition it would generate in products produced by low-wage workers in Mexico and labor's supporters predicted hundreds of thousands of job losses as a result. As the vote on the agreement in the US Congress approached, at the end of the summer in 1993, the outcome looked uncertain at best, bleak at worst. It was not until the actual vote was taken in the US House of Representatives, where the opposition was greatest, in November that the Mexicans finally knew that the agreement actually would go into effect. There was considerable and probably justified fear in Mexico that rejection of the agreement would lead to lowered expectations about Mexico's economic future and the possibility of considerable capital flight.

Foreign investment in the Mexican equity market was opened in 1989 and grew quite rapidly. This investment reached 27.9 percent of the market capitalization in 1993, or more than $54 billion.[14] Foreign investment in government debt was opened the next year, in 1990, and this also grew rapidly. It reached $6.5 billion in 1993, most of it in the form of *cetes* (Certificados de la Tesorería de la Federación), which amounted to 81 percent of the total of all public debt instruments purchased by foreigners.[15] At the same time, because of the uncertainty of the NAFTA outcome and the need for financing the public sector, the authorities turned to an instrument called *tesobonos* (Bonos de la Tesorería de la Federación). The essential difference between the two was that tesobonos, while peso instruments, were indexed to the dollar, thereby providing the purchaser a hedge against currency depreciation. Because the Mexican peso was freely convertible, the tesobonos in effect amounted to dollar instruments. Slightly more than $1 billion of these were sold in 1993, or 15 percent of foreign purchases of government instruments. Foreign participation in the sale of all government instruments reached almost 39 percent of the total in 1993, compared with slightly more than 3 percent when the market was opened in 1990. For better or worse, the Mexican capital markets – for private debt and equity purchases and government debt – were opened widely even before NAFTA. They were further opened under NAFTA, and then even more when the economy collapsed in 1995.

The use of tesobonos did not seem radical because they had been used in modest amounts earlier. The increase in their use in 1993 over the previous year was 286 percent. However, in previous years, tesobono issuance had increased, for example in 1990, and then decreased, as in 1991. However, as it turned out later, the tesobono instrument took on a much more important role in Mexico – the temporary improvisation to tide over the period of uncertainty at the end of 1993 turned into an avalanche in 1994. The inability to meet the large, short-term tesobono obligations when holders wished to cash them in after the December 1994 devaluation was the central reason for the large US–IMF international loans and lines of credit at the beginning of 1995. This gets ahead of the story, however. The key point for now, at the end of 1993, was the resort to a practice that later came to play a major role in the events that unfolded in 1994.

The political–economic interplay

On January 1, 1994, the day NAFTA came into effect, there was an uprising in the state of Chiapas. The Chiapas story, quite naturally, dominated the news in Mexico and outside. The day for the uprising could hardly have been chosen better in that many eyes were on Mexico as it entered into what those who crafted NAFTA hoped would be a new era in Mexico–US relations. Subcomandante Marcos, the leader of the *Ejército Zapatista de Liberación Nacional* (Zapatista Army of National Liberation, or EZLN) proved later that he was an expert at public relations through masterfully written statements for the press, exclusive interviews given to prominent journalists at decisive moments, and the manipulation of signals like the use of ski masks ostensibly to shield the identity of Zapatista leaders. Marcos also sought subsequently to rally civil society in Mexico and outside against the policy of neoliberalism which – while not easy to define in the way seen by the Zapatista leader – includes reduction in the role of the government in economic affairs, great reliance on the market, and the removal of import barriers and impediments to foreign investment. Each of these elements was part and parcel of NAFTA.[16] Mexico has long been a country of regions with highly disparate rates of economic growth and opportunities. Data coming from the Mexican census of 1995 showed that 23 percent of the population of the country as a whole earned less than the minimum wage which, in Mexico City, was the peso equivalent of about $100 a month.[17] In Chiapas, the proportion earning less than the equivalent of a single minimum wage was more than 40 percent, almost twice the percentage for Mexico as whole. For all of Mexico, the proportion of persons earning more than five times the minimum wage was 23 percent and in Chiapas the proportion was 11 percent. The north, in general, has fewer people in absolute poverty than the south and more people earning at least five times the minimum wage than the average for Mexico as a whole. The population of Mexico City is highly divided, with a percentage of its population double the national average in absolute poverty, and also a higher proportion of the population than the national average earning more than five minimum wages. NAFTA could be expected to aggravate these differences by improving the economic prospects of the north and the Valley of Mexico while doing little for the more impoverished south. Marcos played on this reality.

Low-grade guerrilla activities have existed for some time in Guerrero and Oaxaca states, and to some extent elsewhere in Mexico, but did not get out of control or affect the national body politic. The PRI dominated the countryside in Mexico, even resorting to violence to maintain this domination. On the whole, however, Mexico has been a relatively stable country once the predecessor to the PRI came into existence in 1929. The consolidation at that time, 70 years ago, represented a bargain among regional leaders to share the spoils rather than fight over them. The uprising in Chiapas shattered this image of a peaceful country, at least in the impoverished south. It also brought out the relative neglect by successive governments in tending to the needs and providing economic opportunity for the indigenous, largely Mayan, population in Chiapas. This destruction of the myth of a peaceable population across the whole territory of Mexico – the assumption that I'm all right, you're all right – had considerable impact on the way the central government operated and shifted the attention of President Salinas from his economic restructuring to restoring order in Chiapas. There was no assurance that the uprising in Chiapas would remain localized. The poverty that was not attended to and the cavernous inequalities that always were there became the stuff of daily news in Mexico City and across the country.

The events in Chiapas had a profound impact on the work habits of President Salinas. His priorities changed from concentrated attention on economic issues to an effort to manage the Chiapas developments and to minimize their impact on the nation as a whole. I was told again and again by insiders that meetings of the president with his economic cabinet, which had taken place at more or less weekly intervals in 1993, occurred rarely in 1994. The persons interviewed had different recollections about the number of meetings of the economic cabinet in 1994. Jaime Serra Puche, then head of the Secretariat for International Commerce and Industrial Development (Secofi, from its initials in Spanish) and therefore a regular participant, recalled that there had been six in all of 1994, five of which were before May, compared with 57 or 58 in previous years. Santiago Oñate, who was chief of staff of the president from early April until the end of November, recalled that there had been only one meeting of the economic cabinet during those eight months. Fernando Clavijo, who worked in the presidency both when José Córdoba Montoya was chief of staff and after he left and Oñate was appointed, did not recall the exact number of economic cabinet meetings, but he stressed there were few.

The precise number of meetings is obviously not a critical point, but their scarcity was mentioned repeatedly. What had changed was the attention the president gave to economic matters; this altered radically, from the top of his concerns to somewhere lower down the list. One senior insider told me that Salinas' two top priorities in 1994 were to *contain* the Chiapas uprising (knowing he could not end it) and manage the electoral transition to the next PRI president. This did not mean that Salinas did not meet one-on-one with his cabinet ministers from time to time, or that he cut off telephone communication with them, but rather that he no longer sought internal debate to obtain some form of high-level consensus on economic policy. In an administration – indeed, a country – where opinions from outside a small insider group were barely entertained, the lack of economic cabinet meetings reduced the give and take on policy even further.

Mexicans joke among themselves that policy is made by what is referred to as the "Club de Toby." Toby was a character in the comic strip *Little Lulu* and he formed a group, or club, from which girls were excluded. Mexicans differ on the number of persons or families kept informed on economic policy thinking and who have some influence on decisions – the number may be 50, perhaps 100.

But all Mexicans who know about governmental decision-making are aware of the Club de Toby phenomenon.

The consequence, as one insider put it, was that the government was paralyzed at the start of 1994. The precipitating event was the uprising in Chiapas. Weekly, even daily, meetings took place on how to handle this issue. The distraction expanded when the first mediator appointed by Salinas to seek to resolve this issue, Manuel Camacho Solís, played a private political role as well. Camacho, a long-time ally of Salinas, had been the regent, equivalent to mayor, of the Federal District, during the first five years of the Salinas sexenio. He anticipated that he would be named the presidential candidate of the PRI for the 1994 election and, when he was passed over in favor of Luis Donaldo Colosio, he resigned his position amid considerable fanfare. Salinas then appointed him as Secretary of Foreign Relations and, when the Chiapas rebellion occurred, Camacho left this position to become the president's mediator to deal with the problem. For many months, he continued to act as if he might be chosen to replace Colosio as the presidential candidate of the PRI and Salinas took no overt action to suppress this double game until much damage had been inflicted on Colosio's campaign. This maneuvering was an added distraction to the Chiapas troubles as such.

Salinas at this time was being supported by the US government as the candidate to lead the World Trade Organization (WTO), which was formed after the Uruguay Round of trade negotiations to replace the General Agreement on Tariffs and Trade (GATT). When asked whether they thought that Salinas' behavior in the early part of 1994 was influenced by this aspiration, many of the senior persons with whom I spoke were certain that it was. He wished, they believed, to avoid controversial actions – such as military suppression of the Zapatista effort – lest he lose support for his candidacy as director general of the WTO.

The evidence, in sum, is overwhelming that the president of Mexico was distracted in early 1994. His attention was being devoted to issues other than economic policy. These included Chiapas, political intrigue within the PRI, and personal aspirations about his world role after he completed his presidential term. It does not necessarily follow that economic policy would have differed had Salinas given the same attention to this as he had in previous years, but it is clear that the economy was on automatic pilot – at least as far as the president was concerned. Perhaps the apt metaphor is the famous cartoon about "dropping the pilot" when Bismarck was

50 *Financial Decision-making in Mexico*

dismissed as chancellor of Germany by Kaiser Wilhelm II in 1890. Salinas dropped himself.

The direct economic effect of the Chiapas uprising

Mexico's international reserves when 1994 got under way were $25 billion.[18] In the days and months following the Chiapas uprising, reserves actually rose. They reached a peak of more than $29 billion in mid-February and early March. They did not begin to decline by any appreciable amount until after Colosio was assassinated on March 23.

During the first quarter of 1994, capital inflows into Mexico reached $9.8 billion, which the Bank of Mexico stated was the highest level ever of capital inflows for a single quarter.[19] The Bank ascribed this record entry of capital to the confident expectations generated by the entry into force of NAFTA. The bulk of this inflow was portfolio capital, investment in Mexican equity shares and public debt instruments.

During the first quarter of 1994, the value of outstanding tesobonos – in effect, short-term dollar obligations – rose, although by no means spectacularly. The substantial increase in tesobono sales did not take place until after the assassination of Colosio. At the start of 1994, outstanding tesobonos amounted to $1.6 billion; at the end of March, they were $3.75 billion. On January 1, international reserves exceeded the value of outstanding tesobonos by more than $23 billion; at the end of March the excess of reserves over tesobonos outstanding were still close to $21 billion.[20]

The conclusion one can reach about the interplay between the events in Chiapas and expectations about financial stability is that the former did not influence the latter. The data are quite convincing about this. Following the Chiapas uprising, Mexican international reserves rose. The voluntary capital inflows in the three months following the uprising were higher than for any previously measured three-month period of Mexican history. Tesobono sales increased as investors sought a dollar guarantee, but the amounts were modest, certainly when compared with what happened later. The inflow of foreign direct investment (FDI) in the first quarter of 1994 was almost $1.8 billion, more than a third the size of such investment during all of 1993. One can argue as to whether the peso was overvalued before January 1, 1994, but the events on that day and in the subsequent two-and-a-half months did nothing to weaken confidence in the stability of Mexico's exchange-rate. Indeed, the problem faced by the central bank was to prevent excessive *appreciation* of the peso – not depreciation – because of the large capital inflows. The panorama that confronted the economic policy-makers at the start of 1994 looked promising, certainly as compared with the gloomy picture of economic decline in the second half of 1993. The entry into effect of NAFTA inspired confidence both within and outside Mexico. The Bank of Mexico was intervening in the foreign-exchange market accumulating foreign currency. Between January 1 and early March, the accumulated intervention amounted to more than $4 billion. In order to limit the inflationary pressure generated by the injection of such a large amount of pesos into the market, the Bank of Mexico sterilized a large part of the monetary impact of the flows by selling government instruments to re-establish what it considered to be balance in the money market. As a result, interest rates went down; for example, the annualized nominal rate for 28-day cetes was less than 10 percent in February and March. The real annualized rate, after discounting for inflation, was between 1.2 and 3.6 percent for 28-day cetes between January and March. The nominal rate moved up to almost 16 percent in April (10 percent real) when the situation changed. The proportion of the inflows sterilized in the January–March period was only 55 percent of the proportion sterilized in the first quarter of 1993, but the Bank of Mexico did not think the monetary liquidity in the economy was excessive. The peso was stable for most of January and February and did not begin a gradual depreciation within the pre-prescribed flotation band until late February and March.

The merchandise trade and current account situations deteriorated during the first quarter – the current account deficit in the first quarter of 1994 was $6.7 billion, or more than 17 percent greater than in the comparable period of 1993 – but at this stage, the economic decision-makers were downplaying the importance of the current account deficit because overall foreign reserves were growing as the result of the large capital inflows. I was told repeatedly by senior officials dealing with the economy that the current account deficit was healthy in that it permitted the use of foreign savings; and that the capital inflows this time, in 1994, were unlike those of the late 1970s and early 1980s because they were voluntary and initiated by the investors and not by the Mexican authorities, by borrowing from commercial banks. In all fairness, this was traditional thinking of economists, the kind of lesson the key Mexican economic policy-makers learned in their graduate studies.

The Colosio campaign

In addition to the distractions affecting President Salinas' attention from the financial picture and the other uncertainties at the start of 1994, considerable infighting was taking place within the PRI. Some inner turmoil is natural during the final year of a president's six-year term in that the outgoing president increasingly becomes a lame duck and groups within the party maneuver for position and power. This is particularly true in Mexico: there is no re-election of a president; a presidential turnover normally involves considerable shifting of key personnel all across the government; and this takes place within *camarillas*, or cliques, of individuals associated with different potential leaders. Mexico lacks an established senior civil service – with the exception of a few civilian agencies, such as the Foreign Ministry, the Bank of Mexico, and, to a lesser extent, the Treasury and the continuity of professional officers in the military – and the shift in personnel at the start of each new administration is therefore substantial. The choice of potential cabinet officials depends on the person chosen to be the presidential candidate, which is natural in most systems, but the jobs below that level depend predominantly on the *camarilla* that exists. The *dedazo*, the finger pointing to the presidential candidate made by the outgoing president, sets in motion a vast scramble for jobs in the incoming government.

Salinas came to office after a dubious vote count in 1988, but most of this cloud about his legitimacy had dissipated by the start of 1994. He had proved during those five years to be an extremely adept political player and, while there were weaknesses in the economy – relatively low GDP growth, some deterioration in income distribution – his policies had done much to transform Mexico. As of January 1, 1994, Mexico was a member of NAFTA and the structure of the economy had been drastically changed away from preponderant dependence on oil. Mexico was soon to become a member of the Organization for Economic Cooperation and Development (OECD), widely regarded as the club of developed countries. Salinas had developed a worldwide reputation as a savvy leader and a person able to accomplish what he set out to do.

The Chiapas uprising, while it had no immediate effect on Mexico's economy – nor did it dampen expectations that the economic future was promising in the aftermath of the changes wrought under Salinas – did raise questions about the political and social structure of the country. Political reform had been taking place slowly, and it was evident to all those who observe these things that economic transformation came first, political opening only later. The philosophy of Salinas was no secret, to first lock in the new economic model and then – if even then – to embark on real democratization of the country.

Enrique Krauze, among others, commented on this. He noted Salinas' emphasis on the need to first achieve permanence of the economic project. Krauze called attention to the fact that there were political advances during the Salinas sexenio, especially at the end, but they were always reactive, forced on him.[21] Salinas laid out his priorities with respect to economic transformation and political change in his final *Informe*, the president's annual report to the nation, of November 1, 1994: "Thus, more important than debating whether or not political reforms followed the other aspects, it is a fact that they were achieved in time for the most crucial moment of their expression – the elections of August 21, which sum up the headway made during these years and mark our passage toward a better democracy."[22]

There was grumbling about Salinas' selection of Colosio as the presidential candidate of the PRI. This came from Camacho, to be sure, but also from other PRI stalwarts, mainly those referred to in Mexico as the *dinosarios* (dinosaurs). Colosio had held many important posts in Mexico – senator, head of the PRI, and cabinet officer – but was identified within the party as a political reformer and a person interested in social issues. The concern within the party was that he was not sufficiently dedicated to the continuation of the PRI's power. There is substantial evidence that Salinas himself had come to question the wisdom of his selection of Colosio.

The difference between Colosio and others within the PRI was much discussed in political circles in the early months of 1994. The then US ambassador to Mexico, James Jones, sent a classified report to Washington in which he expressed his belief that Salinas wanted to weaken Colosio's candidacy and possibly replace him with Camacho.[23] Colosio made a speech to PRI members on March 6 which was cited repeatedly as his declaration of independence from Salinas and from PRI traditionalists. The speech did not mention Salinas, nor was it overtly critical of the PRI, but its content was definitely anti-*dinosario*. The speech was cleared with Salinas before delivery. Some quotations from the speech can give its flavor:

The times have passed when our political fights could take place essentially within our organization and not with other parties... old practices must be left behind, those of a PRI that talks only within itself and with the government.

Mexico wants democracy and rejects its perversion: demagogy!

Today, before the *priísmo* of Mexico, before the Mexicans, I state my promise to reform the power by democratizing it and put an end to any vestige of authoritarianism.

Reforming power signifies bringing the government to the communities by means of a new federalism.

We all take on these commitments of republican reform, democratic and federal reform; reform of the processes to achieve these, and internal reform of the PRI.

Transparency [of the election] requires the participation of observers, both of our own citizens and international visitors, and not exclusion of those who can provide the most complete testimony.

I declare my deepest commitment with Chiapas... Chiapas is the call to the conscience of all Mexicans.

This is the hour of a new economic impulse; it is the hour to grow, without losing financial or price stability. The economy, beyond the technical needs, must be at the service of the Mexicans.

The great demand of Mexico is democracy.[24]

Colosio was assassinated on March 23 and this speech was delivered only 17 days before. This juxtaposition, plus the clear maneuvers by many within the party to bring down Colosio's candidacy, plus the content of this speech and the indications it gave that he would be a president quite different from Salinas – all these factors together gave rise to the widespread belief in Mexico that his murder was orchestrated by senior persons of the PRI. In addition, the Mexican authorities pursued a number of leads to determine if the person convicted for the murder, Mario Aburto, acted alone, and from time to time released stories about discoveries of accomplices. Now, many years later, we know little more than we did at the beginning. Other than these circumstantial indications, there is no evidence that either Salinas or the PRI was involved in the Colosio murder. This lack of hard evidence, of a smoking gun, did not then dispel popular suspicions, nor has it to this day.

Several years later, on April 2, 1996, the journalist Sergio Sarmiento published a front-page article in the newspaper *Reforma* reporting on conversations he had with José Córdoba Montoya regarding the 1994 events surrounding Colosio.[25] Córdoba had been the influential chief of staff of Salinas until his departure from this post in April 1994, and he said that there were in fact differences of opinion between Salinas and Colosio in the first months of 1994, but that if anyone had opposed the "campaign against the campaign" of Colosio, it was he, Córdoba. Córdoba said that he suggested to Salinas that if he were to make the peculiar selection of Camacho as the government negotiator for Chiapas, this action should be accompanied by a decree making Camacho ineligible to be a presidential candidate. Salinas refused, saying this would be offensive to Camacho. Camacho did not explicitly eliminate the ambiguities about his possible presidential candidacy until March 22. Colosio, according to the news story, told Córdoba on March 15 that he was annoyed and bewildered by the Salinas' excessive tolerance of Camacho's behavior. Córdoba is quoted in the news article as saying that "in the first months of 1994, it was very difficult to reconcile the priorities of the president and the candidate."

One final indicator of the disturbed atmosphere that existed in the first months of 1994 is a letter sent to Colosio by Ernesto Zedillo, then Colosio's campaign coordinator and later the presidential candidate who replaced Colosio.[26] The letter was sent four days before Colosio was assassinated. Zedillo, in the letter, points out that the atmosphere had changed between the time Colosio was nominated as the PRI presidential candidate late in the previous year and January 10, 1994; that until the latter date, Salinas gave the presidential succession his highest priority, but after that he was more focused on social and financial stability. The letter shows considerable evidence of animosity toward Camacho. The main recommendation in the letter is for Colosio to work out an explicit agreement with Salinas under which he offers Salinas his full support and loyalty, but at the same time makes it clear to the general public that he will not be manipulated by the outgoing president. Zedillo was not precise about how to accomplish this dual task. In effect, Zedillo suggested that Colosio make a declaration of independence and demonstrate that he was his own man; and, in fact, his speech of March 6 was interpreted that way by Mexican commentators.

Colosio's assassination

At this point, early to mid-March, while the political pot was boiling, there was little spillover from these events into the real economy. Insiders in Mexico knew that much political infighting was going on, but the general public was indifferent to this. It was more concerned about the need for a recovery from the economic slowdown of the second half of 1993. Some foreign investors knew what was happening, as I learned from speaking with them, but most did not, as I also learned from interviews. Apart from what they said to me *ex post*, the evidence from the record capital inflows in early 1994 is decisive – expectations about the Mexican economy were buoyant. There was concern within the US government about the overvalued exchange rate, but not alarm. The serious misgivings about the use of tesobono sales as a substitute for exchange-rate and foreign-reserve policy did not come until later.

This atmosphere of complacency changed radically after March 23, the day Colosio was assassinated in Tijuana. The event was shocking; Mexico had not experienced this kind of political violence at the presidential level for more than half a century. The murder had immediate economic consequences and, as one looks back, a profound effect on Mexico's political culture. A number of informed Mexican commentators – Sergio Sarmiento, in *Reforma*, for one – have remarked that Mexico's political history would have been different had Colosio become president and carried out what his initial campaigning implied.

Zedillo was chosen by Salinas as the new PRI candidate on March 29 almost by default. The practice then in Mexico was to choose a cabinet officer as the PRI presidential candidate, but the constitution specified that the candidate had to be out of office for at least six months before the date of the election.[27] Zedillo met these requirements. He had been Secretary of Education starting in January 1992 and left that post in November 1993 to be the general coordinator of Colosio's presidential campaign. Camacho also met these criteria – he had been regent of the Federal District and briefly was foreign secretary, and he left the latter in January 1994 to take up his duties as official mediator for Chiapas – but given his ambiguous behavior in relation to Colosio during the previous months, his selection as the PRI presidential candidate was unthinkable. Zedillo was not considered a strong candidate. He was a technocrat who had never had held elective office, but neither had Salinas before him, or De la Madrid, or López Portillo, or Echeverría before that; more to the point, however, was that Zedillo was not clued in to the thinking and maneuvering of the mainstream of the PRI. These deficiencies became clear during the campaign and again in his first years as president.

Mexico's foreign reserves were $28.3 billion on March 23, and had been reasonably stable in the weeks before that. They began to decline immediately after the assassination – to $27.4 billion on March 25, to $24.4 billion at the end of the month, and down to $17.3 billion at the end of April. This was an $11 billion loss in a period of five weeks. The loss was double the reserve gain in the earlier weeks of the year, the time that Mexico enjoyed abnormally large capital inflows that were converted into reserve gains. The reserves stabilized for a time after that. The general public and even the money markets did not know immediately the precise changes in reserves because the practice of the Bank of Mexico was to publish these figures only three times a year – in the *Annual Report* of the Bank of Mexico in the spring, in the address of the governor of the Bank at the annual bankers' convention in the summer or fall, and in the *Annual Report* of the president to the Congress in the autumn.[28]

There was discussion in *Hacienda* and the Bank of Mexico about the proper policy reaction to the assassination. The main decision was that credit and exchange-rate policy should not be altered because the murder was seen as a one-time event whose consequences would pass after the initial shock. Ariel Buira, then a vice governor of the Bank of Mexico said this explicitly.[29] This assessment was correct as far as reserve loss was concerned; the reserve level held steady within a narrow range until early November, declining for a while in July and then recovering to about $17 billion, the level to which it had fallen by late April.

A further decision was made to keep the monetary base reasonably steady, again because of the expected transitory nature of the financial fallout from the assassination, but also out of fear of further weakening the already weak banks. This point was made repeatedly in discussions with Bank of Mexico officials, including

Agustín Carstens, the director of economic research and Buira, and in interviews with others in *Hacienda* and the presidency concerned with economic policy. The weakness of the commercial banks, quite clearly, limited the flexibility of the government to conduct monetary policy.

The decision-making at the end of March was determined by a combination of considerations. These included the heavy influence of inertia, the unwillingness to make a radical change in a policy that was working to keep down inflation, coupled with the economic recovery that was developing in the early part of the year from the poor performance of the second half of 1993; the expectation that the Colosio assassination was a transitory shock; and concern that raising interest rates would further weaken the fragile financial situation of already weak private banks.

These were not unreasonable considerations. A currency devaluation in the immediate aftermath of a political assassination could well have made the crisis worse. However, the argument that reserves held steady for some seven months omits the reality that the kind of capital inflows that led to reserve increases in the early part of the year did not resume. Investors, both Mexican and foreign, never fully recovered their earlier confidence in the financial–political stability of Mexico.

Just about all the Mexican insiders who ventured opinions, publicly and in private conversations, accepted as eminently natural that there was a run on reserves after such a cataclysmic event as the murder of the probable next president of Mexico. Just about all, but not everybody. One senior official said to me that in order to understand the tacit and almost universal acceptance that a political shock would lead to financial uncertainty requires knowledge of the Mexican context. Political uncertainty stimulated knowledgeable Mexicans to run for cover, as they had done quite consistently at the end of presidential terms since the 1970s. Mexico, he argued, was predisposed and Mexicans were conditioned to expect the worst from political uncertainty. "In Israel, the prime minister was assassinated and nothing happened to the exchange rate," he said. It is not surprising that Mexicans were the first to run for cover by sending dollars out of the country. They knew the situation more thoroughly than foreigners. They were acting rationally, based on their earlier experience.

The thinking of Mexican policy-makers at the end of the first quarter of 1994 was one of deep concern, but not panic. A horrible event had occurred, but its effects were expected to erode with time. Policy was designed, therefore, to stick with the basic model and ride out the storm. The thinking of private asset holders was to defend their positions, at least until they knew more about what the storm would bring. The president of Mexico was distracted as a result of the combination of events that began with the uprising in Chiapas on January 1, and this was aggravated by his falling out with the presidential candidate he himself had chosen.

Policy, really, was marking time to see how long the fund withdrawal from the assassination would last and how the political situation would develop in an election year.

4
The Second Quarter of 1994

Ernesto Zedillo was chosen as the presidential candidate of the PRI on March 29, a bleak moment in Mexico's financial and political situation following the events of the tumultuous first quarter of the year. Foreign reserves were still falling; they were $25.3 billion on that day and did not reach their nadir for this period, $17.3 billion, until the end of April. Zedillo was not unknown – he had served in the Bank of Mexico, as a researcher in relative anonymity, but also in two cabinet-level posts, as Secretary of Programming and Budget and later Secretary of Education – but he certainly was not well known. Had they been left to their own devices, the political kingpins of the PRI would not have chosen him. Zedillo was the archetype *técnico*, an economist with a PhD from Yale University, and without intimate familiarity with the political workings of the PRI. Colosio, by contrast, had been a federal senator, president of the party, as well as a cabinet member. The choice of Zedillo was Salinas' and the probability is high that he later came to regret this, just as he had misgivings about his earlier selection of Colosio.

A victory by the PRI candidate, particularly one as little known to the general public as Zedillo, was no longer a sure thing. Salinas himself had won the presidency in 1988 with just 50.5 percent of the vote, the lowest percentage of any PRI presidential victory since the party was founded in 1929 (under a different name). In addition, Zedillo faced what on paper were two formidable opponents, Cuauhtémoc Cárdenas of the Partido de la Revolución Democrática (PRD), on the left, and Diego Fernández de Cevallos of the Partido de Acción Nacional (PAN), on the right.

Salinas' emphasis was largely on politics during the second quarter of 1994. A PRI victory, to assure that Zedillo would be the next president, took priority over all other issues. I was told this repeatedly by Mexican insiders, even those whose primary interest was to maintain economic stability. The fact that a political party and its *de facto* head, the president of the country, focused on winning the next presidential election is hardly remarkable; it would have been had this not been the priority of the political leadership.

What I was told again and again, however, is that economic policy – including policy at the nominally non-political, independent central bank, the Bank of Mexico – was deeply influenced by the imperative to assure Zedillo's victory. This is adamantly denied by the then governor of the central bank, Miguel Mancera, and some of the vice governors, including Jesús Marcos Yacamán in a personal interview. The facts and the judgments of close observers will be set out on this issue.

The priority of politics has many sub-plots in addition to the role of the Bank of Mexico. Some of the following actions may have had a sound rationale regardless of the upcoming election – and some surely not – but there is evidence that presidential political motivations entered into the calculations as well. These actions include:

- the increased use of development banks as intermediaries for off-budget government expenditures
- the resignation of José Córdoba Montoya, Salinas' chief of staff and perhaps his most important non-cabinet advisor on economic issues, and on political matters as well
- the discarding of any possibility of currency devaluation before the election because this would be politically devastating
- the growing sales of tesobonos as a signal to the market that there would be no pre-election devaluation
- and the action taken to prevent interest rates from rising more than absolutely necessary after the Colosio assassination.

Peter Smith, a respected US observer of the Mexican scene, emphasized in his dissection of the events of 1994 that "political logic prevailed over economic logic."[1] The upshot of his analysis is that in the crunch of that crisis-laden year in Mexico, politics invariably trumped economics – and this certainly was the case during the second quarter of 1994 when the presidential campaign was building to its crescendo of the actual election on August 21.

Actions of the Bank of Mexico

The Bank of Mexico was accused by many observers, inside and outside Mexico, of handling the fallout from the Colosio assassination more with the political situation in mind than the economic one. I was told this explicitly by a number of senior Mexicans, many still in official positions – including in the Bank of Mexico. The uncertainty of the electoral outcome was cited repeatedly in these conversations, including with officials of the Bank. Their reasoning was that there would be time to resolve the underlying economic issues once Zedillo's election was an accomplished fact.

It is worth noting at this point, however, that the analysts at the central bank turned out to be wrong. The economic situation was not dealt with in the period immediately following the election; it was not dealt with until the badly handled devaluation of December 20 of that year, when Zedillo was president and not president-elect. This outcome will be taken up in later chapters.

There were two main reasons for the failure to take more drastic economic measures – particularly to deal with the exchange rate – in the period following Colosio's assassination. These were the deep conviction that a peso devaluation just prior to a contested presidential election would be fatal for the PRI; and, second, that an alternative of sharply rising interest rates might have the same fatal political outcome, while simultaneously weakening the already fragile banking sector.

It would be naive to treat the political arguments lightly. Governments are political entities and, as one US observer has noted, the only sustainable policies are those that keep policy-makers in office.[2] Yet, governments create independent central banks precisely to divorce them as much as possible from current politics. There are perhaps no other institutions that play as important a role as central banks in the success or failure of economic policy that are similarly removed from normal political accountability in full-fledged democracies. The German central bank, the Bundesbank, is renowned for its dedication to anti-inflationary policies, even if the short-term cost is low economic growth.[3] The US Federal Reserve Board deserves as much, if not more, credit than the elected governments for the sustained, low-inflation, economic growth in the United States in the late 1980s and 1990s. In Great Britain, as a way of building confidence of the business community, and, hence, of bolstering the political support of this community, the Bank of

England was given greater independence after the Labour government came to power in 1997.

Put differently, no observer is surprised when political figures, such as presidents or cabinet officers, act politically, but the question of integrity does arise when a nominally independent central bank – which has been deliberately removed from politics and any direct public accountability – acts politically. This was why in 1993, effective at the start of April 1994, the laws and the appropriate constitutional provisions governing the Bank of Mexico were changed, giving the Bank more autonomy from the government and setting out as the Bank's primary objective the maintenance of the purchasing power of the national currency – that is, to control inflation. Whatever else one can say about the priorities of Miguel Mancera, the governor of the Bank during this period, he was true to this objective; reducing inflation took priority in his policies over augmenting growth and he was supported in this policy by Pedro Aspe, the Secretary of *Hacienda* (Treasury). There was more tension between the Bank and *Hacienda* after Zedillo became president and Guillermo Ortiz was the Secretary of *Hacienda*; the tension revolved around the interplay between economic growth and containing inflation.

Nevertheless, the question raised by Bank's critics during the second and subsequent quarters of 1994 was just how independent the Bank was in practice. The independence was constrained from the very outset in that Mancera was part of the economic cabinet of the president, which evidently is a political role. Mancera participated in meetings of the pactos, where economic policy was discussed by government, business, and labor representatives – and this surely removed some of the Bank's independence. This participation made the governor of the central bank part of a team rather than an independent actor removed from daily political pressure. Mancera was present at the critical meeting of the pacto in December 1994 when the decision to devalue the peso was taken, and this was a major breach of the Bank's independent role. However, the best way to evaluate the charge that the Bank acted politically is to examine what policies it carried out. This will be done in the following section for the three months of the second quarter of 1994.

Bank policies during the second quarter

The Bank was constrained in the actions available to it during the second quarter. The US Federal Reserve had already raised short-term US interest rates twice in the first quarter, in February and again in March. The Fed again raised short-term rates twice in the second quarter, in April and May. The four increases totaled 1.25 percentage points. These increases added to the attractiveness of investment in US instruments, a point that became important during the outflow of capital from Mexico in the aftermath of the Colosio assassination. The Fed's action reinforces a truism about US relations with Mexico – that the most important US policies that affect Mexico, favorably or unfavorably, are those taken with little or no consideration of their cross-border impact. The recovery of the Mexican economy in 1996 and subsequently owed more to the sustained GDP growth in the United States than it did to the existence of NAFTA.

During the first quarter of 1994, when capital inflows into Mexico were soaring, the peso stayed close to the floor of the band established with the dollar. Reserves accumulated to their peak for the year in mid-February at more than $29 billion. The Bank argued in its *Annual Report* for 1994 that it would have made no sense in these circumstances to have increased the daily slide in the peso (the *desliz*, as it was called) to more than the 0.0004 new pesos a day, a devaluation crawl level that had prevailed since October 20, 1992. Increasing the slide, the Bank argued, would have aggravated inflation. It might, also, have helped to reduce the overvaluation of the peso at a time that was relatively favorable for doing this. The inflows in the first quarter owed much to US congressional approval of NAFTA and it was unclear, even than, that the stimulus this gave to capital movements into Mexico would be long-lasting. Beyond that, the Bank did not concede at that time that the peso was overvalued.

The situation changed abruptly after March 23, when Colosio was assassinated. Instead of entering, capital left Mexico. During this period, the peso did depreciate within the established band. There were 3.1063 pesos to the dollar at the end of January 1994; this depreciated to 3.3598 at the end of March; and to 3.3918 at the end of June. The peso reached its lowest (most depreciated) level before the December devaluation at the end of November, when it was 3.4498 to the dollar. These figures translate into a 9 percent nominal devaluation *within the band* from the end of January to the end of June; and 11 percent from the end of January to the end of November.[4]

The phrase, "within the band," is intended to highlight the limits to devaluation that were permitted. When the action was taken in December 1994 to alter the value of the peso, this was not at first called a "devaluation" by the then Secretary of *Hacienda*, Jaime Serra Puche, but rather a raising of the ceiling (thereby providing flexibility for greater depreciation of the peso). It was, of course, a devaluation – explicit, in that pre-existing criteria were dramatically altered. The Bank of Mexico had no authority during the second quarter to raise the ceiling of the band; it had no authority to depreciate the peso outside the pre-established band. The critical vote in the decision-making body for that step was formally in the hands of the Secretary of *Hacienda*. More exactly in the real world, it rested with the president of Mexico. Even had he wished to devalue the peso during the second quarter – which he clearly did not – neither Mancera nor the *junta*, the five-member board of the Bank, had that authority.[5] There is a legitimate argument that devaluation in the midst of the political crisis after Colosio's assassination would not have been salutary, but instead would further highlight the political instability that existed in Mexico.

The amount of tesobonos sold to the public, both to Mexicans and foreigners, was another instrument of policy, but this was in the hands of *Hacienda* rather than the Bank. Tesobono sales were a major instrument of financial policy during the second quarter. Outstanding tesobonos were $1.6 billion at the start of 1994; $3.8 billion at the end of March; and $13 billion at the end of June. At the end of the day, tesobono sales led to financial tragedy when they had to be cashed in, but at this point in the unfolding of policy, in the second quarter, they were a crucial instrument. Other capital was not entering Mexico and US interest rates were rising and the use of tesobonos permitted Mexico to pay lower interest for borrowed capital because of the dollar indexing; and, in these circumstances, the tesobonos substituted for an actual devaluation of the peso, which had been ruled out for the time being.

This left the Bank to deal with the situation with a limited number of instruments: intervention in the exchange markets to control the degree of depreciation within the preset band; sterilization of capital inflows and outflows to deal with the monetary aggregates and interest rates; and management of the monetary base.

In order to keep the value of the peso with respect to the dollar within the preset band, either intervention in the exchange market or allowing a sharp rise in short-term interest rates was necessary. The Bank intervenes in exchange markets in order to facilitate Pemex operations and to affect cross-rates with currencies other than the dollar, but the main reason is to control the value of the peso. The Bank's policy was to intervene only within the band. When the peso was strengthening, as was the case during the first quarter, intervention served to protect the floor of the band and, in the process, to accumulate dollar reserves. After the assassination of Colosio, dollars were sold out of reserves to buy pesos and thereby protect the ceiling of the band. Accumulated intervention – buying dollars – from the start of 1994 until the beginning of March was more than $4 billion, and foreign reserves during this period rose from $25 billion to $29 billion.[6] During March and April, accumulated intervention – this time, the sale of dollars and other foreign reserves – amounted to $10.8 billion, and foreign reserves declined to $17.5 billion. Thereafter, the peso stabilized and there was only modest intervention for the rest of the second quarter. Total intervention – sales of dollars – from April 22 to June 30 amounted to less than $1 billion and led to a level of reserves at the end of the second quarter of $16 billion.

The Bank of Mexico's argument was that the loss of reserves, and the requirement that it was compelled to intervene in the exchange market to protect the ceiling of the peso band, was forced almost exclusively by political events in Mexico. This is the position also taken in the widely cited article written by two prominent bank insiders, Francisco Gil-Díaz, a vice governor, and Agustín Carstens, general director of economic research.[7] Another vice governor, Ariel Buira, took this same position – that the problems were political – in a piece he wrote on events in 1994.[8] The Bank, in its 1994 report, provides a graph that was designed to relate foreign reserve losses to specific political events;[9] the murder of Colosio was shown as the reason for the reserve loss in March and April and then, in June, the resignation of the Secretary of the Interior (*Gobernación*), Jorge Carpizo, over what he felt was undue limitation of the unfolding political opening, is given as the basis for the more modest reserve loss. President Salinas did not accept Carpizo's resignation.

Intervention in the exchange market to protect the ceiling of Mexico's exchange-rate band was made necessary by the unwillingness of the Bank of Mexico to allow short-term interest rates from rising too much. Critics of the Bank do not fault its behavior in intervening in the exchange market rather than devaluing the peso because the Bank lacked authority to do this. There was much more discussion about the decision to sterilize the effects of the dollar loss as opposed to allowing interest rates to rise more than they did, but this was a Hobson's choice: rational analysts can come down on either side.

The sacrifice of $12 billion of reserves from the time of Colosio's assassination until the end of the second quarter would not have been necessary if Mexico had instead adopted a more flexible exchange-rate regime earlier – say, in the first quarter when conditions were relatively favorable. There were reasons, largely political, for not adopting a less managed exchange-rate policy. The Bank, and those who supported its actions, defend the intervention by pointing out that the reserve hemorrhaging did cease in April and then again in July, when the reserve loss was modest, and did not resume again until November and December of 1994. The Bank's argument was that continuation of the kind of political turmoil that occurred after the exchange market was stabilized at the end of June and the beginning of July was uncertain. What all of this meant, however, was that when further shocks did occur later in the year, the Bank of Mexico had fewer foreign reserves with which to protect the peso under the regime that had been adopted.

Critics focus much more on the related policy of sterilization adopted by the Bank. When the Bank intervenes in the market, it either adds pesos when it buys foreign exchange, or removes pesos when it sells foreign exchange. The purpose in either case – buying or selling foreign exchange – is to manage the value of the local currency. "Sterilization" refers to neutralizing the effects of these liquidity changes. The argument in favor of sterilization is to limit the disturbances in the domestic credit market stemming from capital flows.

By sterilizing the reserve losses, the Bank limits the extent of interest rate rises. Short-term interest rates, nevertheless, did rise significantly in March and, with modest fluctuations, stayed high throughout the second quarter. The real interbank rate (tasa de interes interbancaria promedio, or TIIP) averaged 11.24 percent in March and rose to an average of 18.89 percent in June. Other short-term interest rates, such as on 28-day cetes, had similar increases.

In its 1994 *Informe*, the Bank notes that the argument can be made that it could have allowed interest rates to rise much more and this might have avoided the devaluation that took place in December. This line of reasoning is rejected on the grounds that it would have led to even more turbulence in the markets. The *Informe* is less explicit about the concern that higher interest rates would have aggravated the position of the already weak banking structure, but this was general knowledge among informed Mexicans and the point was made explicitly in the interviews I had with Bank officials. The final argument of the *Informe* on this issue is that the Bank did retain a relatively high level of reserves until mid-November (between $15 and $16 billion), when renewed political disturbances put further and unexpected pressure on the Bank.

Two comments can be made at this point. The first is that while further foreign reserve losses did not occur between July and November, neither did capital inflows resume. This should have been a sign that confidence in Mexico policy was eroding. The second comment is more of an aside at this point – that is, holding the discussion until Chapter 5 dealing with the third quarter and the leadup to and aftermath of the August 21 election – namely that interest rates fell sharply in July and most of August. This is the main basis for the charge that the Bank acted politically in its monetary policy. In the light of its primary objective of achieving price stability, the Bank pointed out that it used the monetary base as its intermediate variable. In 1994, under the essentially fixed exchange-rate system in effect, the monetary base had two important sources, the Bank's own market interventions and variations in domestic credit. The Bank argued that monetary policy in 1994 was geared to limiting excessive expansion of the monetary base in order to moderate inflationary pressures.

These developments – the related intervention, sterilization, monetary, and interest-rate policies – are laid out in the Bank's 1994 *Informe*. However, in an effort to explain its policies to the important US and foreign audiences before the issuance of the formal report, Mancera submitted a column which appeared in the *Wall Street Journal* editorial page on January 31, 1995.[10] His purpose was to insist that Mexico had acted prudently in 1994. "Mexican monetary policy," he wrote, "should not be faulted for not having contemplated a series of political shocks that were entirely unexpected, and indeed, that had been unknown in Mexico for several decades."

Commentary on Bank policy

There is abundant evidence that the three key economic policy-makers in Mexico were committed, at almost any cost, to maintaining the exchange-rate structure that existed before the election. President Salinas, according to the Mexico City newspaper *Reforma*, had obtained a commitment from Pedro Aspe, when he invited him in 1988 to become Secretary of *Hacienda*, that there would be no "abrupt devaluation" of the peso.[11] Aspe and Mancera were of one mind on this point, certainly during the first half of 1994. In a series of articles in *Reforma* dealing with decision-making prior to the December 1994 devaluation, which appeared on three consecutive days in May 1995, the investigative reporter Rossana Fuentes-Berain, referred to Aspe and Mancera as "*almas gemelas en lo económico*" (twin souls in the economic arena) and "*el binomio*" (hyphenated or connected name) Aspe–Mancera.[12]

There was thus no give at the top of the decision-making hierarchy about exchange-rate policy, and, I was told repeatedly in the interviews I conducted, there was little disposition to hear contrary views from subordinates on this issue. Several informants told me that Guillermo Ortiz, then the Subsecretary of *Hacienda*, was excluded from many meetings on economic policy precisely because he was known to favor a more flexible exchange-rate policy, or at least a different approach to economic policy than the exchange-rate-based anti-inflation program that was the anchor of Mexican economic policy at this time, and had been since late 1987.

The motives of the three leaders were not necessarily identical. Salinas was concerned at this time about politics, getting Zedillo elected and thus assuring PRI continuity. Later in the year, after this was accomplished, his concern shifted to his place in history. He did not wish to repeat the performance of Echeverría and López Portillo, both of whom devalued the peso as they left the presidency and are remembered for it. He was the US candidate to head the newly established World Trade Organization (WTO) and was concerned that the failure to maintain the value of the peso would prejudice this.[13] These points were made repeatedly in my conversations with government insiders. In any event, there were few meetings of the economic cabinet during the first half of 1994, or even later in the year, and dissident policy views could not emerge in this context. Salinas did meet regularly one-on-one with Aspe, but these meetings were unlikely to bring out divergent views on exchange-rate matters. Aspe, in turn, met at lunch on Tuesdays with Mancera, and this could lead only to reinforcement of the economic policy position of these two kindred souls on exchange-rate matters.

There were, however, divergent views lower down in the hierarchy – or if not divergent, a willingness to question first principles.

In early 1994, the research group at the Bank of Mexico solicited a study by two Israeli economists and a vice-president of JP Morgan to critique Mexico's economic policy. The main conclusion of this examination was that Mexico should shift its nominal anchor from the more or less fixed exchange rate (the band) to an inflation-target anchor. This recommendation would have led to more flexibility in exchange-rate matters.[14] The existence of this study was by no means secret and was known outside the Bank. Indeed, senior, non-Bank, government officials recommended that I read it. The study was prepared before the crisis. Two of its authors prepared another after the crisis. One of their conclusions was that much of the crisis could have been avoided by tighter monetary policy and an earlier shift of the nominal anchor – say, in the first quarter – and relying less on targeting the nominal exchange rate in a narrow band.[15] The argumentation of this analysis goes along the following lines: confidence could be maintained as long as investors believed the exchange rate could be maintained and capital inflows continued to sustain the current account deficit; yet a finite stock of foreign-exchange reserves underpinned the strategy; finally, with the exchange rate at the top of the band for almost a year and erosion of foreign-exchange reserves, confidence was lost and the large deficit in the current account was regarded as unsustainable.[16]

Another study first called to my attention by senior research officials of the Bank – who sent it to me before it was formally published – was by a British analyst, Stephany Griffith-Jones.[17] This is a well documented study. She makes several points about Mexico's economic policy in the Salinas years – for example, that the sequence and timing of liberalization in the capital account and privatization in the financial sector could have been more gradual and less simultaneous. This is a point that was made repeatedly to me by private-sector leaders, even those who prospered from this policy. In a meeting with the *cupula* (pinnacle) of the Monterrey business community – those whose firms were doing well in the international marketplace – I was told that it was a great error to open the economy to imports as rapidly as was done.

Griffith-Jones also argues that the devaluation was too late. An important element of her critique is that the economic authorities based policy on the assumptions that the current account deficit was temporary and capital inflows permanent, both high-risk assumptions, as many observers inside and outside Mexico said at the time. The Bank's 1994 *Informe* goes to great pains to stress that many other countries – Singapore, Malaysia, and Thailand were cited specifically – had large current account deficits and high growth rates, without adverse exchange-rate consequences.[18] If they could, why not Mexico? Many observers, including Griffith-Jones, have pointed out that Mexico also financed its current account deficit largely by short-term and volatile capital inflows, which made the policy doubly vulnerable.

One further outside commentary on Bank policy at this time will be given. Two analysts at the Federal Reserve in Washington, in a careful econometric study, cautiously concluded that interest rates were not raised sufficiently during the second quarter to avoid a later devaluation, probably because this policy would have required a change in thinking at a time of concern about weak economic activity and an unhealthy banking system. It is not surprising, they conclude, that the authorities allowed only moderate interest rate increases even though this led to a sharp decline in reserves and eventual abandonment of the exchange-rate policy.[19]

The development banks and fiscal policy

An issue that, at first blush, would not enter into the discussion of the financial and economic crisis that Mexico experienced in 1994 is the budgetary treatment of development banks and funds. These institutions are designed to promote development in particular regions or sectors with limited access to commercial credit, and to stimulate activities that require large lumps of capital at the outset because of the long time it takes to reach maturity.[20] The three most important development banks are Nacional Financiera (Nafin), Banco Nacional de Comercio Exterior (Bancomext), and Banco Nacional de Obras y Servicios Públicos (Banobras).[21]

The activities of these banks do enter into the discussion of economic matters in 1994 because, as of 1993, their operations were taken out of the calculations of the balance of the financial budget of the public sector, and, by coincidence or otherwise, their deficit (credit outstanding) in 1994 came to between 3 and 4 percent of GDP.[22] Put differently, had they been included, the public-sector budget, would not have been more or less in balance – as was reported in official releases and touted as evidence of the stringency of Mexico's budgetary management – but in significant deficit.

The principle of removing the activities of the development banks from the formal financial budget is an arguable matter and reasonable people can come down on either side of the issue. An OECD report on Mexico referred to this change as bringing Mexico's public-sector accounting into line with international practice.[23] The reason for the change, as set out in a document from the presidency, was that the major part of the credit from the development banks consisted of second-tier operations (*segundo piso* in Spanish) – that is, the lending was channeled through commercial banks, reducing their risk and largely eliminating their dependence on the federal budget.[24] In his report on banking reform, Guillermo Ortiz noted that in 1988 development bank credit was 66 percent as first-tier banks (that is, direct lending to the borrowers), and the rest second-tier; but that in 1992 the proportion of direct lending had diminished to 37 percent and second-tier lending had increased to 63 percent.[25] These proportions only partially bear out what the presidency said in explaining the shift from on-budget to off-budget because first-tier lending was still significant.

The argument for removal of the development banks from the financial budget conceded that any government subsidies to these banks should not, in principle, be removed. In practice, these subsidies were removed from the on-budget accounting as well. The most pervasive case of subsidies was Banco Nacional de Crédito Rural (Banrural), which absorbed 95 percent of the subsidies in 1992 and continued to operate largely as a first-tier bank – that is, as a direct lender in the agricultural sector.[26]

There was considerable internal debate, at least at the staff level, when the shift was under consideration in 1991 and 1992. The main technical argument against taking the operations of the development banks off-budget, even if there were no subsidies, was that they increased aggregate demand operating through official channels. This permitted the kind of official discretion that does not exist when commercial banks provide credit to borrowers. Several informants pointed out to me that when President Salinas visited communities around Mexico, he promised lines of credit to small and medium-sized industries, when the development banks were both on-budget and off-budget. The operations of Banrural and to a certain extent Banobras (which finances activities of states and municipalities) are particularly subject to this kind political manipulation.

The purpose here is not to rehearse the technical validity of taking development banks off-budget, but rather how this affected the public accounts in 1994. Jonathan Heath, a highly regarded economic consultant, argued the decision to take the development banks off-budget was technically correct, but the expansion of their use of intermediaries for government expenditures in 1994 was unfortunate.[27] The operations of development banks were not kept secret, but there was little awareness, even in financial circles, of how their operations affected the public sector as a whole. Had the public-sector financial deficit been visibly larger rather than being partially hidden in the off-budget operations of the development banks, the Bank of Mexico might have been forced to lean against the wind much more vigorously than it did to offset the larger public deficit. Non-Mexican economic analysts might at the time have been more cautious in their statements about fiscal stringency in Mexico. When these analysts realized what had taken place, they revised their earlier assessments about Mexico's fiscal discipline.

Was the growth of the deficit of the development banks deliberate? Did it happen in 1994 out of sheer coincidence when the economy was subjected to other shocks? I was told repeatedly by knowledgeable informants that the growth of the development bank deficit was not accidental. It was higher in 1994 than in 1993, when the change was made in budget accounting, and higher in 1993 than in 1992. The concern of the political leadership was intense at the end of 1993, when the economy fell into recession, and this apprehension was aggravated by the slow growth that had prevailed in Mexico from 1982 through 1993. One should not forget that 1994 was a presidential election year and the long period of dominance of the PRI rested to a great extent on delivery of high economic growth. Acceleration of the rate of economic growth was by no means certain in 1994.

I was told by several officials from *Hacienda* that the increase in development bank lending in 1994 was intended to help overcome the recession by lending freely. A senior official of an important foreign embassy gave the opinion that the behind-the-scenes intermediation through the development banks helped to sink the government. His reasoning was that funneling money through the development banks became a key instrument of macroeconomic policy, and Mexico therefore did not have an austere budget, but a rather loose one. When the realization outside of Mexico sunk in that there was more profligacy than stringency in the fiscal sector writ large – including both on-budget and off-budget measures – this led to considerable disillusion about the sincerity of statements by the Mexican authorities.

The departure of Córdoba

It is impossible to understand the change that took place in the decision-making process in Mexico in 1994, the final year of the Salinas sexenio, compared with the first five years, without factoring in the departure in early April 1994 of José Córdoba Montoya, who ran the coordination office of the president. The buildup of problems in the first five years and the policies adopted to deal with them, and then the events themselves in 1994 coming like a series of unending plagues – the uprising in Chiapas, the assassination of Colosio, the rash of high-profile kidnappings, the murder of José Francisco Ruiz Massieu, and the periodic increases by the Fed of US short-term interest rates, are just some of these – all contributed to the crisis atmosphere in 1994. After Córdoba left, Salinas lost a trusted advisor who managed the presentation of complex cross-cabinet deliberations for the presidency. Córdoba was replaced, but the role he played was not filled by anybody else.

The president's coordination office was established in 1988 at roughly the same time that Salinas assumed the presidency.[28] Joseph Marie Córdoba Montoya, who directed this office, was born in France in 1950, the son of Spanish exiles, received his master's degree in philosophy from the Sorbonne and completed all the work except the dissertation for his PhD in economics at Stanford University. While at Stanford, he roomed with Guillermo Ortiz, who was Subsecretary of *Hacienda* during the Salinas years. When he came to Mexico in the latter 1970s, Córdoba taught for a short time at El Colegio de México, joined the PRI in 1980, and held various jobs in the party and the government, frequently as an advisor to Salinas. He was naturalized as a Mexican in 1985.[29] Córdoba's non-Mexican history is germane to the story of his departure from the president's office of coordination.

Córdoba does not have a voluble personality and, for the most part, played a modest public role. He almost never made high-profile speeches and did not make himself available for media interviews. He was thus something of a black box to the general public, touted frequently as the *eminence grise* behind Salinas, although this reputation was based not on solid information, but lack of knowledge by the press. Senior officials in Washington got to know him during difficult moments in the NAFTA negotiations, when he was sent as an intermediary to work out problems as seen from Mexico.

Córdoba had independent views on a number of issues, but I

was told by insiders familiar with cabinet meetings that he mostly acted precisely the way a powerful president would want a chief of staff to behave – he kept the president informed about the views of his key cabinet officers, while staying in the background himself. It already has been noted that the economic cabinet met roughly once a week before 1994 and these sessions were organized and the background prepared by Córdoba's office. Córdoba was known to disagree with Aspe on exchange-rate issues, but the views that prevailed were Aspe's – or perhaps those of Salinas himself. Sergio Sarmiento, who writes a daily column for the newspaper *Reforma* and has a political commentary program on Televisión Azteca, reports that since 1992, Córdoba together with Ortiz, who was Aspe's deputy, were recommending a more rapid slide of the peso (a faster depreciation of the currency) to arrest the growing current account deficit in the balance of payments, and this was rejected.[30] In this same column, Sarmiento reports that Córdoba recommended against the choice of Manuel Camacho as the negotiator with the insurgents in Chiapas shortly after the uprising, and this too was rejected. This latter recommendation illustrates that Córdoba provided advice to Salinas on political as well as economic matters.

According to Sarmiento, the only public speech that Córdoba gave during the sexenio was to a meeting of the Mexican Bolsa de Valores (stock exchange) in 1992 where he recommended a devaluation of the peso, a position contrary to that of both Aspe and Salinas.[31]

Córdoba submitted his resignation a week after Zedillo was selected as the presidential candidate after Colosio was assassinated, and left his job in early April. He left Mexico shortly after that to be Mexican executive director at the Inter-American Development Bank in Washington, DC, a position for which he was surely overqualified. This assignment got him out of Mexico and, therefore, less subject to attacks. He later become a resident consultant for the World Bank, before returning to Mexico, where, among other things, he taught economics at the Instituto Tecnológico Autónomo de México, a private university in Mexico City.

Córdoba left his position in the presidency because he had become a political liability, for reasons which are not fully clear. In a book written about him, *El asesor incómodo: Joseph-Marie Córdoba Montoya*, the author, Carlos Ramírez, engages more in speculation than in solid information, and therefore clarifies little.[32] Luis Rubio, a highly respected commentator on the Mexican scene, thought that many attacks were lodged against Córdoba as a proxy for attacking Salinas when doing the latter directly was either risky or inconvenient.[33] Rubio also makes the point that Córdoba was a good target because he was a foreigner. Sarmiento also notes the xenophobic tone of Ramírez's book, which he says is characteristic of Mexico's politics.[34] Juan Rebolledo, subsecretary in the *Secretaría de Relaciones Exteriores* (the Foreign Ministry, or SRE), who had worked previously in the presidency both when Córdoba and his successor were there, but was not then a part of the inner circle, thought the campaign against Córdoba had elements of press resentment at the lack of access to him, plus xenophobia.[35]

A number of opposition politicians intimated in public statements that Córdoba, somehow, was implicated in the murder of Colosio, for which they provided no evidence. Cuauhtémoc Cárdenas did precisely this and he and some of his colleagues were sued for libel by Córdoba. In writing about this lawsuit, Córdoba indicated that he thought the real target was Salinas and that he, Córdoba, did not appreciate being accused of being an assassin simply because of the "deep rancor" (*gran encono*) Cárdenas had against Salinas.[36]

A well documented analysis of Córdoba's role during the first five-and-a-quarter years of the Salinas administration would be most welcome because of his interesting background and his influence on the policies of his adopted country. This also could bring out the nasty xenophobia that most observers believe played such a large role in making him so inconvenient (*incómodo*) in the early part of 1994. The intent here is not to do this, but instead to highlight how decision-making suffered when Córdoba left his position as presidential advisor. Salinas was left without an independent, informed, non-threatening interlocutor with whom he could speak on a daily basis.

Ulises Beltran, a technical advisor to the presidency when Córdoba was there, told me that there was an absence of solid discussion of key economic issues at the presidential level after Córdoba left.[37] Fernando Clavijo, who served in the presidency until the end of the Salinas administration, noted that in the few cabinet meetings he attended, Córdoba spoke last and summarized the various economic interventions, something that his successor could not do.[38]

Santiago Oñate, who succeeded Córdoba in the presidency, told me the same thing.[39] Oñate, a lawyer with a strong labor background, had taught at the National Autonomous University of Mexico (UNAM in its Spanish initials), was a federal deputy, ambassador to the Organization of American States, secretary of labor, and head of the PRI – an impressive curriculum vitae. But, as Oñate told me, he was not an economist and resisted the appointment as chief of staff. Salinas, Oñate said, assured him that he would attend to the economic matters himself. Oñate said he was present at only one economic cabinet meeting in his time at the presidency (April 8 to the end of November) – but there were few such meetings in any event during this period. The paucity of such meetings probably was related to Córdoba's absence, but also to the distraction of the president with other issues, particularly the elections.[40] Salinas had many meetings alone with Aspe, Oñate said, and was on the telephone every day, sometimes many times each day, with Mancera. The old pattern of economic discussions between the president and many senior participants in the same room had broken down.

The views noted here about the change in decision-making after the departure of Córdoba are typical of those of many others with whom I spoke. An analysis of policy in Mexico by economic technicians would not normally get into the role of an economic advisor who shunned the limelight. Yet, the departure of Córdoba made a big difference in economic decision-making in Mexico in 1994. Who knows whether different decisions might have been made in the course of the year if Córdoba had stayed and provided his independent assessments to the president, particularly those on exchange-rate policy, which differed from the prevailing model?

Tesobonos and foreign investors

The tesobono issue arises at almost every point in a discussion of economic policy in Mexico in 1994. The total outstanding at the end of June was $13 billion and international reserves at that point were $16 billion. The outstanding tesobonos did not overtake the level of reserves until July 18, but this gets ahead of the story. However, a relevant development during the second quarter was the activity of what came to be called the Weston Forum, which was organized by the Weston Group, a New York investment bank that was brokering peso security trades for mutual funds.[41] The Forum members, according to the *Wall Street Journal*, included the Weston Group; Fidelity; Trust Company of the West; Scudder, Stevens & Clark; Oppenheimer Management; Putnam Funds Management; Soros Fund Management; Salomon Brothers; and Nomura Securities International. This was a formidable group.

Once again relying on the *Wall Street Journal*, the group met at least twice with senior Mexican officials, in Washington, DC, on April 8, with Guillermo Ortiz of *Hacienda*, Ariel Buira, a vice governor of the Bank of Mexico, and Agustín Carstens, director of research at the Bank, and later on April 20 in Ortiz's office in Mexico City.

The Forum made six policy suggestions, which included reducing the speed of the daily devaluations of the peso, insuring investors against currency exchange losses if the peso exceeded the upper limit of the band (that is, depreciated more than the band prescribed), authorizing commercial banks to increase their foreign-currency liabilities, issuance of longer-term tesobonos, increasing swap lines with foreign banks, and using international reserves to strengthen the value of the peso from its level on April 21 of 3.36 to the dollar to 3.15–3.21. The argument of the investment bankers was that these measures would assist Mexico to obtain more investment, whereas a devaluation of the peso would lead to economic deterioration. The *New Republic* article gives a different spin, that the "suggestions" were not really negotiable and obviously did not come from disinterested bystanders.

The pressure is troublesome in that it calls into question the sovereign independence of Mexico to establish its own financial policy when confronted by such a powerful group of foreign investors at a time when capital inflows were considered essential. These investors were pushing themselves into the most delicate and important issues of national economic policy in Mexico. Their suggestions were not necessarily bad – although I question the soundness of many of their demands – but they surely were overbearing. When the moment of truth came later, after the December devaluation, the investment bankers bailed out, leaving the Mexican authorities and population holding the bag. If ever moral hazard was in play, it was in this pressure of foreign investment bankers asking Mexico to adopt far-reaching and debatable policies that would protect the money of the banks' clients.

Peter Smith quotes Guillermo Ortiz as saying it was one thing to listen to "these guys" but quite another "to follow their policy recommendations."[42] Some of the measures that the Weston Forum advocated did take place – such as increased tesobono sales and increased swap lines with the United States and Canada – but these were in the works in any event. Tesobono sales had been replacing cetes for some months. The swap line was a reaction to the capital flight after the Colosio assassination and the loss of reserves that Mexico suffered in trying to limit the fall of the peso.

5
The Third Quarter of 1994

Ernesto Zedillo was elected president of Mexico on August 21, 1994, in what was considered the most credible presidential election in Mexico in this century – perhaps ever – by both national and foreign observers.[1] Based on data from the Federal Electoral Institute (IFE), Zedillo, the candidate of the Partido Revolucionario Institucional (PRI), received 50.2 percent of the vote, Diego Fernández de Cevallos of the Partido de Acción Nacional (PAN) 26.7 percent, and Cuauhtémoc Cárdenas of the Partido de la Revolución Democratica (PRD) 17.1 percent, with the remainder going to candidates from a variety of other parties. The percentage distribution of votes for the parties in the election for the Chamber of Deputies, the lower house of the Congress, was roughly similar, and, based on the mixture of first-past-the-post decisions and proportional representation, the PRI captured 300 of the 500 seats, the PAN 119, and the PRD 69. The Senate was enlarged and the PRI ended up with 95 of the 128 seats in the expanded upper house.

Two concerns that existed before the elections were expressed repeatedly to me by officials I interviewed: that necessary changes in the economic model, particularly the exchange-rate anchor against inflation, could occur only after the election; and that a Zedillo victory was necessary to assure the change–continuity economic policy paradigm they wanted. There was continuity in the remainder of the third quarter after the election, and well into the fourth quarter, but not the changes many had hoped would take place. Exchange-rate policy remained the same during this period. The key economic policy instrument continued to be the sale of tesobonos, thereby perpetuating the assurance that exchange-rate policy would not be modified for the time being. Nothing was done in the immediate aftermath of the election to deal with the growing deficit in the current account of the balance of payments. In effect, economic policy was put on hold until Zedillo was actually sworn in as president on December 1. The expectation of many officials that Salinas would take the political hit and alter the exchange rate during his watch, and thus provide a clean slate for his successor, did not occur.

It was generally accepted by most Mexicans that basic changes in the economic model would not take place in the runup to the election, but not that there would be inertia afterwards. The third quarter was thus a most intense period, first a focus on politics in governmental policy-making to avoid prejudicing a PRI victory, then an avoidance of making changes in economic policy even after the political outcome was favorable. Much outside advice was sought before the election on policy changes needed, but there is little evidence that the main decision-makers gave them much heed during the third quarter.

Pre-election economic policy

Denise Dresser, a *politólogo* (a person who analyzes the political situation) who teaches at the Instituto Tecnológico Autónomo de México (ITAM), argues that the crisis that erupted later in the year "was rooted in the conflicting imperatives of economic adjustment and political survival."[2] This view is accepted by most observers in Mexico and outside and explains the lack of corrective action before the elections. It does not, however, explain the inaction after the elections, after the PRI had secured continuity for six more years.

The interest rate on 28-day cetes, after reaching a peak in April following the assassination of Colosio, followed a modestly declining path in July and August – really right through much of November – as did the interbank rate, the TIIP. Sebastian Edwards noted that the Bank of Mexico around this time, in July, did not accept the high yields demanded by prospective buyers at auctions of cetes and refused to sell the full amounts that were planned.[3]

Instead, the authorities increasingly dollarized Mexico's public debt through continued, large sales of tesobonos, which simultaneously kept interest rates low and delayed the pressure to devalue the peso. Tesobono sales from June 30 through August 19, the last day before the elections on August 21, amounted to roughly $6 billion.

The tesobonos outstanding on August 19, $18.8 billion, exceeded foreign reserves on that day by more than $2.5 billion. If short-term dollar obligations – tesobonos – are subtracted from the reserve level, Mexico by then had substantial negative reserves. No senior official in Mexico thought precisely in these terms of comparing tesobonos outstanding with reserves in hand, but I was told by a senior official at the Bank of Mexico that the tesobono buildup was discussed repeatedly when the Bank board met. The Mexican authorities did not relate the two because it was not contemplated that it would be impossible later – after the December 20 devaluation – to roll over just about *any* of the tesobonos.[4]

There is a revealing passage in the Spanish version of the Bank of Mexico *Informe 1994* about the shift from peso to dollar debt.[5] The discussion goes along the following lines: because of the growing perception of foreign investors that there was a large exchange risk in Mexico, they demanded dollar instruments in place of those denominated in pesos; had the government refused to issue more tesobonos, it was highly probable that the Mexican public itself would have demanded foreign exchange as their cetes expired, putting pressure on foreign reserves and the exchange rate; what the authorities did was logical in order to get by what was considered to be a transitory situation; monetary policy in 1994, therefore, was largely conditioned by the situation in the exchange market.

It is unclear is why the monetary authorities thought that the pressure on the exchange rate would run its course. The demand for tesobonos was not abating, as it did after NAFTA was approved by the US Congress at the end of 1993, but accelerating. If anything, this meant that skepticism, both in Mexico and outside, that the value of the peso could be maintained was getting ever more profound. The failure to attract new capital inflows other than through tesobono sales and thereby augment foreign reserves was further evidence that uneasiness about the stability of the exchange rate had not abated.

Miguel Mancera, the governor of the Bank of Mexico, insisted in a conversation with me that there was no pre-election pressure on him regarding the course of monetary policy – "nada."[6] Vice-governor Jesús Marcos Yacamán said much the same, that "as a member of the junta [I] never felt political pressure."[7] Other vice governors made much the same point. I have no basis for questioning these statements. One must distinguish between what the government – the presidency and *Hacienda* – did from the actions of the Bank.

The main criticism that can be documented that the Bank's policy was politically motivated is that it did not counterbalance the politically motivated economic policy mix of the government during 1994.[8]

Post-election policy

The most salient question to address for the post-election period in the third quarter – and, indeed, for the remainder of the year until the devaluation was forced by the dwindling foreign reserve position – is why there was inaction. Perhaps the better way to phrase this is not "inaction" but, rather, continuation of the previous action that made the country so vulnerable. The inevitable question that is asked by many outside observers – including me – is: "How can such smart guys make such dumb mistakes?"[9] This question can be asked most forcefully about the period between the election and the inauguration of Zedillo as president.

At the request of Mexican authorities, the World Bank prepared 18 policy-option papers in anticipation of the change of administration and a meeting on these with Mexican and World Bank officials in attendance was held in Cuernavaca, which is about an hour's drive from Mexico City, in August. The papers dealt with a variety of themes, such as education, labor, environment, and included the issues under discussion here – exchange-rate, fiscal, and macroeconomic policy.[10] The World Bank recommended a macroeconomic environment more conducive to economic growth and, in this context, suggested a depreciation of the peso and lower interest rates. According to the most senior World Bank official regularly concerned with Mexico, its "advice on exchange rate policy was not acted upon."[11]

A number of persons from within the Mexican hierarchy made similar recommendations. Arturo Fernández, now the rector of ITAM but then an advisor to Jaime Serra Puche, the Secretary of International Trade and Industrial Development (Secofi), sent a memorandum to Serra in which he was joined by Ignacio Trigueros, a respected economist at ITAM, recommending a change in exchange-rate policy in conjunction with other related changes.[12] It was expected even then that Serra would be the next secretary of *Hacienda*. This was in August and, in a meeting in September with Serra and his key advisors, this recommendation was rejected. Serra's other colleagues in Secofi were not convinced that a policy change was needed then and thought that the economic situation would calm down, at least until 1995, with the advent of the new government in December. Fernando Clavijo, then in the presidency, told me that in September he and Guillermo Ortiz recommended in writing that the exchange rate should be depreciated and that the memorandum was not well received.[13] Clavijo believes that one reason, perhaps the main reason, why Ortiz was not selected to succeed Aspe as *Hacienda* secretary in the original Zedillo cabinet was that the recommendation in this memorandum would alienate many powerful financial leaders.

The decision to retain the old policy was publicly confirmed when a new pacto, the succession of agreements that started in late 1987 under which the government, business, and labor jointly set forth economic policy for the coming period – usually a year – was released on September 24. The pacto continued the exchange-rate policy, including the daily slide in the band of four centavos. Zedillo, then president-elect, supported the pacto.[14] Zedillo made this position clear in a statement made to the Spanish journal *ABC*, published on August 25.[15] This was an interesting position in that Zedillo had not been a partisan of the policy that had been pursued in the previous several years and his advisors believed that exchange-rate policy should be more flexible. I can only speculate on why Zedillo took the position he did with respect to the September pacto; he did not wish to offend Salinas, who was still president, and he assumed there was time enough once he became president himself to alter economic and financial policy.

In my interview with President Zedillo he said that the government could have acted on the exchange rate any time between September 1 and November 20, not by an abrupt change, which would have been disruptive, but by beginning a gradual correction.[16] His consistent concern with economic policy in earlier years was with the falling savings rate, which began around 1990, and was reflected in the growing current account deficit – that is, the growth of imports reflecting growing consumption and a decline in national savings. This was a position he had taken publicly and which he said he raised repeatedly in cabinet meetings. (As an aside at this point, the Mexican savings rate did increase after Mexico recovered from the disastrous depression of 1995.)

The US Federal Reserve Board was becoming concerned that overvaluation of the peso, especially in the context of other developments in Mexico, was becoming an increasingly risky strategy.

The most senior officials of the Fed said this to the Mexicans during a visit to Washington in October when informed that the transition team had decided not to make any changes for the time being, but this view that the situation in Mexico was unstable had been developing for months in the Fed.[17] What the Mexican transition team told the Fed was essentially confirmation of the decision taken when the pacto was renewed in unchanged form in September. The US ambassador to Mexico at that time, James Jones, said that many officials told him they favored changing exchange-rate policy in September or October and he also thought that if this had been done together with consistent ancillary measures, the issue probably would have been resolved.[18]

September, as it turned out, was not a tranquil month. On September 28, José Francisco Ruiz Massieu, the secretary general of the PRI, nominally the second highest official in the party hierarchy, was murdered in downtown Mexico City. Ruiz Massieu had been governor of the state of Guerrero from 1987 to 1993 and was a federal deputy at the time of his assassination. The assassination had only a minor visible impact on the economic situation – between September 23 and the end of the month, foreign reserves fell by some $500 million to a level just above $16.1 billion – but it was another indication of political instability in Mexico. There was more visible confidence deterioration later in the year, on November 23, when José Francisco's brother, Mario Ruiz Massieu, resigned his job as assistant attorney general alleging that the investigation of his brother's murder was being obstructed. Mario fled to the United States and was later charged with accepting drug money.[19]

It is clear what happened in the third quarter with respect to modifying prevailing economic policy. The answer is: precious little. Explaining why this was so is more difficult. The evidence is that the resistance to changing the model – that is, keeping the exchange-rate band and the daily *desliz*, continuing the issuance of tesobonos, living with the growing current account deficit, and the other consequential aspects of policy – came largely from two people, President Salinas and Pedro Aspe, the secretary of *Hacienda*. The motives of the two men may not have been the same, and neither was available for substantive discussion with me.[20]

Salinas, I was told repeatedly by persons close to him, was concerned with his reputation. He did not want to repeat the experiences of two of his predecessors – Luis Echeverría and José López Portillo

– who are remembered, among other things, for the large devaluations that took place as they left office. In the case of his immediate predecessor, Miguel de la Madrid, the devaluation came earlier during his time in office. Many Mexicans felt that the more honorable action would have been to take the hit while he still was in office and thus free his successor from the opprobrium. I was told this repeatedly. Salinas might have consented if Aspe had favored an exchange-rate change, but I don't know; and, to be fair to Salinas, it is probable that he – like Aspe, Zedillo, Serra Puche, and others – felt that the adjustment could be made smoothly in the new year once the new administration was established. Many Mexicans argued that the new year would also have been more convenient for the investment bankers engaged in Mexico, because then the devaluation would come after they received their year-end bonuses.

It is hard to know how much Salinas' desire to become director-general of the World Trade Organization (WTO) influenced his behavior as his administration came to an end. I asked Santiago Oñate about this because he was chief of staff when the issue of Salinas' candidacy was at issue.[21] Oñate said he wasn't sure about the depth of Salinas' desire to head the WTO during the third quarter when the president was occupied with other issues – first the election, then emotional problems concerning his marriage, and in September, the murder of José Francisco Ruiz Massieu, who had been married to Salinas' sister. Salinas, I was told, had been counseled by Miguel de la Madrid, his predecessor, that it was not appropriate for an ex-president of Mexico to serve other leaders. By November, when it was evident that Salinas did want the head job at the WTO, it was too late. It was not clear even earlier that he could have secured the job, despite US backing, because Salinas did not have solid support from other Latin American countries. The WTO issue is more interesting in what it says about the great admiration for Salinas in the US government just a month or so before the ceiling fell in on his economic policy than as an explanation of Salinas' position on the exchange rate.

Aspe's motives appear to me to have been exactly what he said they were, that the primary objective of economic policy should be to lower inflation and complete the successful diminution of inflation indexes which began with the pactos in late 1987. He did not believe Mexico could have a successful, "small" devaluation of 15 percent without losing credibility and foreign confidence.[22] He also argued that a peso devaluation should never be done in isolation but be accompanied by a comprehensive economic policy package. I will return to Aspe's position when reviewing events of the fourth quarter, but his letter cited in n.22 is relevant because it is the most explicit explanation of Aspe's thinking.

There are rationalizations in the Aspe letter that were not relevant to the discussion taking place in the third quarter and in November. I know from interviews with US actors in the Treasury and investment banks who were engaged in Mexican affairs that Aspe was on the telephone frequently assuring bankers that the peso would not be devalued. This was also the implicit message of the continued large issuance of tesobonos. There is a certain transference in Aspe's explanation of his position in his 14 July 1995 *Wall Street Journal* column, written well after the December peso collapse, about a 15 percent raising of the band and doing this in isolation from other complementary measures. Before the events of December 1994 – say, in late August or in September, while Aspe was still *Hacienda* secretary – he could have prepared a comprehensive package to accompany an exchange-rate change, had he so wished. Based on his actions, or inaction, he obviously did not wish to do so. There were options other than a 15 percent raising of the band that were available in the third quarter and into November. One must conclude that Aspe was confident he could manage the situation until the new year when any necessary changes, if any, could be made. Many Mexicans believe to this day that had he remained in office, he probably would have been able to manage the transition. It is by no means clear why, for Mexico's well-being – disregarding Salinas' pride and the interests of foreign investment bankers – it was so important to wait until 1995 to make the necessary changes.

The other major player was Miguel Mancera, governor of the Bank of Mexico. To be comprehensive, one should include the entire *junta* of the Bank since the four vice governors supported Mancera's anti-inflation priority. However, while Mancera's voice counted for much, any decision to alter the exchange rate was not his to make. The decisive vote to do this, had it come to that in the board established for this purpose, was Aspe's.[23] The Bank's mandate, after all, was to maintain the purchasing power of the currency – to keep down inflation.

Investment bankers in the money centers were an influential group because Mexico needed the capital inflow from portfolio investment to finance its large current account deficit. The viability of the total policy was premised on the assumption that these inflows would continue to come because they were voluntary and not borrowed at Mexican initiative, as was the case in 1982 when the previous financial collapse occurred. We know that the investment bankers and their clients supported maintenance of the existing rate. The Weston Forum members wanted even more, as their request in the second quarter made clear, namely, to strengthen the peso within the band. It is hard to know how decisive this pressure group was in the decision-making process in the third quarter, or even right up to the devaluation on December 20. They clearly had great influence, however. Does this explain the decision to put off the crucial exchange-rate decision until 1995? Perhaps.

Aspe was attentive to the players in this group, and he was trusted by them. He was on the telephone with them frequently; he assured and reassured them that there would be no devaluation. As one observer put it to me, Aspe could be arrogant in his dealings with people, particularly those with whom he disagreed, but he spoke to the lowliest people in the financial community. This observer told me that, by contrast, Serra Puche, who succeeded Aspe in *Hacienda*, was more straightforward, but had a loftier view of those with whom he spoke. Many investment bankers were livid when the devaluation actually came because they felt that the Mexican government "tricked" them.[24] They are among the strongest believers that the devaluation would have been avoided, certainly in 1994, had Aspe been allowed to remain secretary of *Hacienda*.

There is much discussion among informed Mexicans of the wisdom of such close relations between the secretary of *Hacienda* and foreign investment bankers. The trust that was developed served Mexico well in keeping the necessary portfolio capital coming – although it took a dollar-indexed instrument to accomplish this. On the other hand, this closeness with the investors may have removed substantial freedom of maneuver on the exchange rate. Had the peso been devalued, whatever form this took, while Aspe was still in *Hacienda*, the charge of trickery or double-dealing would have been much more harsh.

Mexico gambled by not acting to remove what all the relevant players were convinced was an exchange-rate risk when they invested in Mexico. The Bank of Mexico's *Informe 1994* is quite explicit that this was so. Salinas, Aspe, Mancera, and their supporters gambled – and so did Zedillo by going along with this when he was president-elect – and the country lost. It is proper to ask whether the gamble was necessary and whether the outcome would have been less disastrous had Mexico changed its policy course earlier.

Expert views on the policy model

It is useful to recall that the economic policy model under which Mexico was operating was adopted at the end of 1987 in order to deal with the growing and unacceptable inflation. In that year, consumer prices rose by 159 percent (December-over-December), accelerating from the levels of the two previous years of 63 percent and 105 percent. The pacto technique was adopted then and this was started with a sharp devaluation of the peso of about 140 percent. The peso, in other words, was deliberately undervalued in 1987 to leave room for subsequent real appreciations as Mexico's inflation exceeded that in the United States without a comparable adjustment in the peso–dollar rate. There were subsequent modifications in the model, such as changes in the daily level of peso depreciation, but the basic apparatus remained the same.

The exchange rate thus became the anchor for the anti-inflation policy. It was depreciated only modestly in order to keep prices in Mexico from rising too rapidly. There were complementary understandings on government fiscal policy, monetary policy of the Bank of Mexico, price policy by private businesses, and labor restraint in wages. One innovative aspect was to gear wage adjustments not to the previous year's inflation, but to the projected price rise in the coming year, with the result that real wages declined over the period. The program was successful in terms of achieving the primary objective to reduce inflation; the consumer price index rose by only 7 percent in 1994. All this turned out to be illusory after the economic breakdown that began in December and the consumer price index jumped by 52 percent in 1995.

There was a tradeoff, however, in order to meet the anti-inflation objective. In the years from 1987 through 1994, those during which the pacto and exchange-rate anchor were in effect, GDP growth was anemic, particularly coming out of long period of recession after 1982. Depending on the base one uses, real GDP growth over these six years of the pacto model averaged perhaps 3 percent a year, or barely 1 percent per capita. Similarly ominous, gross domestic saving fell sharply in these years, reaching a low of 14.6 percent of GDP in 1994.[25]

There was considerable discussion within the government when the model of using the relatively rigid exchange-rate band was adopted. One insider in the discussions then and subsequently told me that the motives of the actors who designed the policy were mixed. Some had eventual floating of the peso in mind and others hoped it would lead to a decision to fix the rate. The idea of establishing a currency board was examined in the intervening years. Setting up the band removed some freedom of action from the Bank of Mexico and a currency board would have removed much more. What I was told was that, in general, the cabinet-level officers favored coming to a fixed rate, while the professional staff working for the relevant cabinet officers hoped the band would lead to a floating exchange-rate system. Francisco Gil-Díaz, when he was a vice governor at the Bank of Mexico, told me that at one time he supported a currency board, but he doubted that the Mexican body politic would accept this and he therefore favored a largely free float.[26]

The most adamant critic of the policy of using the exchange rate as the anchor for economic policy was Rudiger Dornbusch, of the Massachusetts Institute of Technology. His persistent argument, presented in both lay and technical terms, was that while an exchange-rate anchor to combat inflation, combined with incomes policy, which is what the pactos were, were helpful at the start of the stabilization process, neither should have been kept too long. "The trouble is this," he said, "somewhere along the way, a U-turn must come to restore competitiveness – otherwise the currency ultimately goes over the cliff."[27]

In 1995, two US economists, in examining the durability of fixed exchange rates or exchange-rate bands, applied their analysis to the Mexican situation. The general conclusion of Obstfeld and Rogoff was that many efforts to peg exchange rates within narrow ranges ended in spectacular débâcles, citing not just Mexico in 1994, but earlier in Sweden and then in Great Britain when it tried to defend the pound's position in the currency grid of the European Monetary System (EMS).[28] The main lesson they drew from the Mexican model was that decision-makers faced an ever-worsening dilemma, whether to stand by the exchange rate and tolerate the depressing effects of overvaluation and high interest rates, or to ratify expectations, reaping some short-term gains in output but sacrificing long-term inflation credibility.[29] Until January 1995 – that is, until after the devaluation – the interest rate differential between three-month tesobonos and US Treasury Bills of similar maturity was between 1.75 and 3 percentage points, which was a measure of the risk investors placed on tesobono default. The gap between one-year tesobonos and cetes of similar maturity was higher, ranging between about 4 and 7 percentage points in 1994, which was an indication of the expected peso depreciation of the dollar.[30] It is hard to reach any conclusion other than one that portrays Mexico as being on knife edge and having created what was practically a no-win policy once the expectation solidified inside and outside the country that the peso could not hold its value with respect to the dollar.

Jeffrey Sachs and his colleagues concluded in a 1995 analysis that after the government ran down gross reserves in an effort to prop up the peso and ran up short-term dollar debt, expectations generating a panic became self-fulfilling.[31] The analysis lists three factors that complicated policy-making in Mexico: the political cycle; uncertainty about the course of future capital flows; and financial sector vulnerability.

Arnold Harberger, in a study prepared for Bancomer in Mexico, focused on what he calls the "real exchange rate" – that is, the peso adjusted by a price index in relation to a dollar of constant purchasing power. He gives much stress to the bad luck Mexico faced during the first half of the year, but then concludes:

> Still, I feel that it is likely that the authorities would have been somewhat more cautious, somewhat "tighter" in their policies, if 1994 had not been an election year, and if some banks were not experiencing problems with delinquent loans.[32]

It may be more informative to look at what Mexicans were thinking and doing as the events of 1994 progressed because they were closest to the scene. Mexican residents, based on an IMF analysis, were the first to put pressure on the country's foreign exchange reserves.[33] These were people acting rationally to protect their assets and those who could did so by getting out of pesos into dollars and other foreign currencies.

Since 1976, when the currency was sharply devalued at the end of the Echeverría administration, there has been a drop in the value of the peso at least every six years. Mexicans were conditioned to expect this again, especially in 1994 when there was general skepticism that the value of the peso could be maintained. Every Mexican who had reached the age of financial reason by 1976 – in effect, every Mexican who was about 20 then and was in his or her latter 30s or early 40s in 1994 – had experienced only repetitive currency depreciations. My impression, based on years of conversation with younger Mexicans, is that they believe hardly anything the government or the Bank of Mexico says about the currency, and turning this mental attitude around represents a major challenge for the Zedillo government as it comes to the end of its term and for future Mexican governments. Decades of conditioning to expect the worst about the national currency must be reversed if the authorities wish to prevent the expectation from becoming self-fulfilling.

Commercial bank fragility

The precarious position of Mexico's commercial banks during 1994 was both common knowledge and a major constraint on the monetary policy options pursued by the Bank of Mexico. The central bank did not want to aggravate the weakness of the banking structure by allowing interest rates to rise too much, even as the peso was under strain. A number of corrective actions to deal with non-performing loans were taken starting in 1992, but the situation continued to worsen.[34] By 1998, when the government concluded it must act forcefully rather than operate at the margins of the problem by controlling interest rates, the estimated cost of taking over the bad loans of the banking system were 17 percent of the 1997 GDP.[35] This figure could come down, depending on how many of the non-performing assets the government proposed to incorporate in its own portfolio could be sold, and at what price, and the cost was more likely to exceed the official estimate. This became a highly contentious issue when the government submitted legislation in 1998 for dealing with the bad loan problem in a manner roughly equivalent to what the United States did during the savings and loan (S&L) rescue in the Bush administration, of taking over the questionable assets and selling them at the best prices that could be obtained. These assets were held by the Fondo Bancario de Protección al Ahorro, or Fobaproa – roughly a deposit insurance fund. The main difference between the US S&L rescue and the proposed assumption of bank debt in Mexico is the scale, at least five times larger in Mexico in relation to GDP.

It is evident that the Bank of Mexico was reluctant to raise interest rates after the 1994 election, just as it was before the election, out of concern about worsening the problems of the banking structure.

Interest rates were not raised – indeed, they were "manipulated downwards."[36] One might have concluded that the fear about bank fragility would have reinforced the case for an exchange-rate depreciation to relieve the interest rate pressure. However, the authorities did nothing about the exchange rate; they decided to wait for another moment. It is hard to escape the conclusion that, as the third quarter came to an end, the Mexican financial officials chose the worst of all worlds – although they did not know how bad the outcome would be until three months later.

6
The Fourth Quarter of 1994 and Beyond

The conclusion of key policy-makers at the beginning of the fourth quarter – those from the outgoing administration and the incoming one as well – was that they could mark time for a few months on the related issues of peso overvaluation and the growing current account deficit. This was the essence of the decision taken in the pacto meeting of September 24 – that corrective action could wait until the new administration was in office. As the authorities learned to their everlasting chagrin, they were wrong.

Nevertheless, the end of a presidential electoral year is a busy time in Mexico. The outgoing president, Carlos Salinas, had to give his sixth and final *Informe* (state-of-the-nation address) summarizing his accomplishments while in office, and the new president who would be inaugurated on December 1 had to think about his cabinet.

By the start of the fourth quarter, it was clear both outside and within the government that the status quo was not durable. Capital was not flowing into Mexico, except via the continued sale of tesobonos – short-term debt with a dollar guarantee – which was a reflection of market distrust that the peso–dollar rate could be maintained. Inflation was coming down, but economic growth was weak. The US Federal Reserve further complicated the situation by raising short-term interest rates again on November 15, this time by 0.75 percent, the sixth increase in 1994, making it even more difficult for Mexico to attract foreign capital. Interest rates in Mexico were relatively high at that time, but were not raised further for several weeks. Concern persisted about the weak condition of commercial banks.

During the last year of almost every administration in Mexico, there is discussion of how much influence the outgoing president will have over his successor. This was certainly the case during the final months of the Salinas administration, in the light of the manner in which Zedillo was chosen to be the PRI candidate – not only by the traditional *dedazo* (finger pointing) by the incumbent president, but by a second Salinas *dedazo* after Colosio was assassinated. Many thought that Zedillo's lack of experience in internal PRI politics would leave him vulnerable to manipulation by Salinas. In actual experience, each new Mexican president almost always becomes an independent actor, a near-dictator for six years and then, with rare exceptions, a secondary figure in Mexico's high politics after he leaves office. Salinas, because of events at the very outset of the new Zedillo administration, became a political liability to the PRI and voluntarily absented himself from Mexico in March 1995, eventually to take up residence in Dublin.

The events of the final quarter of 1994 turned out to be more dramatic than anyone, even the most avid thrill-seekers, could have anticipated. There were further runs on Mexican reserves, starting in November and then accelerating in December. The peso was devalued a mere three weeks into the new administration and this precipitated a dramatic weakening of the currency. Mexico knew that it was subjecting itself to a possible exchange loss when it gave a dollar guarantee to tesobono holders and consciously factored this risk into its decision, but did not contemplate for a moment that the outstanding tesobonos could not be rolled over at all.[1] The "beyond" in the title to this chapter is to cover the period in early 1995 up to the point that the United States, in conjunction with the International Monetary Fund (IMF) and a number of central banks, provided massive support to permit Mexico to meet its obligation to redeem tesobonos as they became due.[2] The year 1995 turned out to be the worst year for the Mexican economy since the great depression of the 1930s, or perhaps since the country became enmeshed in its bloody Revolution and subsequent civil war.

The public face of the authorities

Mexico held its 58th national banking convention in Cancún in mid-October and the senior officials of the government concerned with economic policy addressed the assembled audience, as did the governor of the Bank of Mexico and the president of the Mexican Bankers' Association.[3] These speeches provide a good indication of what the business and banking communities, and by extension the public as a whole, were being told about the economic situation of Mexico as a change in administration was approaching.

President Salinas' remarks were perfunctory. He stressed the reduction of inflation that had been accomplished during his administration and said that the effort was to make low inflation permanent. He took credit for bank privatization, but gave little indication of the troubled state of many of the privatized banks. His central theme was that "ya vemos el futuro con la confianza... que podemos... ir más lejos." (We already see the future with the confidence that we can go much further.)[4]

Pedro Aspe's speech was a paean to the accomplishments of the previous six years – inflation brought down to less than 10 percent in 1994, 3 percent real economic growth, an increase in employment and real wages – and came to the conclusion that despite the tribulations of 1994, the reactivation of the country was "solid" and "permanent." Aspe praised the reform of the financial sector and the strengthening of financial supervision. In his peroration, he also asserted that as a result of the transformations of the previous six years, the Mexican economy had achieved considerable stability. He was effusive in his praise of Salinas.

Miguel Mancera focused first on the accomplishments of 1994, citing the launching of NAFTA, Mexico's acceptance into the Organization for Economic Cooperation and Development (OECD), the autonomy that was granted to the Bank of Mexico, and the continuation of the structural changes begun in 1987 with the pactos. He attributed the large current account deficit to capital inflows and he argued that the size of the deficit was less important than how the capital was used. This was the standard Bank position, enunciated in many speeches and Bank reports.

The most interesting parts of the speech were his references to the interest rate flexibility that had been followed and the "massive" placement of tesobonos, which diverted the shocks of the year to these instruments. He noted the frequent Bank intervention in the exchange market, but insisted that solidity still existed in that $17 billion of foreign reserves remained at the time of the convention. "El presidente Salinas deja un legado de congruencia en el gobierno de la economía que, estoy seguro, la historia habrá de reconocer." (President Salinas has left a legacy in the management of the economy that, I am sure, history will have to recognize.)[5]

In view of later events, it is worth quoting the opening sentences of the final paragraph of the speech by Roberto Hernández Ramírez, president of the Mexican Bankers' Association:

> Así es México hoy dia. Más que preocuparnos del déficit de la cuenta corriente, ocupémonos en trabajar con eficienca, en atraer capitales y en sentar las bases de un desarrollo sano en lo político y con un marco jurídico e institucional adecaudo. El déficit es incidental.[6]
>
> [Such is Mexico today. More than preoccupying ourselves with the current account deficit, we should engage ourselves in working with efficiency, to attract capital and to establish the basis for healthy political development, with an adequate juridical and institutional framework. The deficit is incidental.]

Only one of two possible conclusions can be drawn from this set of remarks: either those in charge of crafting financial and economic policy were whistling in the wind; or they were withholding the problematic side of economic policy from the general public. Just about every person I interviewed who was familiar with the proceedings of the banking convention – other than those who made the speeches – remarked on the fatuousness of the key speeches in light of what was taking place in Mexico.

The most important public speech during the fourth quarter was President Salinas' sixth *Informe* to the Congress on November 1.[7] The *Informe* usually contains a laundry list of events and accomplishments in many fields – national security, foreign relations, internal politics, macroeconomic and monetary policy, sectoral issues, juridical matters, education, health, poverty alleviation, among other themes – and this one was no exception. Because this was Salinas' final *Informe*, it also set forth what he believed were the main accomplishments of his sexenio, during which, mostly in the first five years, he was an activist chief executive. The discussion here will focus on the economic–financial content of the speech.

Among the accomplishments Salinas cited were the entry into force of NAFTA, the conclusion of other trade agreements, the reduction of inflation, the recovery from the economic problems that erupted in 1982, and the balanced public-sector budget. He did not mention that while the public-sector budget would be in balance or surplus in 1994, there were substantial extra-budgetary expenditures through the development banks. He made much of Mexico's ability to borrow in foreign markets and said that the natural counterpart to this surplus in the capital account was a deficit in the current account. On this, he said much the same as Mancera had at the banking convention, that the inflow of foreign capital had been used to finance private investment, an assertion that, by and large, was inaccurate. Exchange-rate policy, he said, provided an atmosphere of certainty fostering investment and served to maintain the competitiveness of the economy even as it helped to bring down inflation. This, as the unfolding events demonstrated, was not the case. It would have been quite a feat to have accomplished all of these objectives simultaneously – constraining inflation and augmenting competitiveness – by steady real appreciation of the peso with respect to the dollar over a six-year period.

The tone of the speech, in its economic and other aspects, is that all is well in Mexico. Further changes will be needed, but the reforms of the past six years put Mexico on the right track. This kind of optimism may be the inevitable nature of a state-of-the-union address, particularly one that comes at the end of a six-year period of considerable change. However, the speech did little to alert either the congress or the general public to the real problems that Mexico faced as Salinas was getting ready to turn over the reins of government to Zedillo.

Behind the scenes

Both Salinas in his *Informe*, and Mancera in his speech to the banking convention in Cancún, highlighted the fact that the level of Mexico's foreign reserves, at more than $17 billion, was adequate to defend the value of the peso. The actual reserve level on October 19, when Mancera spoke, was close to $17.3 billion, and on October 31, the day before the Salinas *Informe*, it was $17.2 billion. The reserve level started to go down on November 3, almost as a sign that the reassurance of the president was a signal to get out of pesos. However, the Bank of Mexico did not begin intervening in the market to protect the peso until November 14. Total intervention between that day and the end of November was $3.2 billion and reserves at the month's end were down to $12.5 billion.[8]

The Bank of Mexico, in its *Annual Report* and other literature, attributed the large reserve loss in mid-November to the resignation of Mario Ruiz Massieu as assistant attorney general and his allegation that he did this because the investigation of his brother's assassination was being impeded by his superiors. Much of the reserve loss in November followed the Mario Ruiz Massieu resignation, but by no means all; the full reserve loss in November was $4.7 billion and the drop in reserves following the resignation was $3.7 billion. The Bank's effort to link each case of large reserve losses during the year to some exogenous incident – the Colosio assassination in March, the aborted resignation of the secretary of *Gobernación* (Interior) in June, Ruiz Massieu's charges in November, and then the report of renewed hostilities by the EZLN (Zapatista Army of National Liberation) in December – has the flavor of Wall Street analysts explaining the behavior of the stock market based on daily events, but omitting the larger picture of underlying strength and weakness of the economy. The Bank was being disingenuous by blaming all the troubles on outside, non-economic and non-monetary, matters.

The rapid deterioration of the situation after considerable stability in the level of foreign reserves from the third week in April to mid-November prompted the leadership to meet on November 20 in President Salinas' private residence to discuss the situation. Those present included President Salinas, President-elect Zedillo, Pedro Aspe (Secretary of *Hacienda*) Jaime Serra Puche (then Secretary of Secofi, the foreign-trade ministry), Arsenio Farell (an elder statesman whose judgment was respected by most of the key players), Miguel Mancera (Governor of the Bank of Mexico), and Luis Tellez (earlier a subcabinet official the agriculture department and who was to be Zedillo's chief of staff).[9] The occurrence of this meeting has been reported extensively. In his interview with me, Serra Puche said that the general view of the assembled group was to devalue the peso, and that Salinas said this was acceptable if deemed necessary.[10] Serra said that the discussion covered a variety of techniques for carrying out a devaluation, including but not limited to raising the upper limit of the band. A communication by Aspe to the Mexican press and repeated later in a column in the *Wall Street Journal*, confirmed that the discussion covered a " 'small' devaluation of 10 percent to 15 percent," a free float, or a drastic rise in interest rates to obviate the need to devalue.[11] But Aspe contradicted the view that the meeting ended with consensus. He stated that:

1 Much of the capital flight was due to the perception that Mexico was not willing to bear the cost of defending the exchange-rate band.
2 The peso had depreciated considerably within the band, but the Salinas administration had never carried out an abrupt movement of the band. Mexico could not succeed in carrying out a

"small" devaluation because this would surely lead to additional devaluation in less than 24 hours.
3 Any decision on exchange-rate policy should not be carried out in isolation but be accompanied by a global economic package.
4 If President-elect Zedillo would ratify the existing pacto, which contained the promise to defend the exchange-rate band, this in all likelihood would stop the attack on the peso; and if this did not work and international reserves fell below $10 billion, the group would meet again to decide on a new strategy.

Zedillo, he noted, ratified the pacto that night and this stopped the attack on the peso and, in fact, the peso appreciated slightly within the band from November 21 to November 30.

In my interviews, I found many persons who found the letter self-serving and others who thought it was "absolutamente fiel" (absolutely faithful) in its description of the meeting. These differing views are largely influenced by the interlocutor's opinion on the decisions made in the course of 1994 and on each person's regard for or disagreement with Aspe. On the facts, Aspe is correct that the reserve level stabilized on November 21 and remained stable until mid-December, by which time the new administration was in place and Aspe had been replaced as *Hacienda* secretary by Serra. The reserve level did not go below the $10 billion level that Aspe set as the marker until December 21.

Zedillo suggested at or immediately following the November 20 meeting that Serra leave his position as Secofi secretary and move to Los Pinos, the presidential residence and office, as financial advisor to the president.[12] By this time it was known that Serra would replace Aspe in *Hacienda* in the new government. Aspe reportedly responded that if this were to be done, why not name Serra finance minister immediately rather than leave him – Aspe – there as a lame duck. I was told – not by Serra – that Serra objected to Aspe's suggestion because if he were named *Hacienda* secretary then, before the transition, only to carry out a hurried devaluation, this would destroy his entire tenure.

I was told by several informants that Aspe, in fact, tried to remain for a time as *Hacienda* secretary in order to manage the transition. The information given to me was that he asked to remain for an additional three months after Zedillo became president and he would provide a signed letter assuring his resignation after that. This was not accepted. Aspe, I was told, was offered another cabinet or cabinet-level position, but not *Hacienda*, but he refused the offer. I was told further that the *cúpula* of the private sector (literally, the dome or vault, but as used here, the peak level) lobbied quite hard with Zedillo to retain Aspe as *Hacienda* secretary, not just for three months but for at least a year. This group had little confidence that Serra had the experience or temperament to be an effective head of *Hacienda*. There is an important body of opinion in both Mexico and outside the country that the *fracaso* (calamity) that occurred with the December 20 devaluation would have been avoided had Aspe remained. Who can say?

The new administration

Ernesto Zedillo assumed the presidency on December 1. The transition from the Salinas administration was not smooth and the start of the new government was not auspicious.

I was told repeatedly by insiders that the briefings of the new cabinet secretaries by the outgoing ones were largely superficial. Part of the responsibility rests with Zedillo in that much of the incoming cabinet was chosen late. This was not the case, however, for Serra, who was chosen early. Yet, informant after informant told me that Serra did not know many of the key details that surrounded his main responsibilities. I cannot say whether this was because of Serra's failure to seek this information or Aspe's reluctance to provide it. A senior person in a position to know put it this way: "Uno no preguntó, y el otro no contestó." (The one did not ask and the other did not answer.) The general impression among insiders was that relations between the two men were cool – that they were seen as rivals. Serra found no contingency plan when he took office, although the implicit understanding of Aspe's description of the meeting on November 20 was that a Plan B would be carried out if foreign reserves fell below $10 billion.

Many senior officers below the cabinet level said they were convinced that Zedillo himself received only scant briefing on key issues before he took office. He knew about many problems because he had been part of the government earlier, but not in the year before the final decision-making power became his. The elaborate transition structure that has become common in the United States when administrations change does not exist in Mexico. The transition was difficult in 1976 and again in 1982 and costly in 1994 because of the delicate situation in the country's financial structure and the waning confidence in government policy.

Serra, when he spoke with me, said that he believed that Mexico needs an improved built-in transition mechanism, particularly now that the country's democratic opening might bring in a non-PRI president. Serra added that the timetable for submission of the new budget to the congress when a new administration assumes power is December 15, an unreasonable two weeks after entry into office. Serra's focus on his budget presentation when he came to *Hacienda* was subjected to considerable criticism – that he was fiddling while the financial system was burning – but more on this below. Many of the key subordinates in *Hacienda* left that ministry when Serra arrived and he thought that the information gap that resulted from this experience could be mitigated if there were a more permanent civil service, at least in that ministry.

Zedillo's cabinet was not well received. A phrase that captures the disappointment is that it was a cabinet of *subsecretarios* (vice ministers). Private-sector leaders and Zedillo dined together at the Anthropological Museum in Mexico City on December 2, the day after the inauguration. One participant told me that it was an icy affair and then, in a separate discussion afterwards, Zedillo said that when he was nominated, there were capital outflows and a fall in the stock market (*bolsa*); when he won the election, the reaction was similar; and after his inaugural address, the same thing happened. This may be apocryphal and the facts on reserve and *bolsa* behavior overstated, but the story is an accurate metaphor for the initial relationship between the business community and the new government.

Zedillo's inaugural address was not inspirational.[13] It did not deal with the sensitive financial issues then in play. The beginning of the new administration was still a time of testing between it and the private sector and the initial reaction was that the government should receive a failing grade. The Zedillo government, as several informants phrased it, did not enjoy a honeymoon.

Serra devoted much of his time immediately after he took over *Hacienda* working on the budget that he was required to submit to the congress and then getting detailed briefings for his congressional testimony. This meant that he had less time for what turned out to be more pressing matters, such as the financial collapse that took place just five days after the legal deadline for the budget submission. The question arises as to whether this mattered. The decision already had been made to defer exchange-rate decisions until the new year and Serra might not have given more thought to this issue even if the budget submission were not required. However, it also meant that Serra had less time for discussion with dissenters about policy dealing with the most important economic issues facing the country. An issue like capital flight and the value of the peso with respect to the dollar could not be set in concrete – or should not have been – subject to no reconsideration during the critical period at the start of a new administration.

The budget, when submitted, was considered so unrealistic as to be ludicrous. One of Serra's closest advisors and defenders of his later actions at the time of the devaluation, Pascual García Alba Iduñate, told me that the handling of the budget and its content was an error.[14] The budget, he said, can be approved in general and have built-in flexibility depending on the revenue that is received. Another informant said the same thing in slightly different words, that the submission could have been more tentative and still have met the legal requirement, and that this would have been acceptable because everyone knew the government had just come into office.

One of the most devastating commentaries on the budget, as submitted, was a cartoon in the newspaper *Reforma* showing a department store Santa Claus broken up by laughter, with Serra on his lap holding a scroll with the words: "1995: inflation 4 percent, growth 4 percent, 800 000 new jobs."[15] The budget document, on which Serra worked so hard, seriously damaged his credibility and the full fallout from this came a week later when the peso was devalued. This reaction, that his intensive focus on the budget showed that Serra did not have his priorities right, was one that came up repeatedly in my conversations about the first days of the new government. The tendency of senior officials to avoid outside contacts apparently prevailed even when officials of one government were leaving and the top team of the new government took over.

Foreign reserves, which had been holding at about $12 billion from the time of the November 20 meeting, fell below that level on December 15. This was almost certainly unrelated to the budgetary submission, which had not really been taken seriously by the informed public. Heavy intervention in the exchange market began on December 15, when the Bank of Mexico sold $119 million, then $855 million on December 16 (a Friday), and $701 million on the following Monday, December 19. Foreign reserves on December 19 fell to less than $10.5 billion, close to the arbitrary $10 billion that Aspe felt earlier was the critical level that should call for a reconsideration of policy.

There were reports that same day that Zapatista rebels had occupied 38 municipalities in Chiapas – a report that later turned out to be false. This false report made the reserve position even more precarious, and questions about financial stability even more urgent.[16] The budget, which already was dead on arrival, now had another stake put through its heart. There was no longer any doubt that job one was to restore some credibility to financial policy.

The pacto meeting, December 19–20

The rationalization that the foreign reserve level was sufficient to defend the value of the peso no longer existed. The decision, therefore, was made to call a meeting of the pacto to discuss the next steps on macroeconomic policy, and particularly the exchange rate. The pacto had become the instrument through which economic decisions were made. This form of corporate decision-making came naturally in any event to Mexicans in light of the history of corporatism since the 1930s. Beyond this, several informants told me that Serra wanted the approval of the pacto members as reinforcement when the exchange-rate structure was changed, and it was evident that this outcome would result from the pacto meeting. I was told that he originally hoped to have the full pacto membership present, about 60–75 people, but in the end a truncated group was invited, although still about half that number. Serra consulted with Mancera before calling the meeting and he obviously had the consent of the president. Zedillo was out of the city, in Sonora, when the meeting was held.

Using the pacto, with its private-sector membership, as the vehicle for deciding on the exchange rate drew little open criticism in all the years after 1987, when the pacto structure was designed, but this procedure was criticized by many for the December 19 meeting. This was essentially a meeting that would lead to a radical exchange-rate shift, something that had not been the case previously, except at the first pacto meeting, which also led to a sharp devaluation.

There were interested private parties at the pacto meeting whose personal or institutional situations would be vitally affected by the outcome and there were questions about this special position on a matter of universal, national interest. In addition, the representative of the commercial banks at the meeting was influential – perhaps, decisive – in changing the outcome from the initial position of the governmental and central bank actors to one that took the situation of the banks into account. Andres Oppenheimer quotes Jesús Silva Herzog, a former *Hacienda* secretary and ambassador to the United States during the Zedillo administration, as saying that "You don't discuss a devaluation with anybody . . . not even with your wife."[17] This was a sentiment I heard repeatedly from *Hacienda* and Bank of Mexico officials and Mexican scholars who study financial issues.

Would the criticism of using the pacto meeting to negotiate the form that devaluation took have been as harsh if the aftershocks had not ensued? Probably not. But the repercussions of the December 19–20 decision were catastrophic and it was thus natural that the questionable manner in which the decision was made was censured.

Santiago Oñate, who was then Secretary of labor, told me that Serra started to call him early in the morning of December 19, about 9.30 he recalled, and he added that cabinet officers usually don't start calling until about 11 a.m., after they have reviewed the morning's intake.[18] Oñate was in his office early that day, about 6–6.30 a.m., because he had to deal with an incipient mining strike. Serra, he said, clearly was upset about the report of events in Chiapas and planned to call a meeting of the pacto that afternoon. Oñate's responsibility was to get the consent of Fidel Velázquez, the long-time labor leader, to the expected announcement that night of a devaluation and Don Fidel, he said, assured him that he would support the president.

The meeting got under way in the afternoon of Monday, December 19, and did not adjourn until the early hours of Tuesday morning. The opening position of the Bank of Mexico, supported by all the key government players there, was to allow the peso to float and find its own level.[19] This also was Serra's favored position and, he told me, that of President Zedillo. The key government player at the meeting was Serra because the decisive vote was that of *Hacienda*. Mancera had a bad cold and was not at his best. Serra said that the first reaction of the private-sector participants to the idea of floating was negative. They were concerned with the psychological fallout and were convinced that the situation could be handled with only a minor adjustment. The discussion was lengthy.

José Madariaga Lomelín, then President of the Mexican bankers' association, argued in favor of raising the band by 15 percent rather than floating.[20] In the end, that was what was done. Serra said he and Mancera consulted with each other and then called Zedillo, who consented to this outcome. The announcement of the decision was made the next morning on the radio by Serra.

Mexico was then full of assertions and rumors about the decision to lift the band rather than float. Ignacio Trigueros, a senior research economist at the Instituto Tecnológico Autónomo de México (ITAM), told me he believed the banks could cover their dollar position with the peso at 4 to the dollar[21]; the market rate was then less than 3.5 pesos to the dollar and a 15 percent increase in the band, assuming the peso moved all the way to the top of the band but no more, would have left the peso at about 4 to $1. Others, both in the private sector and in the Bank of Mexico, were suspicious that the motive of the banks was to buy time to cover short positions in dollars before the peso depreciated too much. There was much discussion as to whether the insiders at the pacto meeting could cover their positions between the time the meeting ended, about 3 a.m., and the announcement about 4 hours later. The Mexican market was closed, but not European markets; and covering themselves need not have required selling pesos to directly acquire dollars, but could have taken the form of purchases of other securities. I tried to verify whether this was done, but the evidence was inconclusive. I am unable to state for certain that insiders at the meeting took advantage of the knowledge of devaluation they had before it was available to the general public, both inside and outside Mexico, but giving this opportunity to selected interested parties must inevitably raise suspicions.

For the first day after the announcement, the money markets were calm, but then all hell broke loose. The Bank of Mexico, on December 21, used $4.5 billion of its already meager reserves to intervene to protect the new ceiling. On that day, the reserve level fell to $5.8 billion. On the following day, December 22, the foreign exchange commission agreed to float the peso. This did not end the speculation against the peso, which continued well into 1995.

Did the decision to raise the band, in isolation from other reinforcing measures, lead to more panic than would have been the case if the peso had been allowed to float instead? It is hard to say with confidence what the road not taken looks like. Mancera, in his interview with me, would say only that with the benefit of hindsight, it would have been better to have floated immediately.[22] President Zedillo said that he thought that this discussion is largely irrelevant, that once confidence was destroyed, the outcome would have been the same under immediate floating and raising the band.[23] Arnold Harberger, in an evaluation from the outside, thought that it was a "great mistake" not to allow the currency to float because the continued existence of the exchange-rate band, even with a higher ceiling, assured speculators that there would be no downside risk.[24]

Pedro Aspe's assertion, as reflected in his public position on the discussion at the November 20 meeting, turned out to be right – Mexico was unable to pull off a "small" devaluation. We do not know if the outcome would have been better if the change in the exchange rate – whether raising the band or floating – had been accompanied by complementary macroeconomic measures. When I put this matter to Zedillo – why was the action on the exchange rate taken in isolation – his response was that the devaluation was not a measured decision of straightforward political-economy theory, but a necessary action that had to be taken immediately. If not, he said, Mexico would have been out of reserves, perhaps in a matter of hours. Delay until January, which is what he said he had hoped for, was simply not possible.

The fallout

By the end of the work week, on December 23, the sales of tesobonos were brisk. When the ceiling of the exchange-rate band was raised on December 20, outstanding tesobonos were a little more than $20 billion. Three days later, they were in excess of $22 billion. The way it was put to me by Arturo Fernández, who had earlier been an advisor to Serra, was that those who had not already discovered the hedging value of tesobonos did so after the devaluation.[25] Those who wanted to protect their peso assets had a ready instrument for shifting to dollars.

One reason for the delay in the panic reaction of market players, particularly outside the country, was that the existence of the large, outstanding stock of tesobonos finally was noticed.[26] The level of outstanding tesobonos was not kept secret, but the New York market players were not paying attention to this.[27] The financial houses knew that foreign reserves were low – although not all knew how low – but for some reason little attention was given to the excess of short-term tesobonos outstanding as compared with reserves in hand until after the devaluation. On December 20, reserves were $10.4 billion and tesobonos outstanding were $20 billion, a difference of $10 billion. The difference between the two widened on December 23 to more than $16 billion.

Serra went to New York, where, on December 22, he received a cold reception. He insisted there, as he did in Mexico when he announced the exchange-rate change, that the act should be referred to as raising the ceiling of the band and not a devaluation. He was mocked in media articles in Mexico for systematically avoiding the word "devaluation" in radio interviews on the morning of December 20.[28] This hair-splitting, as they saw it, also annoyed the New York bankers who met with Serra.

Serra, together with others, also saw Alan Greenspan and other Fed officials in Washington a few days later and this led to some Fed purchases of pesos to strengthen the Mexican currency. Even then, however, the full dimensions of the financial and economic fallout from the December 20 devaluation had not been fully absorbed. One persistent complaint of New York investment bankers was that Serra did not respond to their telephone calls after the devaluation was announced. James Jones, the US ambassador in Mexico, heard this over and over from the bankers and he told me that it took Serra a day to answer even his telephone calls.[29] Jones puts great stress on this lack of communication as an element in the economic breakdown.

Serra's version of this charge is different.[30] He said he was appearing on radio programs constantly on the morning of December 20 because his first obligation was to inform the Mexican people. His subsecretary took telephone calls, and then he took them when he completed his radio interviews. The most frequent question asked in these calls, he said, was along the lines: "Why didn't you tell me in advance about the devaluation?" Part of the problem here was the fact that Mexican bankers and businessmen knew about the devaluation several hours in advance from the pacto meeting. This is obviously a sensitive point for Serra. He responded to a survey on Mexico that appeared in the *Economist* on October 28, 1995, which contained the phrase that he had "pre-announced his devaluation to a coterie of leading Mexican businessmen."[31] His letter to the *Economist* argues that its assertion misrepresents what happened in that it ignored the existence of the pacto, a key part of the stabilization program.[32]

Serra submitted his letter of resignation to President Zedillo on December 25. He told me that Zedillo at first resisted and said that it was too quick for a cabinet change, but then accepted it on December 29.

Serra became the fall guy, the person who was sacrificed as the new Zedillo government moved on to deal with the damage that resulted from what turned out to be disastrous policies. He was blamed for much – for not having the experience and savvy in dealing with money market players in New York and elsewhere, reacting too slowly to fast-breaking market developments in the financial sector because he had become too used to dealing with slower-moving trade matters, for using the pacto to decide on exchange-rate issues (even though this mechanism had been so used for seven years), for being too certain of his knowledge and therefore not open to other opinions, and simply because he was in charge when the whole house of cards came tumbling down. In a sense, this is just; those in charge of public matters must take responsibility for calamities that occur during their watches. In other respects, this calumny is unfair; Serra inherited a problem that both he and President Zedillo thought could be dealt with a few weeks later. The broader theme – why did honest, well trained, intelligent people, Serra included, make major errors of judgment – will be revisited at greater length in Chapter 9.

"El error de diciembre" (The error of December)

The question of whether the disaster that befell Mexico was the result of incorrect actions taken in December or the consequence of inadequate policy decisions throughout 1994, and even earlier, was revived within Mexico by former President Salinas a year later. He sent a statement, dated December 3, 1995, which was widely circulated in the Mexican media.[33] Salinas used two phrases, which he said were not original with him, which have since become embedded in political folk language in Mexico. The first is that he was made Mexico's "favorite villain" (*villano favorito*) by groups that had particular grievances or some special interest. He used this expression as a takeoff to review the accomplishments of his administration.[34] Salinas highlighted how both the economy and the politics of Mexico had been opened during his sexenio; his practice of "social liberalism" that, as he put it, was clearly different from neoliberalism; and the fact that when he left the presidency, the Bank of Mexico still had $12 billion of foreign reserves.

Some of this recitation is undoubtedly true, particularly that the economy was opened during his administration and this changed the direction of Mexico's development policy. Some is self-serving, in that "social liberalism," his phrase for the Solidarity program he initiated, among other measures, did little or nothing to reverse the profound inequalities and poverty in Mexico. Some is too clever by half, such as the fact that foreign reserves during his last year in office fell from a high of more than $29 billion. And some is more inaccurate than factual in that he deliberately held back political opening as best he could in order to carry out his economic opening.

The second phrase is more germane to the discussion of Mexico's financial and economic policy. He was not responsible, he said, for the "error of December" – that is, the devaluation of December 20. He had, he said, always fought to avoid abrupt devaluations. During his tenure, he added, the *desliz*, or daily crawl, depreciated the peso by more than 50 percent. The problem with the tesobonos, which he said were always publicly announced, did not come solely from their magnitude, but also because foreign investors lost confidence in this instrument after the December 20 devaluation.

Salinas' statement on the error of December epitomizes the debate that exists to this day in Mexico, whether the buildup of problems – the drawing down of reserves, the growing short-term, dollar-indexed debt, the large current account deficit – or the handling of the exchange-rate change was the main culprit in the economic disaster that befell Mexico. To a large extent, this is a false dichotomy. The vulnerabilities were created during the Salinas years and the final shock that set off what has been referred to as the inevitable crisis came a few weeks after he left office. The two are not fully separable.

The general sentiment of economic observers is that Mexico had little choice on December 20 to take some action to deal with its disappearing foreign reserves. This, however, is not a universal sentiment. Robert L. Bartley, the editor of the *Wall Street Journal*, argued in an editorial column two years after the event that it was this very mindset that Mexico had to correct its "real exchange rate" that brought disaster.[35] By his count, he says, there are three Mexicans who are willing to challenge the basic argument that one can determine the real exchange rate and that the effects of "overvaluation" or "undervaluation" from this dubious base are doleful. One can also count three American sources that believe that Mexico should not have devalued, or once this was done, should have taken action to restore the old value – the *Wall Street Journal* editorial page, the Republican presidential hopeful Malcolm (Steve) Forbes, Jr., and the actual vice presidential candidate of the Republican Party in 1996, Jack Kemp. Bartley had a reprise to his arguments later when he argued: "Toying with a little devaluation sooner or later leads to a lot – and is a scourge to be avoided."[36]

Mexico's immediate response

It took some time before the sizeable effects of the reaction to the December 20 devaluation sank in, either in Mexico or the United States. On December 22, when Serra was still in charge at *Hacienda*, Mexico's swap lines with the United States and Canada of US$6 and C$1 billion, respectively, were activated, presumably because all parties thought this amount of resource support would provide some market confidence. It did not and the peso continued to depreciate, reaching a low in December of 5.7 to the dollar, more than a 65 percent nominal depreciation from the rate that existed at the end of November. Mexico canceled its scheduled auction of tesobonos on December 27. The financial support package was enlarged on January 2, 1995, to $18 billion, of which $9 billion was from the United States. This was an expansion of $3 billion from the earlier swap line. The other contributors to the package were $5 billion from various governments operating through the Bank for International Settlements (BIS), C$1.5 billion from Canada (about US$1.1 billion), and $3 billion from international banks.

Guillermo Ortiz Martínez was appointed to succeed Jaime Serra Puche as *Hacienda* secretary on December 29. Ortiz had been the principal subsecretary under Pedro Aspe and had a long career in the Bank of Mexico and at one point was Mexico's executive director at the IMF. When Zedillo first named his cabinet, Ortiz was made Secretary of Communications and Transport. As Ortiz was shifted to *Hacienda*, talks were opened with the IMF and the World Bank.

The Mexican authorities at this time announced measures to liberalize foreign participation in commercial banks, something which had been quite limited earlier. This limitation had been reflected in the NAFTA provisions; I was told by Sergio Ghigliazzi García, then the director of the Center for Monetary Studies of Latin America (CEMLA), headquartered in Mexico City, that Mancera had long been opposed to a large foreign participation in Mexican banks.[37] Ghigliazzi had been a senior official of the Bank of Mexico and served on a number of advisory commissions to the Bank dealing with foreign exchange, general credit, and other issues. The key Mexican dealing with financial issues in the NAFTA negotiations told me the same thing, that the Bank of Mexico officials wished to limit foreign participation in the banking sector in order to better control monetary policy.[38] Now, in light of the emergency, these restrictions were eased. The opening to foreign banks led to substantial change in the structure of banking in Mexico. Of the 18 banks that were privatized in 1991–2, four were controlled by foreign capital in mid-1998, five were controlled by the original owners, eight were merged or no longer existed, and one was seeking a foreign partner.[39]

On January 3, Mexico announced a new economic program. It had an inflation target of 19.5 percent, a growth target of 1.5 percent, and a reduction in the current account deficit from the $29 billion of 1994 to $14 billion. The IMF endorsed the program. The program was wildly unrealistic.[40] It was only later, on January 12, after the United States indicated that it would seek approval of a $40 billion rescue package from the Congress, that there was full recognition of the seriousness of the Mexican economic crisis.

7
Back in Washington and New York

When, on December 20, 1994, the Mexican financial and monetary authorities raised the band within which the peso was permitted to fluctuate by 15 percent, the expectation in Washington was for a short-lived shock, some economic adjustment, and then back to business as usual with a modestly devalued peso. Mexico, after all, had a history of currency devaluations, particularly during transitions from one administration to another. Beyond that, Mexico was not a world monetary powerhouse and its exchange-rate gyrations would not normally attract great or sustained international attention.

The action, instead, turned out to be an economic disaster for the Mexican people – it was not back to business as usual – and an object lesson of the disinterested cruelty of players in the international financial market when they conclude that a nation's economic policy is not worthy of respect. The Mexican experience took on milepost significance; students of the monetary system and players in the financial market now talk of what happened in Mexico in before-and-after terms – before the devaluation and the global consequences afterwards. When the financial and economic crisis erupted in East Asia in 1997, it became clear that financial crises that build slowly and erupt abruptly were not unique to Mexico.

The Mexican experience led to many changes in the way official international financial institutions do their business. The International Monetary Fund (IMF) secured international commitments to enable it to raise substantial funds rapidly for use should there be another Mexican-type blowout. Dissemination of information on economic variables of countries has been strengthened. Mexico, along with other countries, now has a web site where this information is available reasonably currently. Private financial institutions, like pension funds and investment houses, now pay more attention to variables they largely ignored earlier, like the growth of short-term tesobono sales by the Mexican authorities. The financial authorities did what is normal in the aftermath of an unexpected tragedy – they prepared themselves to fight repetitions of the last débâcle, but were still unprepared for the East Asian meltdown that moved rapidly from country to country in 1997.

The US Treasury and the Federal Reserve Board in Washington tracked developments in Mexico quite closely in 1994. So did the IMF and the World Bank. Private financial intermediaries had an obligation to protect the assets of their clients. When the blowout occurred, all these foreign actors, public and private, had to react. Many did in panic, others entered as rescuers.

This chapter deals with this foreign component. The questions asked here are similar to those made familiar during the Watergate investigation in the US Congress: What did the foreign actors know, when did they know it, and what did they do? The rescue operation mounted jointly by the US government and the IMF, with contingent backup from many central banks operating through the Bank for International Settlements (BIS), made whole most investors in tesobonos. This highlighted the issue of moral hazard, of why governments and international institutions should rescue investors seeking relatively high returns, and how this issue will be treated in the future.

The public record to assess these issues is far from complete, but much documentation is available, particularly of the thinking and actions of US government agencies. The international financial institutions are more secretive, but not completely so. The published material has been augmented by conversations with key policy actors and private market players, who will be identified unless a commitment was made not to do so in order to elicit frank opinions.

The presentation that follows covers thinking outside Mexico of events and policies within Mexico that preceded the December 1994 devaluation, actions that were taken (or not taken) on the basis of this analysis, reactions that followed the devaluation, and then the motivations for the peso rescue package.

Tracking events before the US and international rescue package

Much has been written about how surprised foreign governments, international financial institutions, and private investors were by the sudden and drastic collapse of confidence in the peso. There had been expressions of concern coming from outside Mexico as early as 1993 and throughout 1994 about what was felt to be the increasing overvaluation of the peso and growing deficit in the current account of the balance of payments, but for the most part these were low key. The general sentiment was that some corrections were needed, that they probably would come in due course, and that would be that. On the whole, the management of economic policy in Mexico was given high praise. Carlos Salinas, the president, and Pedro Aspe, the Secretary of *Hacienda*, were the darlings of official foreign institutions and market investors. Even the most severe critics did not foresee the extent of the collapse that would follow the raising of the exchange-rate band on December 20, 1994.

The chronology of key events (p. xviii) will ease the tracking of events in Mexico for the reader up to the time of the rescue package.[1] The listing contains the main developments to which officials and traders were reacting.

The US Treasury

The material that follows is presented from the public record, which is then amplified from statements obtained in personal interviews. Contextual commentary is interspersed with the description of the events, and concluding commentary is provided as well.

Lawrence Summers, then Undersecretary of the Treasury for international affairs and the senior US official dealing on a regular basis with the Mexico economic situation, has said that as the year 1994 progressed his assessment of the outcome in Mexico became progressively more pessimistic. He started the year by comparing the Mexico situation with what had happened in Argentina a few years earlier, that there would be an exchange-rate adjustment with a temporary adverse effect on economic growth, but in the end the country would emerge with a more stable currency and economic recovery. In later months, he compared Mexico with the situation in France a year earlier, when the country faced serious exchange-rate problems, but manageable in a technical sense. Just before the crisis erupted, his comparison was with the experience in the United Kingdom not many years before, and he feared that Mexico was headed for a crash.[2]

The public record

This exercise in increasingly dire comparisons was *ex post* reconstruction of Summers' mood during 1994, but it conforms well with the story portrayed in internal Treasury documents – with one exception. The one aspect that looks more like rationalization than expectation is that the Treasury as a whole did not expect the severity of the crash that occurred after the exchange-rate band was lifted. Discussions with other Treasury officials revealed that the professional staff engaged in a speculative pool on how much the peso would depreciate – whether the full 15 percent provided for by the Mexican action on December 20, more than that, or less. The mean appraisal was that the peso would depreciate by 9 percent – that is, would remain within the new band – and hold there for a while.[3] This would not have been a catastrophic outcome, but rather almost business as usual with the added advantage of a more properly priced peso. That benign assessment was proved inaccurate almost immediately and the Bank of Mexico, after losing about $4 billion of its already dwindled reserves trying to protect the ceiling of the new band, allowed the peso to float on December 22.

In a series of memoranda starting early in 1994, the Treasury professional staff exhibited what is best described as low-key concern about the economic situation in Mexico.[4] Thus, Jeffrey Shafer, then Assistant Secretary for international affairs, on February 10 advised Summers who was traveling to Mexico a week later, that the two operational issues on his agenda were the enlargement of the swap line with Mexico and the formation of a consultative mechanism. The motive of these initiatives was to improve financial cooperation in the wake of NAFTA, which had gone into effect just a month earlier. Summers also was advised to tell Aspe, Mexico's Finance Secretary, that he was concerned that maintaining the peso at its then nominal level would "at some point" erode Mexico's trade competitiveness.[5] Yes, there was concern about the exchange rate, but it clearly was perfunctory. Other issues had higher priority.

The Treasury at this time was receiving bi-weekly reports from its attaché at the US embassy in Mexico City. The report of February 15 raised the issues of the fragility of Mexico's balance-of-payments situation because of the "large dependence on portfolio investments which are potentially volatile," and the almost sole reliance on interest-rate rather than currency adjustments to attract continued capital inflows. The comment was interesting because in the same report, the embassy noted that the rate on 28-day Mexican Treasury Bills (cetes) had fallen the week before to their lowest rate ever.

The US Federal Reserve began its program of steady increases in the federal funds rate on February 4. Shafer, in a memorandum of

March 8, noted that rising US interest rates, coinciding with historically low Mexican rates, were leading to a falloff in capital flows into Mexico. Somewhat more concern became evident after the assassination of Luis Donaldo Colosio on March 23. On the following day, the managing director of the IMF, Michel Camdessus, sent a letter to Lloyd Bentsen, the Secretary of the US Treasury, with a copy to Alan Greenspan, Chairman of the Federal Reserve Board of Governors, noting the uncertainty this created and suggested initiatives to provide Mexico with a secondary line of reserves. The tone of the letter was calm, stating that Mexico has "dealt with these pressures." The generally relaxed attitude of the Fund to economic developments in Mexico in 1994 will be covered below.

An internal memorandum to Shafer at about this time noted that the Bank of Mexico had intervened in financial markets every working day from March 23 to April 5, selling $5.2 billion of its foreign reserves. The interventions slackened after that, but as of April 15, reserves had fallen from $29 billion earlier to $20.2 billion. This memorandum added: "In our view, Mexico's current exchange rate policy is sustainable." This, in general, was the view of the international institutions as well, even if not always of the academic community. Rudiger Dornbusch, of the Massachusetts Institute of Technology, in a memorandum for the New York Federal Reserve, argued, as he had elsewhere then and later, that the "exchange rate-based stabilization strategy has led to an overvaluation, a potentially precarious financial situation, and a lack of growth."

Between April and September, many of the concerns stimulated in the United States by the events in Chiapas and the murder of Colosio were put on the back burner. At the end of April, international reserves were $17.3 billion and they were back to that level by mid-October, with only modest variations up and down in the interim. The murder of José Francisco Ruiz Massieu on September 28 had no immediate impact on the reserve level. The Mexican presidential election of August 21 went in favor of the PRI – that is, of the establishment – and this also calmed external observers. The loss of reserves did not recur until November. Nevertheless, the Treasury staff on October 27 advised Secretary Bentsen of their concern over exchange-rate policy. The peso was trading close to the ceiling, the weakest level of the band, with little room to accommodate additional pressures.

The heightened nervousness of the Treasury – which presumably reflects the deepening pessimism that Summers said he felt as the year 1994 proceeded – became evident in November. Shafer, on November 18, alerted Bentsen to the weakness of the peso and renewed intervention. In a memorandum of December 5, Summers and Shafer were advised that Mexico's reserves were only slightly above the "critical" $10 billion threshold. The memorandum did not make clear why that was the critical level; it was the floor that Aspe had given in the November 20 meeting discussed in Chapter 6 at which exchange-rate policy should be reconsidered . The memorandum also noted that the current account deficit at that point was close to 7 percent of GDP. (This deficit for the whole year was 7.9 percent of GDP.) Further increases in US short-term interest rates, the memorandum stated, "would hurt." (The US Fed did not act again to raise rates until February 1995.)

In its bi-weekly report to Summers and Shafer on December 20, the professional staff noted the lifting of the band earlier that day by 15 percent, or 53 centavos, to 4.0016 pesos per dollar. The memorandum continued: "There probably will be considerable volatility in the foreign exchange markets for a short period of time, followed by some strengthening of the peso." The memorandum also concluded that increased inflation in Mexico, which normally would be a concomitant of currency devaluation, might not rise in 1995 by much more than 1 percentage point, that is, to about 8 or 9 percent. In fact, the consumer price index in 1995 (December-over-December) was more than 27 percent.

On December 22, the swap line to Mexico under the North American Framework Agreement (NAFA) was activated at $6 billion. This was a response to the Mexican situation but, as it turned out, a feeble one. The severity of the situation still was not recognized. It was, however, by January 12, 1995, when President Clinton requested approval from the Congress for a $40 billion loan guarantee program, for which he obtained the concurrence of the congressional leadership, Bob Dole in the Senate and Newt Gingrich in the House. The size of the credit was large, about double what was thought would have to be used, in order to provide an extra degree of assurance to money market operators.

The situation required much more public candor from the Treasury than was the case earlier. As the General Accounting Office (GAO) pointed out in its report, the Treasury felt it could not publicly express its concern earlier for fear than this would provoke capital flight.[6] On an instinctive basis, it is hard to quarrel with this judgment but, in fact, the capital flight came anyhow. Beyond that,

118 *Financial Decision-making in Mexico*

the evidence is that while the Treasury was concerned about many of the economic policy measures in Mexico, there was never any expectation of a crash. Had there been, the decision not to go public might have been different. This, of course, is speculation, but not unreasonably so. In any event, in remarks on January 20, Summers did say that, viewed in retrospect, Mexico made "critical errors" in macroeconomic policy during 1994. The major error he cited was Mexico's "unsustainable" exchange-rate policy.

An aside may be warranted at this point. The December 4, 1995, statement by former President Carlos Salinas about *"el error de diciembre"* (the error of the previous December) was designed to embed in the public mind that the problems were caused not by the macroeconomic policies earlier in the year when he was president, but by the ineptitude of Zedillo and his cabinet in handling the exchange-rate change. The remarks by Summers are based on a more conventional interpretation, that the developments in December, inept or otherwise, were the culmination of earlier policy errors.

The Clinton administration used many arguments to convince Congress to authorize the $40 billion line of credit. In testimony before the House committee on banking and financial services on January 25, Robert Rubin, the Secretary of the Treasury, said that what was at stake for the United States was continued growth in US exports, the prevention of augmented illegal immigration from Mexico, and avoidance of financial spillovers across the globe. None of these arguments carried the day, and on January 31, President Clinton announced that the United States would provide credits of up to $20 billion from the Exchange Stabilization Fund (ESF). The ESF was established in 1934 "for the purpose of stabilizing the exchange value of the dollar." It has been used ever since to buy and sell foreign currencies, engage in swaps with foreign countries, and provide guaranties for foreign obligations. ESF usage is normally for reversible and short-term transactions of up to 6 months, but renewable for additional short periods. Many in Congress challenged the legality of its use and its large size for what they referred to as the Mexican "bailout." The GAO, in its report, stated that it had "no basis to disagree" with the Treasury's conclusion that ESF resources could be used for the assistance to Mexico.[7]

The $20 billion assistance was contained in three separate packages, short-term currency swaps, medium-term swaps of up to 5 years, and guarantees for up to 10 years. The interest rates varied according to the term of the loans. The ESF credit was one element of a much larger package that in theory amounted to $52.5 billion; the United States achieved the overkill that had been built in to the earlier $40 billion legislative proposal.

Interviews

These confirm the impression obtained from the public record that the Treasury mindset was to expect some adjustment problems in Mexico, but not the catastrophe that occurred. Treasury analysts were concerned about the overvalued exchange rate, the large current account deficit, the loss of reserves, and, at various points, the relatively easy monetary policy in the face of rising US interest rates. Little attention was paid to the buildup of tesobonos. It was only after the crash that Summers himself raised the issue of "net" reserves – that is, calculating reserves not merely by subtracting borrowed reserves, but subtracting as well short-term dollar (or dollar-equivalent) obligations that could be cashed in as long as the Mexican authorities did not impose capital controls. Summers said he did not recall any contemporary prominent public writings calling attention to the tesobono problem in this light.[8] In the end, the 1994–5 crisis turned into a debt crisis, not unlike the 1982 crisis, according to Summers. The origins were different and the contexts were quite disparate, but the crash of 1995 resulted from the desire of most holders of tesobonos to cash in these dollar-indexed instruments.[9]

Summers was Undersecretary, not the Secretary of the Treasury. He of course knew and met from time to time with Pedro Aspe, the Finance Secretary of Mexico, but he told me that his main point of contact was Guillermo Ortiz, his counterpart. Hierarchy has its own protocol, particularly in a society as formal as that of Mexico. Aspe's main contact in the US Treasury was Lloyd Bentsen, the secretary. Bentsen knew the issues and was well clued in to the US political scene. Nevertheless, there was something of a disconnect in this arrangement. Aspe, in addition to his political position, was a trained economist, a *técnico*. So was Summers, but not Bentsen.

Would it have made a difference if the discussions had been held regularly between technician and technician, given the highly technical nature of the Mexican economic model? There can be no sure answer to this hypothetical question, but the answer may be "yes." Summers had some contact as well with the governor of the Bank of Mexico, Miguel Mancera, but the main discussions here were between the two central banks. This was technician-to-technician discussion, Alan Greenspan and Miguel Mancera at the top and also at secondary levels. These contacts did not change the outcome, but the key policy-maker in the Mexican government, other than President Salinas himself, was Pedro Aspe.

Summers has stated that, at its core, he did not have much more information than was available to market players and analysts. He also does not believe that Treasury should be in the business of issuing alerts to investors. As already has been noted, the market players also missed the tesobono dangers.

The final assessment by Summers is that the "bailout" (his word) was correct, as can be seen in retrospect. Mexico was able to enter private markets within months of the crisis, not years, as was the case after 1982. The economic decline in 1995 was sharp, but so was the recovery in 1996. As to the problem of moral hazard, Summers said this troubled him, but he doubted there would be similar bailouts in the future; he was wrong about this. There is a disconnect here, too. The IMF is now gearing itself to respond rapidly to future crises – that is, to bail out countries that get into balance-of-payments problems owing to capital flight. This, to some degree, almost surely must involve some moral hazard, even if not identical to that faced in the Mexican case. After the Asian crisis, Secretary Rubin gave much more prominence to the moral hazard issue. After a trip to Asia, he told reporters that "what we don't want to have is a situation where people can do unwise things and not pay a price for it."[10]

The views of Summers are generally supported by the Treasury professionals who dealt with the Mexico situation. In interviews with a number of senior officials, there was open acknowledgment that the instinctive judgment of the Treasury following the assassination of Colosio coincided with the Mexican view. The murder was seen as a one-time political event and the fallout from it would probably subside. These officials were quite explicit that the political repercussions from a single political event should not normally drive economic policy. In fact, as the Mexican foreign reserve data show, market reaction to the Colosio assassination did run its course after about a month.[11]

The Treasury staff, as the written record shows, was concerned then and later about the overvalued peso and the relatively low Mexican interest rates. These officials noted that the reserves lost after the assassination did not return and they felt they would not return without a more attractive interest-rate incentive.

While there was instinctive agreement with the Mexican financial decision to treat the Colosio assassination as a temporary setback, there was less understanding of the Mexican decision not to take some action to recover reserves following the August elections. Tightening monetary policy at this point would have been welcome. So, too, would have been a decision to let the exchange rate float during, say, September in the interregnum between the election and the assumption of the presidency by Zedillo on December 1. Many Mexican scholars and officials felt the same way. What happened instead was that monetary policy actually eased during that period. Treasury officials also commented that during that period, Aspe personally assured foreign bondholders that Mexico would not devalue. The unease of the Treasury increased later in the year, in November in particular, when there were internal discussions in Mexico on exchange-rate policy. The decision after the November 20 meeting at Salinas' house was to continue existing policy.[12]

The Treasury officials involved in making policy toward Mexico now admit that they were myopic in not following more closely the buildup of tesobonos and in not fully grasping the significance of this development. It was only after the peso débâcle was transformed into a liquidity crisis by Mexico's inability to refinance outstanding, short-term tesobonos under acceptable conditions that Summers and others at the Treasury stated that the concept of "net reserves" should have taken account of the outstanding tesobonos.

The net reserve concept refers generally to gross reserves, *minus* borrowed reserves that must be repaid. There had been no expectation that the tesobonos would have to be repaid as they matured over the course of 1995, but rather that they would be turned over by issuing new tesobonos. It was only in January 1995, when refinancing was not possible, that the Treasury realized that the calculation of net reserves should also include short-term public debt instruments, especially those indexed to the dollar.

What was said earlier merits emphasis: It was not part of the mindset of the US Treasury, just as it was not of the Mexican *Hacienda*, that refinancing under acceptable conditions would suddenly become impossible. It was only after this realization that the idea of a bailout entered into US policy thinking. Mexico, by then, was experiencing two financial crises, one of the banking system and the other of national liquidity. The US Treasury had experience in dealing with a banking crisis – indeed, had just gone through one in the domestic savings and loan (S&L) crash. By contrast, there was less experience in dealing with the more basic national liquidity problem in Mexico. The decision was made to deal with the national liquidity crisis first – hence the proposal for legislation for a $40 billion credit and ultimately the use of the ESF facility for $20 billion – and leave action on the banking crisis until later.

The Treasury knew by December 23 that its earlier assessment of what would follow the devaluation of December 20 was wrong because calls came from the Mexican *Hacienda*. The use of the expanded swap lines was not working. The bureaucratic issue in the US government was complex. There was no confirmed Treasury secretary because Bentsen had resigned and Rubin had not yet been confirmed by the Senate.

The Treasury, by early January, concluded that a peso rescue package was necessary. This judgment was supported by Alan Greenspan, the Fed chairman, and this was significant in that he was not seen as having a partisan political motive. The Treasury concluded that it had two options for raising the support package, either by legislation or use of the ESF. The legislative route was chosen because the Treasury felt that the ESF could not support more than $20 billion of credit and that at least double this figure was needed to convince the markets that the Treasury intended to succeed. The larger amount was achieved only when the IMF agreed to contribute to the support package.

The motive for and the handling of the rescue package will be discussed later, but it was seen then as a major action. The amounts were huge, certainly compared with previous rescue packages for Mexico or other developing countries. Going ahead with the package, both the failed legislative effort and the ultimate use of the ESF, took considerable courage, something evident from the failure of the legislative proposal despite the support of the leadership of the Republican party in the Congress. The liquidity crisis in Mexico was seen as serious, both in terms of its consequences in Mexico and the potential repercussions in the United States.

The Federal Reserve

The other key actor in the US government was the Federal Reserve System, in particular the Board and its staff in Washington and the New York Fed, which was charged with market dealing and therefore had to keep abreast of foreign currency and economic developments. Both bodies kept a steady watch on Mexico. The policy responsibility for dealing with Mexico on economic matters rested primarily with the Treasury, but Fed officials had the advantage of dealing more non-politically, as technicians to technicians. This should have stimulated more candor from the Fed than from the Treasury, and in fact this seems to have been the case in internal memoranda.

The public record

The Federal Reserve in Washington had senior staff with longer experience on Mexican affairs than did the Treasury. In addition, one staff member with decades of experience, Yves Maroni, was called back from retirement for temporary service when it appeared that the Mexican economic situation was getting dicey. Maroni wrote a lengthy internal memorandum dated January 28, 1994 (after Chiapas, but before the Colosio assassination and the onset of foreign-reserve losses) in which he traced the history of peso movements starting in April 1954, when the peso was devalued from 8.65 to 12.50 pesos to the US dollar. By most reckonings, that devaluation was successful; the 12.50 rate endured until 1976 and Mexico enjoyed solid economic growth in excess of 6 percent a year over that 22-year period. The 1976 devaluation had been years in the making, but came at the close of the sexenio of Luis Echeverría after years of growing fiscal expenditures designed to reduce income inequalities but which resulted instead in large public-sector deficits, mounting inflation, and a growing current account deficit.[13]

Maroni's discussion is quite complete and provided considerable information for persons new to the Mexican economic scene. It describes the currency band within which the peso was permitted to fluctuate, plus the existence since June 1992 of a narrower band which was communicated daily to commercial banks so that they would know the limits at which the Bank of Mexico would intervene in the markets. He characterized the Mexican authorities as being satisfied with the exchange-rate setup. He did point out, however, that Mexico's growth rate might become hostage to exchange-rate management because the need to attract foreign capital restrained Mexico from lowering interest rates to stimulate the economy. Mexico's economic growth performance during the Salinas years was, in fact, pedestrian.

After listing and discussing what he thought were the exchange-rate options available to Mexico, Maroni concluded that "the present regime is the most appropriate at the present time and for the foreseeable future."

Concern was expressed in an internal memorandum at the Federal Reserve Bank in New York at about this time, on February 3, 1994, that the capital flows coming into Mexico to finance the current account deficit "appear to be financing consumption rather than a domestic investment boom."[14] The fear was that this could lead to a debt crisis similar to that of the early 1980s. This commentary, unfortunately for Mexico, turned out to be accurate. A later internal memorandum at the New York Fed, dated June 3, estimated that the peso was overvalued by about 20 percent and that while it was possible that the then existing band could be maintained in the near term, the situation was precarious. An internal memorandum on Mexico's exchange-rate options prepared by the staff of the Washington Fed on August 17 concluded that Mexico might look to the post-electoral period to consider a change in exchange-rate policy. Another analytical memo of the Washington Fed of August 19 explored the exchange-rate issue and the probability, under various conditions, of a tesobono default. This was most prescient.

An analyst at the New York Fed on September 28 commented on the pacto renewal the previous weekend and the fact that it stuck to the anti-inflation priority and made no change in the exchange-rate regime. The pacto continued the peso slide of 0.0004 pesos per day, or 4.3 percent on an annual basis at the then exchange rate of 3.0512 to the dollar at the lower (stronger) end of the band. This rate of depreciation was sufficient to keep the peso from further real appreciation with respect to the dollar, but did nothing to correct existing overvaluation. The peso was then trading less than 2 percent below the upper (weak) end of the band and there was thus little room for maneuver. A Washington Fed memorandum of September 29 commented on the pacto as follows: "in the absence of adjustment to a more competitive level, the peso probably will remain vulnerable to the types of political shocks we have seen take place with dismaying frequency this year."

From what is available on the public record, the Fed, both in Washington and New York, showed increasing concern over the course of 1994 that Mexico's exchange-rate policy, and the growing level of tesobonos, would come to no good end. The language in the internal memoranda refers to "vulnerabilities," not to certainties. When Summers commented privately that there was no public record of warnings about the danger of the buildup of tesobonos – that the private markets and analysts were no more farseeing than the public analysts – he probably was unaware of some internal fears at the Washington Fed.

It is unclear just how much and how forcefully these concerns were transmitted to the Bank of Mexico where the counterparts of the Fed operated, but the views of the Fed were known in Mexico. The emphasis in Mexico remained on reducing inflation; overcoming the overvaluation of the peso, and the issue of reversing the relatively low level of economic growth that was a concomitant of this, kept being deferred to the future. The problem, in the end, was that the future came earlier than the Mexican authorities, and even their US counterparts, anticipated.

Interviews

The most senior officer (other than the governors) at the Washington Fed dealing with this issue during all this period was Edwin M. (Ted) Truman, staff director of the Board's division of international finance. Truman had some two decades of experience tracking Mexican financial issues, longer than any other person of comparable rank in the US government. Truman said he alerted Summers, when the latter was nominated to be Deputy Secretary of the Treasury when Robert Rubin moved up to be Secretary, that he would have to deal with the Mexican problem. Summers undoubtedly did not need the warning. One response to this concern was the conclusion on April 26, 1994 of the North American Framework Agreement (NAFA) making permanent the $6 billion swap line established earlier, plus the Canadian swap line of C$1 billion. One of the ground rules of this line was that it was not to be used to support the peso, but it is not evident that this stricture was followed.

When NAFTA was under consideration by the US Congress in late 1993, the uncertainty about the outcome put pressure on the peso, which it withstood quite well. As the Fed saw the situation after NAFTA went into effect on January 1, 1994, the financial requirement in Mexico was for a large devaluation, a faster crawl, or a wider band. The upcoming elections in August meant that definitive action probably would have to wait until later in the year. These reflections were shared with officials of the Bank of Mexico, including the governor, Miguel Mancera. One big mistake, as seen from the Fed, was that Mexico did not act in September after Zedillo had won the election.

Fed officials met with Mexican authorities in Washington in October. The Mexicans included Pedro Aspe, the *Hacienda* Secretary, and Luis Tellez, who was part of the transition team for incoming President Zedillo and who would later be named the president's chief of staff in Los Pinos, Mexico's equivalent of the White House. These visits are referred to in the GAO report.[15] According to Fed staff, Chairman Greenspan was blunt in his conversations that the Mexican financial situation was becoming precarious.[16] Aspe reportedly responded that he hoped to defer action on the exchange rate until the first quarter of 1995, using either a free float or a hard peg of the peso, perhaps via a currency board. There was no sense of imminent disaster on the Mexican side.

The Fed felt that another miscalculation was made in November when the market knew that the Fed once again would raise interest rates, which it did by 0.75 percentage points on November 15. This provided an opportunity for Mexico to act; instead, another auction of government debt came on the same day.

In his highly publicized letter recounting the meeting at the home of President Salinas on November 20, Aspe states forcefully that it was at his insistence that the peso was not devalued by 15 percent at that time. However, there was a sense at the Fed even then that the most adamant opposition to a devaluation came from President Salinas himself. Salinas later gave credence to this instinctive belief when, in an interview published on three successive days in February 1997 by the Mexico City newspaper *Reforma*, he stated that he had obtained a commitment from Aspe in November 1988, when he invited him to become the Secretary of Finance, that there would be no "abrupt devaluation" of the peso.[17] There is other evidence, however, that Salinas would have gone along if the November 20 consensus had been for action then on the exchange rate.

After the devaluation, both the Mexican and US authorities tried to deal with the consequences in traditional ways. These involved activating swap lines and seeking additional lines of credit from US and Canadian banks. None of this worked and the delay in realizing the extent of the fallout and taking immediate forceful action proved costly. Officers at the Fed (not Truman) told me that they asked themselves if the crisis that eventuated could actually have been avoided if the United States had acted more quickly. Truman did comment, however, that the issue was treated as a financial and not a macroeconomic problem. He noted that the expenditure of swap money to support the peso only made things worse. The idea of a large loan, what later became the combined effort of the US Treasury, the IMF, and many central banks, was considered only after much damage was done and after Guillermo Ortiz came to Washington to ponder the next steps.

The IMF and the World Bank

These two multilateral institutions had long played a significant role in supporting Mexico's financial and development policies. Of the two, the IMF was the more important for the kind of short-term financial support required after the December 1994 devaluation. The Bank's function is essentially long-term in nature, but not exclusively so.

International Monetary Fund

The GAO interviewed officials of the IMF in preparing its report. There is, therefore, some public record of IMF thinking about Mexico for the period leading up to the December 1994 devaluation and also of the role of the Fund in contributing to the peso rescue loan. In addition, the documents released by the US Senate Banking Committee under the chairmanship of Senator Alfonse D'Amato contained a few papers from the IMF. One of these was an excerpt from the Fund's annual report for the year ending April 30, 1994, which, in the anodyne language that can be called Fundspeak, points to concern over a number of points: the large current account deficit; the vulnerability of Mexico to a sudden reversal in capital flows; the need to augment public and private savings in Mexico; and the fact that continued appreciation of the peso could pose risks to export expansion. To those familiar with interpreting Fundspeak, the understated language bespeaks some heated differences about the situation in Mexico at the time this discussion took place in the executive board in February 1994.

In March 1994, after Colosio's assassination, Michel Camdessus, the Managing Director of the Fund, assured Lloyd Bentsen, the US Secretary of the Treasury, that Mexico, in the view of the Fund, was "pursuing fundamentally sound economic policies." At about this time, a reportedly secret audit of Fund activities indicated that material that the Mexican government considered inconvenient was excised from the report on the Article IV consultations (the consultations summarized in the *Annual Report* noted above).[18]

This is not the place to get deeply into Fund practices. If Fund reports were completely frank, governments would be reluctant to cooperate. In addition, the reports themselves could trigger damaging reactions that preclude the kind of corrective action the Fund is seeking. The other side of this dilemma is that secrecy deprives the international public, including market players, of the unvarnished opinions of an institution charged with lending billions of dollars of funds that have public guaranties. The conundrum is not conceptually different from that faced by the US Treasury. Had the Treasury openly stated its belief that Mexico had to devalue its currency, this could have triggered a run on the peso. If the Fund openly stated that Mexican policy needed some fundamental changes, this too could have led to a financial crisis.

The IMF, therefore, relies on Fundspeak. The informed public is literate in this language. In the event, of course, the financial crisis came anyhow and was probably worse than if it had been faced squarely earlier. In this constant struggle between secrecy, which in part has a market rationale and in part merely protects negligent government, and openness, the compromise is usually to open just a tiny bit more after years of discussion. The opening is generally grudging and usually insufficient.

Personal discussion with officials of the Fund more or less corroborate the main points of what is on the public record. The IMF worked closely with Mexico over many years, particularly after the debt reschedulings in the 1980s. The Article IV consultations took place at the end of 1993. The dialogue was difficult. Government officials from just about all countries seeking IMF support often accuse Fund officials of arrogance; fund officials dealing with Mexico make the same charge against Mexican officials. There was concern in the Fund that information on key Mexican variables was being made available only with a lag. The Fund, as 1994 proceeded, raised a number of issues, such as the use of development banks to carry out off-budget lending, which meant that fiscal policy was not as tight as advertised; and, it goes without saying that the Fund was concerned about the overvalued exchange rate.

There was considerable tension in economic circles in Mexico before the August election. There was a slight possibility that a non-PRI candidate could become president (Diego Fernández de Cevallos, of the National Action Party, or PAN) and much uncertainty about what policies would follow if he were elected. Things calmed down when Zedillo won what most observers felt was a legitimate victory.

The IMF, like the US Treasury, was aware of the growing issuance of tesobonos and indicated some nervousness about this, but the expressions of concern were low key. The extra vulnerability of the short-term nature of Mexico's public debt was not fully assessed. But the Fund, like other observers, was not contemplating disaster. The Article IV consultations for 1994 were actually delayed from November to December by mutual agreement because a new team was taking over in Mexico. When the band was widened on December 20, Mancera, the governor of the Bank of Mexico, immediately notified Stanley Fischer, the Deputy Managing Director of the Fund. The staff told the board of the Fund that it thought the devaluation would work. As we now know, it did not.

The Fund sent a small mission to Mexico City during the last week of December. There was some discussion of a new IMF program, but Mexico was reluctant to agree. By then, however, the situation in Mexico was spiraling out of control. The Fund staff hurriedly, overnight, prepared a report for management stressing the lack of support funds either from the Fund or the US Treasury. By the end of January, with some urging from the US Treasury, the Managing Director decided to advocate what resulted in the $17.8 billion support package from the Fund. Why this figure? It is hard to know, but between the Fund ($17.8 billion) and the ESF ($20 billion), the total came close to the $40 billion that President Clinton initially sought from the Congress. The Fund support was approved, but not without considerable opposition from the executive board, particularly from European directors.[19]

World Bank

The Bank, like the Fund, has had a relationship with Mexico over a considerable period. As was the case with the Fund, the Bank was actively engaged in Mexico following the 1982 crisis. At that time, the Bank's philosophic approach toward emerging countries began to change in favor of promoting more open markets. This was reflected in many Bank publications seeking to demonstrate that countries that had less import protection and were more welcoming to foreign direct investment generally had better economic growth performance than closed economies. This shift in attitude was reflected in dealings with Mexico, where the Bank sought basic structural changes.

These policies were discussed with the Mexican authorities starting with the administration of Miguel de la Madrid (end-1982 to end-1988), and then accelerated when Carlos Salinas became president (end-1988 to end-1994).[20] Three large loans in the $500 million range each were made for structural changes in trade policy, financial matters, and dealing with public enterprises. The Bank later provided assistance to assure that the Brady Plan, providing debt relief to Mexico, worked and even urged the private market players to support Mexican policies. Mexico, in many respects, became one of the darlings of the Bank, as it did for the US government, in the early 1990s.

Yet, some concern was developing in the Bank, particularly after a large turnover of personnel working on Mexican issues around 1992. What the new personnel saw were a rising current account deficit, an appreciating peso, an economy growing quite modestly even as it came out of a protracted depression, a labor force increasing at about 3 percent a year and for which the low overall economic growth was insufficient to provide jobs, and low growth in productivity. Investment was flat even as the current account deficit was growing, which indicated declining domestic savings. The Bank sent an unpublicized mission to Mexico in September 1992 to discuss these misgivings. The Bank concern became even stronger by late 1992 when it saw little improvement in productivity growth or in domestic savings. Most of the capital inflow to finance the current account deficit was going to consumption and not to investment.

The Bank argued from about September 1992 onward that the Mexican authorities should depreciate the peso (increase the daily slide or *desliz*) more rapidly than was being allowed. This may have had some influence because, in October of that year, under the pacto, the daily crawl went back to 0.4 percent of a peso instead of the 0.2 percent earlier. The Fund at this point endorsed the Mexican government position to give greater priority to further reducing inflation rather than dealing more vigorously with the overvalued peso. Mexico, at this time, was mostly sterilizing dollar inflows in order to keep its money supply within money growth targets it had set.

In January 1993, the Bank sent a confidential mission to Mexico to examine the situation. An aide-memoire was prepared which praised Mexico's anti-inflation program, but pointed out that this was achieved in part by substantial appreciation of the exchange rate, a growing current account deficit, and crushing interest rates that had to be kept high to attract capital inflows. The report noted the high failure rate of small and medium-sized firms (SMEs) as a result of the high interest rate. The report also pointed out what by then had become a common refrain of outside observers, that the heavy reliance on volatile capital inflows made Mexico vulnerable to changes in expectations of investors. The report also commented that should a peso depreciation become necessary, the balance sheets of banks and firms that borrowed heavily in dollars would be weakened.

All these fears, unfortunately, became reality in 1994, when there were changes in expectations, a reversal of capital flows, and weakened banks and firms. At the time, however, the Mexican authorities objected to any publication of this critical material and the aide-memoire was not part of the report issued by the Bank. The same question of secrecy of institutions that operate with public guaranties arises here as it did for the Fund and the US Treasury. The Bank is taking steps to reduce the secrecy of its reports, but these measures do not include public disclosure of country concerns as deep as those in the aide-memoire. It is not that the Bank was saying things in the aide-memoire not also being said by others examining the Mexican scene, but there is a difference between privately stated concerns and official statements by funding institutions.[21] Was Mexico helped by the secrecy? It is doubtful that it was. As already stated, the crash, when it came, was surely more severe than had action been taken earlier.

These differences between the Bank and the Mexican authorities were later – much later – made public. Shahid Javed Burki, the Vice President of the Bank for Latin America and the Caribbean, has since written that Bank analysts identified medium-term financial risks in Mexico and communicated these, but the warnings were not heeded.[22] Burki also makes clear that the Bank spoke with two voices – clearly to the Mexican authorities, muted to the financial markets.[23]

The weakness of commercial banks in Mexico was a serious concern at the World Bank. It is an interesting coincidence that on the very day, December 20, 1994, that the Mexican crisis erupted, the staff brought a technical assistance loan to the executive board for support to the commercial banks. The staff sentiment was that in light of what was happening in Mexico, this loan was needed more than ever.

The Bank made known its sentiment throughout 1994 that some action should be taken to reduce the overvaluation of the peso. Early in the year, in February, before the Colosio assassination, the Bank argued that this was a good time to devalue the peso because

Mexico would be acting from a position of strength, when international reserves were high. (They reached $29 billion in February, the high point for the year.) The exchange-rate issue was raised again after the August elections at a conference in Cuernavaca. Once again, the Mexicans resisted altering policy.

The shift in public debt from cetes, which were denominated in pesos but without any indexation to the dollar, to tesobonos, also nominally peso instruments but with a dollar indexation – and effectively, therefore, dollar obligations for the Mexican authorities – grew throughout 1994. The maturities between the two instruments did not differ materially, but the private market was more willing to take the debt risk in Mexico for dollar than for peso obligations. The tesobonos, as is now understood, were, in effect, reserve decumulations. By mid-year, outstanding tesobonos exceeded the Bank of Mexico's foreign reserve holdings and by the net reserve reckoning, Mexico then had negative reserves. Bank officials assert that they were monitoring the tesobono buildup. It is evident that most private purchasers of tesobonos either were not tracking the buildup; or if they were, they showed no concern.

At the request of senior Mexican officials, the Bank prepared a series of policy options in anticipation of the impending change of government and these were the subject of the informal discussions in Cuernavaca in August cited earlier. Most of the discussion related to sectoral issues in Mexico, but the exchange rate was also an important theme. Guillermo Ortiz, then the number two *Hacienda* official, had the reputation in Mexico of being more flexible on altering the exchange-rate arrangement than either of his two superiors, the *Hacienda* Secretary, Pedro Aspe, and President Salinas. As is known, the decision was made not to alter the exchange-rate policy.

There was much speculation in Mexico that Ortiz's position in favor of greater flexibility may have cost him the job of *Hacienda* secretary in the formation of Zedillo's cabinet. Ortiz was appointed Secretary of Communications and Transport at the start of the Zedillo administration, only to be brought back to Hacienda as Secretary at the end of December 1994, when Jaime Serra Puche resigned after the crisis erupted.

The record shows that World Bank officials had concerns similar to those of the Fund and the US Treasury and Fed. This uneasiness on the exchange rate, the growing current account deficit, and apparently the buildup of tesobonos, was made known to Mexican authorities. What is not known is how forceful the Bank was in pressing its misgivings. The evidence is that the Bank *qua* Bank, as opposed to individual analysts, was not very forceful.[24] The Bank had less leverage than either the Fund, whose main business was to deal in exchange-rate issues, or the various organs of the US government, because most of the funds entering Mexico were from private markets, not the Bank.

The market players

Different market players viewed Mexico from their own philosophic and practical vantages. Thus, some advocated maintaining the exchange rate at all costs, others favored setting up a currency board which would reduce the monetary policy discretion of the Bank of Mexico, still others wanted a free float, and others a more aggressive slide. Yet, one can argue that there is a "market" view that is manifested in what the players do. There was something akin to lemming-like behavior during most of the Salinas administration, when portfolio capital streamed into Mexico in huge amounts, enough not only to help finance the large current-account deficit, but also to augment Mexico's foreign reserves until February 1994. The herd behavior moved in the opposite direction when fears of instability set in after the assassination of Colosio in March 1994 and this became a stampede in December of that year forcing the devaluation on December 20.

In an interview with the key person responsible for portfolio investment of one of the largest US mutual funds, some of the reasons for this near-uniform market view, first favorable to Mexico and then adverse, were made clear. One reason was the ability to change holdings of government debt from cetes to tesobonos, which convinced many market players that Mexico had a powerful incentive to keep the peso strong. Beyond that, constant assurances were given by Pedro Aspe that there would be no abrupt peso devaluation. (Aspe, as we know, was no longer *Hacienda* secretary when the devaluation occurred on December 20.)

It seems clear that the adverse view of Mexican policy, manifested in the large capital outflow during 1994, was led by private Mexican holders of portfolio capital, as opposed to foreign mutual funds. The IMF, in a *post mortem* study released in August 1995, argued that the outward flow was precipitated by Mexicans and not foreign institutional holders of fixed-income securities.[25] From a substantive viewpoint, the issue is not significant because one must assume that investors, whatever their nationality, will act rationally. Who acted first is interesting, however, from the aspect of who knew or suspected first what the weaknesses were in Mexican economic policy, nationals of the country or foreigners, most of whom had little background on Mexican history and knew little about the internal infighting. If the IMF analysis is correct, the danger signs were seen internally before they were grasped outside the country.

One of the arguments implicit in the views of this particular market player, who did have considerable information about past Mexican practices, is that the official Mexican authorities did not see themselves, or their actions, as others outside the government or outside the country saw them. The more precise phraseology of this commentary is that the officials did not see their actions the same way as their co-national, more dispassionate, private actors saw them.[26] This private actor was quite cynical about the motives of Mexican economic policy during 1994. His conviction was that some 85 percent of economic policy was driven by politics – namely, the desire to make sure that Zedillo won the presidential election in August of that year. He pointed to the unwillingness of the Bank of Mexico to raise interest rates and the large outlays of the public sector through development banks, that is, off-budget. His conclusion was that Mexico – the PRI, really – will have a difficult time in establishing its credibility in 1999–2000 in the leadup to the presidential election in 2000 because of past experience.

One other investment banker made the following comment about his company's experience in 1994: "We trusted Salinas and Aspe and did not withdraw our funds, but we will not make that mistake again."

There was much criticism of Mexico after the crisis erupted for its lack of timely publication of foreign reserve and other salient figures. The investor interviewed said that he knew, more or less, the reserve position in early December. He added that the Mexican private sector surely knew this even more precisely. He admitted that the private market in the United States was not paying much attention to the size and short-term nature of the outstanding tesobonos; this information was available for those who wished to know it. Nor, he said, were the foreign market players fully aware of the buildup of short-term foreign credit to the Mexican banks.

He said he reduced his company's position in Mexico in the course of 1994, but did not withdraw completely. He added that he did not recognize the seriousness of the tesobono problem on day one, on December 20. His firm lost about $4 billion between December 1, when Zedillo was inaugurated, until full withdrawal could be carried out. When asked whether he was angry about the way the devaluation was handled, or the fact that there was a devaluation at all, he said "No," but he was disappointed.

The decision to raise the band within which the peso was allowed to float was made at the pacto meeting that ended at around 3 a.m. on December 20. The announcement of this action was made by the *Hacienda* secretary, Jaime Serra Puche, in a radio talk at 7 a.m. on December 20. The government argued that there was no evidence that persons who knew of the decision before it was announced took advantage of it by moving capital out of the country. Unfortunately, it is hard to trace the many ways that pesos could be sold or shorted to verify this assertion. Two knowledgeable experts, including this fund manager, said they thought one technique used was to purchase Telmex stock in London and then capture the extra peso return after the devaluation. I was unable to trace such transactions.

A number of outside observers of Mexico were publicly critical that the devaluation was carried out at all. Malcolm (Steve) Forbes, Jr., who in 1996 sought the Republican presidential nomination, was one of these. Jack Kemp, the Republican nominee for Vice President in 1996, took a similar position on the sanctity of exchange rates. David Malpass, director for international economics at Bear Stearns in New York argued that the "Mexican devaluation proved to be a cold shower for devaluationists," and asserted that current account deficits should be seen not as profligacy but that the accompanying capital inflows should be welcomed as sources of investment.[27] The evidence, as noted above, is that these inflows were used more for consumption than for investment.

Jorge Mariscal, an analyst at Goldman Sachs who is well informed about Mexico, compared the situation there during 1994 to a speeding car on a winding road, one that had to slow down before it went over the cliff. His conclusion was that the problem was less the exchange rate – exports were increasing nicely – but rather the growth of imports because of low savings – or, put differently, excessive consumption. He also said that he "pretty much knew" the level of reserves at the beginning of December 1994. Mariscal said that many outsiders did not appreciate the fragility of the banks in 1994 and how this put pressure on the Bank of Mexico not to raise interest rates.

Just about all the private market investors and analysts who were interviewed approved the issuance of tesobonos. Their reasoning was quite straightforward, that it provided a degree of extra assurance against a devaluation. Yet, as noted, few of them followed the rapid growth in tesobonos or the extent to which their outstanding level exceeded the level of foreign reserves. When the devaluation occurred on December 20, the reserves stood at $10.4 billion and outstanding tesobonos at $20 billion. Foreign reserves later fell further and the tesobonos outstanding later rose to a higher level.

Issuing more and more tesobonos became a substitute for other, more fundamental, policy changes. The tesobonos provided an exchange-rate guarantee to investors in lieu of altering the exchange rate for a more durable corrective. They permitted Mexico to borrow from foreign investors at a lower rate than the Bank of Mexico would have to pay to sell cetes, but this did nothing to alter the interest rate situation within the country, as a devaluation would have permitted. The buildup of tesobonos became a substitute for foreign reserve policy in that the tesobonos outstanding went up and up while reserves either declined or stagnated. Because it did not have a floating rate, Mexico needed reserves for emergencies, but the issuance of tesobonos offered no more than a temporary security blanket. In the end, the inability to refinance the outstanding tesobonos falling due – the liquidity problem – was what did Mexico in and brought on the large rescue package that was mounted in early 1995. Alan Greenspan, Chairman of the Board of Governors of the Fed, known more for his elliptical than direct language, was quite explicit about the role tesobonos played:

> The chosen alternative [to maintaining the exchange rate through further tightening of monetary policy and perhaps bringing on a recession] to dramatically tightened monetary policy, borrowing via tesobonos and drawing on reserves to intervene in the foreign exchange market, had a limit. Indeed, the limit was reached on December 20, and the defense of the peso came to an abrupt end.[28]

In the light of this background, it is useful to examine the history of tesobono issuance and the role of foreign investors in encouraging this policy. The Bank of Mexico had issued tesobonos earlier, at least as far back as 1988.[29] The amounts before 1994 were not large. They reached about $3 billion in 1993, when they were used for financing purposes toward the end of the year when the outcome of the NAFTA debate in the US Congress was uncertain and therefore leading to some instability in portfolio flows to Mexico. However, substantial issuance of tesobonos did not take place until 1994 and kept growing as the year went on.

Many US financial houses, investment bankers and brokers, urged Mexico to issue tesobonos as a way out of Mexico's dilemma of not wishing to devalue the peso or sharply raise interest rates. The lead was taken by the Weston Group, which organized a consortium called the Weston Forum which included many leading financial houses.[30] The Weston Forum experience was a rather sobering one because of what it implied for the sovereign ability of Mexico to set its own financial policy. Because of its reliance on portfolio capital to finance the current account deficit, plus the unwillingness to devalue the peso or raise interest rates, Mexico had only a single available policy instrument, the sale of tesobonos. Whether the Weston Forum players were engaged in an ultimatum or a rational discussion of Mexico's options, the Mexican authorities were at the mercy of foreign financial intermediaries and national investors. Each side had self-interested motives, the Mexican policy officials who, by consciously limiting their options, needed the capital inflows; and the financial houses, which clearly preferred an exchange-rate guarantee for their investments over the risk of a devaluation that would reduce the value of their assets in Mexico. Sovereignty needs some redefinition in this circumstance. Who was the sovereign, the Mexican authorities or the financial intermediaries?

Commentary

Henry Kaufman, one of the most respected private monetary analysts and players in the United States, cited shortcomings in the actions of three non-Mexican groups in the period leading up to the crisis: persons in the financial community, whose emphasis on short-term profits compromised their objectivity; the major governments and multilateral institutions, which did not issue even nuanced statements of caution; and the research community, which did not raise "caution flags."[31] A task force of the Council on Foreign Relations came to similar conclusions about the lack of public candor of the multilateral institutions and the US government, who explained these away by the need for secrecy.[32] A front-page article in the *Wall Street Journal* gave a number of reasons for the financial tragedy:

IMF complacency; the pressure from the Weston Forum and Mexico's need to convince foreign investors that there would be no devaluation; the failure of the market players to take note of the tesobono buildup; and the lack of urgency in the concern of the US Treasury.[33]

These are all worthy conclusions. The issue to which I wish to return is that of secrecy. Policy-making in Mexico itself in the period leading up to the devaluation of December 20 was highly secretive. This was the Mexican tradition, generated over decades of one-party rule. Looking outside Mexico to the official groups, those in the US and other governments, and in the multilateral financial institutions, the tradition of secrecy is also well entrenched. The argument that has always carried the day is that critical public statements by these groups lead to self-fulfilling prophesies and should therefore be avoided. We know from the record recounted above that this secrecy was practiced in Washington, that private admonitions were transmitted to the Mexican authorities, but public statements of criticism were avoided.

It is unwise to draw a sweeping conclusion from a single case when secrecy did nothing to avoid the disaster that was impending and probably made it worse. Yet, it is hard to believe that some "nuanced" indication, to use Henry Kaufman's word, of displeasure with Mexico's financial policies would have made the situation worse than it turned out to be.

The conclusion I draw is that secrecy goes too far. The international community, acting through the multilateral financial institutions, has a stake in the massive meltdown of one of its members. The US government has a stake in preventing catastrophe and instability in a neighbor. Governments now speak out on important "internal" issues in other countries, like human rights and democracy. Is international finance more sensitive than these issues? I think not. I hope the Mexican experience has some influence in modifying current practice.

The Mexican rescue package

When the devaluation decision was taken on December 20, Mexico's foreign reserves were $10.5 billion. One day later, on December 21, they dropped to $5.8 billion. The Bank of Mexico squandered $4.5 billion in a vain effort to stop the slide in the value of the peso. A day later, on December 22, the Mexican authorities called it quits and allowed the peso to float. The swap lines with the United States ($6 billion) and Canada (C$1 billion) were activated. Jaime Serra Puche, the finance secretary, came to New York on that day to meet with the financial community; as described by all participants, the meeting was a disaster. The peso kept falling and, a few days later on December 29, Serra resigned and was replaced by Guillermo Ortiz. An economic austerity plan was announced less than a week later, on January 3, 1995, but it was clearly inadequate. Shortly after that, on January 12, President Clinton proposed legislation for a $40 billion loan guarantee program for Mexico to deal with the liquidity problem and the precipitous drop in the peso. The support of the Republican leadership, Newt Gingrich, the Speaker of the House, and Bob Dole, the Majority Leader of the Senate, did not rescue the initiative.

What follows, picks up the thinking that prevailed in the US government and the international institutions, particularly the IMF.

The public record

President Clinton kicked off the loan guarantee proposal on January 18, 1995, with the statement that the financial problem is a danger to Mexico, but is "plainly also a danger to the economic future of the United States." This line of reasoning was the main argument used to justify the $40 billion guarantee legislation, but in the end it did not carry the day. The most important advocate of this position was Robert Rubin, the Secretary of the Treasury. He laid it out initially in an internal White House meeting on January 10 and his argument was accepted by President Clinton later the same day.

Lawrence Summers made a policy speech at Georgetown University on January 20 in which he said that "Mexico made what in retrospect were critical errors in macroeconomic policy during the last year," and added that unless Mexico was able to refinance maturing tesobonos, this would pose dangers for the United States. Rubin made the same argument in testimony before the House committee on banking and financial services on January 25. In addition to the financial risks to the United States from a Mexican default, he raised the specter of an increase of as much as 30 percent in illegal immigration into the United States.

Administration spokesmen were all over Capitol Hill during the next few days. In addition to Rubin and Summers, the congressional witnesses included Warren Christopher, secretary of State. A few additional arguments were made: a Mexican financial collapse would result in a sharp reduction of US exports and thereby lead to a loss of US jobs; the administration guarantee package should be treated on its financial merits and extraneous conditions should be excluded. There was a standard figure on job losses from reduced exports to Mexico – "nearly" or "as many as" 700 000.[34] I have no idea how this number was derived, but it was blatant nonsense in the sense that job losses and gains are not a static number and constant adjustments are made in the US economy.[35] It was clear that administration spokespersons were reading from the same hymnal.

In any event, the Congress gave little credence to the testimony of administration officials. Their words were seen as political. Much more attention was paid to the testimony of Alan Greenspan, who on January 25 told the House banking committee that a Mexican default "would be a tragic setback... for the United States and the rest of the world as well."[36] Greenspan was seen as being independent of the political influence of the administration.[37]

The usual suspects opposed the guarantee proposal. These, it goes almost without saying, included Ross Perot. Malcolm Forbes, Jr., was against the guarantee. His position was a mixture of philosophy and morality. He told the Senate foreign relations committee that when Mexico devalued the peso, "on the advice of US Treasury officials, on the advice of the IMF, and other so-called experts" it gave way "to that temptation of modern economics, the most seductive and destructive of economic drugs, devaluation. Mexico tried to cheat its creditors, and cheat its own people." Later in the same testimony, he stated that devaluation is "immoral" and "undemocratic."[38]

William Seidman, a former head of the Federal Deposit Insurance Corporation and a person respected for his financial expertise, took the position both in congressional testimony and on the op-ed page of the *Wall Street Journal*, that co-signing a $40 billion note with Mexico would bail out investors who made a mistake in judgment by investing in Mexico, and just as they expected to keep any gains, so should they suffer their losses. He asserted that a rescue would surely arouse resentment in Mexico when the United States sought to obtain security for its investment.[39] I will return to Seidman's first point, on the moral hazard issue, because I think it has merit. He was mostly wrong on the second, his prediction of official Mexican resentment.

On January 31, the administration gave up the fight to get legislative approval for the $40 billion guarantee and resorted instead to using loans and guarantees through the Exchange Stabilization Fund (ESF), reinforced by assistance from the IMF, plus a number of central banks. The original $40 billion figure had not quite been picked from a hat. The reasoning was that the amount had to be large, at least double what might really be needed, in order to convince the markets of the US seriousness. The $20 billion credit and guaranties from the ESF was therefore considered risky if it stood on its own. The operation came together when the IMF agreed to contribute $17.8 billion to the rescue package.

There were many risks involved in the procedure chosen. As Seidman, Forbes, and others stated, there was no certainty that any of the funds withdrawn by Mexico would be repaid. The US credit, to be sure, had a number of safeguards, particularly the oil facility. Funds from foreign oil sales by Pemex, the Mexican government's oil monopoly, were to be held in an escrow account at the Federal Reserve Bank of New York and could be used in the event that Mexico failed to make interest or principal repayments on time. There was much discussion at the time of just how adequate or ironclad the oil facility assurance would be, but in practice it never had to be used because there were no late payments.[40]

In addition, the US Treasury imposed a number of conditions which were closely monitored.[41] These were severe, and it was this type of restriction that gave Seidman pause. Just as the IMF is often portrayed as the villain when things go wrong in a country trying to meet conditions imposed when Fund resources are borrowed, so too might the United States be blamed for the shock treatment involved in Mexico's recovery. There was some of this in Mexico in 1995, but the Zedillo administration really bore the brunt of the resentment for the sharp decline in Mexico's GDP that year.

Both the US administration and the management of the IMF took risks in what they did. The administration may have been on safe legal ground by using the ESF, but the size and nature of the operation were unusual. This led inevitably to restrictions on future use of the ESF, a reaction that administration officials said they knew would occur. In the case of the IMF credit, it, too, was large and there were complaints from European allies that it was rushed through without sufficient consultation and could use up funds that might be needed elsewhere, for example, in Eastern Europe and Russia. Six European countries abstained in the vote authorizing the IMF credit.[42]

The combination of US and IMF conditionality, combined with President Zedillo's own convictions about the need for a crash program to bring Mexico out of its economic crisis, did squeeze the Mexican population. The GDP decline in 1995 was almost 7 percent (using a 1980 base for calculating this; or 6.2 percent using an updated 1993 base), and this came on top of modest growth during the previous 12 years, starting with the collapse of the Mexican economy in 1982. An argument can be made that economic opening will lead to political opening as well,[43] but it became evident in 1995 that economic collapse also can result in political turmoil and, in Mexico's case to a transformation of the political scene.

Yet, from a purely economic viewpoint, the shock treatment worked. Mexico's GDP grew by more than 5 percent (1993 base) in 1996, recapturing most of the ground lost in 1995. Overall economic growth continued into 1997 and 1998. Mexico was able to enter international capital markets within five months of the crisis, not seven years, as was the case in 1982.

This ability to borrow was significant. In January 16, 1997, Mexico liquidated its debt to the United States under the rescue package by a prepayment of $3.5 billion *plus* accrued interest. The funds for this prepayment came in large part from other foreign borrowings at lower interest rates than under the rescue package. There was some grumbling from critics of the original credit that borrowing from Europe to repay the United States was merely a wash for Mexico. Yet, refinancing is a normal way for governments to meet obligations, as is evident when one examines how the US government handles its debt. When this alternative financing is at a lower rate, this is gravy and not a basis for caustic comment.

All told, the Mexican authorities used $13.5 billion of the US credit, $3 billion in short-term swaps and $10.5 billion in medium-term swaps. No more than $12.5 billion were outstanding at any one time. Total interest paid under the loan was $1.4 billion, some $580 million more than would have been earned had the funds been invested in US government securities, according to the US Treasury. The sentiment that the credit line had to be larger than the amount expected to be used turned out to be accurate. The Mexican authorities used none of the $10 billion under the potential credits from central banks operating through the Bank for International Settlements (BIS). Mexico continued to draw down funds from the IMF under this transaction.

Interviews

Senior officials of the US Treasury were aware, even before legislation was submitted to authorize the $40 billion guarantee for Mexico, that they had the ESF option. The initial concern was with the amount; the Treasury was reluctant to use more than $20 billion of ESF funds. There were clear sighs of relief, I was told, when the IMF agreed to provide an additional $17.8 billion. The total figure was larger than that, in excess of $50 billion from all sources and this helped appearances, but it was clear from the outset that the two critical sources of support were from the US Treasury and the IMF.

The interest rates on the US credits were carefully designed not to be confiscatory – as they were in the 1982 rescue package[44] – but Mexico was asked to pay a premium rate both to encourage refinancing and to justify to the US Congress and the informed public the risk that was being entered into. Much was made of the fact that Mexico paid more than the Treasury could have earned from its usual investments. Was this unseemly? In one sense, yes, because the premium interest rate took advantage of a desperate nation. In another sense, not really, because measures had to be put in place to encourage liquidation of the loan (or, more formally, the swaps). I was told that the high interest was deliberate to encourage other financing at a lower rate to permit prepayment. When the final prepayment was made, Treasury officials worked the telephone lines to get maximum media attention.[45]

Junior members of the Washington Fed staff wondered aloud in interviews whether the free fall of the peso and the ensuing collapse of the Mexican economy could have been prevented if the United States had acted more quickly. When the United States finally did act, it did so decisively, but it took more than 40 days, from December 20, 1994 to January 31, 1995, to do so. This, in part, was a reflection of the misappraisal of the seriousness of what was about to befall Mexico. Even if the appraisal of market reaction had been accurate, it is not clear that $50 billion could have been generated in the absence of a demonstrated need, and it took time for this to become manifest.

Interviews in the IMF confirm the bitterness and serious disagreements at the Board meeting when Fund voted to approve its large credit to Mexico. The preparations for the Board meeting for that credit took place over one night after the Managing Director concluded that the potential repercussions on the international financial situation required the large IMF participation.

Individual market players and analysts had different views on the merits of the international support. It was a "bailout" to opponents and "peso support" to proponents. On the whole, however, it is obvious that the world monetary markets approved. This was demonstrated by their actions in permitting rapid re-access of Mexico to ample credit.

Commentary

Two generic lines of argumentation were made for opposing the rescue package. One was the moral hazard issue, that governments should not step in to bail out investors, particularly those investing in risky places in order to obtain higher interest rates than they could obtain at home. The second was that the market is sending an unmistakable message when individuals and investment houses rush to withdraw funds, and no favor is done by overriding this message. What is needed instead, so the argument goes, is a costly workout to embed the message that policy errors are costly in order to prevent repetition of these errors.

Allan H. Meltzer, a distinguished professor of political economy at Carnegie Mellon University, made both these arguments in a column in the *Wall Street Journal* on February 2, 1996,[46] a year after the peso rescue package was approved. Meltzer's main points were that Mexico got into trouble as a result of poor policy, the bailout was used largely to pay the holders of tesobonos, while the Mexican population suffered grievously during 1995. Each of these points is undeniable. What Meltzer does not address was whether, faced with the reality of collapse, the outcome would have been worse had Mexico been allowed to default on its debt. Would the Mexican people have been better off in that case? Would the recovery have been as rapid? My own conclusion is "no" to both questions.

David Felix, another distinguished economics professor, in this case at Washington University in St. Louis, wrote a year earlier that the rescue package would merely validate the policy of relying excessively on volatile portfolio capital.[47] Felix's starting point was that Mexico's collapse was like "chickens coming home to roost" for joining highly unequal economies in NAFTA. He does not explain why NAFTA brought on faulty Mexican financial policy, other than to assert that it did not permit Mexico to take retrenchment measures earlier. I don't agree with this.

The moral hazard issue is a troubling one. I asked about it frequently in my interviews with officials from the US government and international agencies. The response was invariably that they did not know how to carry out the rescue package without making tesobono investors whole. Either there had to be a rescue package, with all its defects, or leave Mexico to the unkind devices of the market, with whatever tragic consequences this could have had. Moral hazard was not unique to this case. It arises under deposit insurance; it is a feature of the many commercial bank rescues that are taking place throughout the world; it was accepted in the US government rescue of the Chrysler Corporation. In bank rescues and deposit insurance, a distinction can be made between shareholders, who are not the objects of the rescue, and depositors. Distinguishing among tesobono holders could not be this straightforward, at least not in this case. From my vantage, this was the least satisfactory aspect of the peso rescue package.

Having said this, it should be kept in mind that not all persons rescued were plutocrats. Many families had a stake in the rescue – like investors in mutual funds and pension plans.

Several Mexican bankers said to me privately that paying off US investors was the primary motive of the rescue package. The comment lacks grace. It assumes that President Clinton was prepared to raise a domestic storm for this end alone. It also lacks decency in that many of the very persons who made this comment also were investors in tesobonos.

There has been considerable public commentary praising the rescue package. The most thorough was an article by a trio of experts in the journal *Foreign Affairs*.[48] Their argument was that "the peso support package worked" because the rescue as such did not deal with a "systemic" but rather a "liquidity" problem, and the support permitted Mexico to painfully work its way out of its disastrous situation. David Hale, chief economist of Zurich Kemper Investments, argued that the large foreign assistance package, by preventing a Mexican default, permitted markets to stabilize relatively quickly and enable Mexico to resume international borrowing by June 1995.[49]

Thomas L. Friedman, in a *New York Times* column, advised against listening to demagogues asserting that Mexico's debt is Mexico's problem.[50] "Mexico owes us $100 billion. That's our problem." Mexico, he argues "*is* home" (emphasis his). Friedman also makes the point that many of the people rescued were investors in mutual and pension funds and not just the managers of these funds.

My view is that the rescue package was a stroke of superb statesmanship, and Secretary Rubin and President Clinton deserve credit for leading in the face of determined congressional opposition. My only regret is that had the support come a month earlier, the damage to the Mexican economy would have been less and the "tequila effect" less pronounced; but this probably would have failed in the US context. It was a courageous decision taken by what we now know is a risk-averse US president (at least in political if not personal matters) in the face of public bombast against the rescue. It is fortunate for Mexico and US–Mexican relations that the need for this decision came when it did in Clinton's first term. Had the crisis arisen during the electoral year 1996, we can be confident that Mexico would have been allowed to stew in its own errors. This was evident during the electoral campaign when Clinton was unwilling to defend NAFTA, or free 'trade in the Americas, both inherently less controversial issues.

The predictors of doom, that the loan would not be repaid, were proved wrong. The rescue package has largely disappeared from view because it did work and the critics, therefore, mostly fell silent. The main disparagement of the rescue comes from those who believe the market must always be allowed to solve economic problems, whatever the hardship involved; or from those who argue that the nominal exchange rate of any currency must be maintained whatever the circumstances. We now know from the Asian crisis that the issue of moral hazard must be resolved somehow to "bail in" the private banks and investors rather than to "bail them out."

8
The Aftermath

Once the gravity of the fallout from the devaluation was fully grasped, realistic policies to deal with the situation were devised. The new program was not unveiled until March 9, 1995, and even then the extent of the economic collapse was underestimated.

The press release of *Hacienda* when the program was announced projected that the decline in gross domestic product (GDP) for 1995 would be 2 percent – it turned out to be 6.9 percent (using a 1980 base in both cases). Inflation for the year was forecast at around 42 percent – it turned out to be 52 percent (consumer prices, December-over-December). The current account deficit was expected to fall from the $30 billion registered in 1994 to $2 billion in 1995 – it turned out to be less, meaning that the fall in domestic demand was greater than anticipated. The decline in 1995 in what the Bank of Mexico referred to as "domestic absorption" – public and private consumption and investment – was a massive 15.9 percent. Because of the sharp rise in exports, which proved to be the main savior of the situation, aggregate demand fell by less, by 10.2 percent, after rising by 4.9 percent in 1994 – a turnaround of 15 percentage points.[1]

These cold numbers jump out to economists who crunch them for a living, but do not necessarily capture the hardship they entailed for the majority of the Mexican population. The minimum wage in Mexico, which varies by region, fell, on average, in real terms by 18 percent during the year. The fall in earnings of workers in manufacturing was similar, measuring from November 1994 to November 1995.[2] These earning declines in 1995 came on top of a persistent drops, particularly of the minimum wage, in most years after 1982.[3] To put a number on what is being said here, the minimum wage in Mexico City and the surrounding area was 20.15 pesos a day in December 1995, about 121 pesos for a six-day week, or the equivalent of less than $16 a week at the then exchange rate of 7.56597 to the dollar. About 15–20 percent of the working population earns no more than one minimum wage.

Figures on the increase in unemployment are inexact. By one measure, the number of people enrolled in the Mexican Social Security Institute (IMSS), the largest of the systems, fell by 629 000 in 1995.[4] Enrollment is a proxy for changes in employment, a plus figure demonstrating employment growth and a minus figure employment loss. The recorded decline in the IMSS is surely understatement of the total picture, in that there are other social security systems and not all persons are registered; the consensus estimate is that the increase in unemployment was about 1 million during the year.

The number of street vendors and others in the informal or black economy grew visibly as the hardships of the year continued. The OECD estimated the size of the informal economy at 35 percent of non-farm employment, and, by the end of 1995, the figure was 5–10 percentage points more than that.[5]

The suffering was great and it was widespread; and the experience certainly will remain in the psyche of all who experienced it. It has affected the way Mexicans look at their government and accelerated the realignment of political parties that was under way even before the crash.

However, there is another side to the aftermath of the events in 1994 – namely, the speed with which the recovery was effected. The drop in the economy started modestly in the first quarter of 1995, peaked in the second quarter, and then declined at somewhat lower rates in the two succeeding quarters of the year. In 1996, the following year, GDP *grew* by 5.1 percent.[6] Two principles that guided financial and economic policy in 1995 contributed both to the substantial one-year crash and to the rapid recovery. These were the president's insistence on paying the external debt; and his conviction that a crash program and not gradual changes were essential to achieve the turnaround.[7] Zedillo was quite explicit on the need for a crash correction at various points during 1995, arguing that as severe as the hardship would be, the cumulative, drawn-out effects of a gradualist model, such as that used to deal with the 1982 debt crisis, would be worse.

The underlying policy principles

Each of the two basic tenets that were used to devise policy for 1995 can be debated. Mexico need not have met the full obligations of tesobonos at their expiration dates – and, indeed, certainly would not have done so if the US rescue package had not been put in place. In that case, the best that Mexico could have done was to give an IOU and delay payment until dollars or other hard currencies were available; and delay would have been tantamount to default. This would have been the outcome had President Clinton not used his executive authority under the ESF and had the IMF not joined the rescue effort.

Moral hazard was a relevant concept for the US government and the IMF – they were bailing out many investors – but had Mexico not met its obligations, the issue would not have been moral hazard but straightforward default. In that case, the credibility of the Mexican government would have been severely compromised. As it was, the credibility of the Zedillo government was given a substantial boost. It is noteworthy, as the Bank of Mexico points out in its report on the year 1995, that Mexico regained access to international capital markets within five months of the December devaluation, whereas it had taken almost seven years to accomplish this after the 1982 crisis. The terms and interest rates at first were not especially favorable – in May and June, the terms on foreign borrowings were a little less than one year and the interest rate was 549 basis points over Libor – but the conditions improved later in 1995 and in 1996.[8] The US rescue loan could not have been repaid as quickly as it was had not Mexico been able to borrow under increasingly favorable conditions in world money markets, especially in 1996. In that year, the Mexican government reached an all-time high in placing securities in foreign money markets and was able to lengthen maturities by issuing bonds.[9]

Economists, for the most part, have concluded, based on experience with gradual versus crash adjustments, that the latter are not merely faster, but succeed more often. The fact that President Zedillo was a trained economist surely influenced his decision. Guillermo Ortiz, the *Hacienda* Secretary, also was trained as an economist. It is speculation to ask whether the adjustment process would have been as rapid had the educational and experiential formation of the President and his Finance Secretary been in politics, but there is evidence that it would not have been. This will be noted later in the reaction of the Partido de la Revolución Democrática (PRD) to the peso rescue loan. One cannot say with certainty what the results would have been – and where Mexico would be today in its economic recovery – had the adjustment effort been a gradual one.

Key elements of the adjustment program

Economic policy in 1994 included the following elements: unwillingness to alter the exchange-rate structure; reliance on tesobonos; insistence that a large current account deficit was not dangerous as long as the funds came voluntarily from private investors; a willingness to retard economic growth over an extended period, using an overvalued exchange rate to do this, in order to drive inflation down to a low, single-digit level; and a kind of morbid resistance to make economic data public on a current basis. The shock after the December devaluation changed all of that:

1 Mexico, on December 22, 1994, abandoned the currency trading band and floated the peso.
2 Mexico ceased issuing tesobonos and in 1995 amortized $29 billion of these obligations (99.1 percent of those outstanding at the end of December 1994).
3 The current account deficit in 1995 was 0.6 percent of GDP compared with 7 percent in 1994. It is unlikely that, for the foreseeable future, any serious Mexican policy official will make light of the vulnerability to the country of a large current account deficit, say one exceeding about 4 percent of GDP. The danger signals will be perceived well before that level is reached.
4 While reducing and maintaining low inflation remains a priority – indeed, this is the main priority of the independent Bank of Mexico – the absolutist nature of rock-bottom inflation rather than economic growth, was abandoned. The use of an exchange-rate anchor for keeping inflation down is unlikely to be practiced again over too long a period, as it was from the end of 1987 to the end of 1994.
5 Financial and monetary data are now released on a timely basis. Today, this goes beyond financial data and there are web sites covering all relevant Mexican agencies. (This still does not go so far as releasing minutes of discussions of the *junta* of the Bank of Mexico on a timely basis. In the United States, summaries of meetings of the Federal Open Market Committee are released on the Friday after the subsequent meeting, a delay of about 2 months.

When I asked senior officials of the Bank of Mexico whether this practice, or one similar to it, might be adopted to let the informed public know about the thinking of members of the *junta*, I was told more than once that this was "unthinkable.")

Both the IMF stabilization program and the US support package were conditioned on Mexico taking steps to have a budget surplus, refraining from the use of development banks as an alternative means for public expenditures, tightening monetary policy, and achieving greater transparency in the management of public economic policy. It was a program of austerity – "stringent" was the word used by Michel Camdessus, the Managing Director of the IMF.[10] It was, in fact, the kind of stabilization program that many critics of the IMF abhor in that it deepened hardships as the basis for achieving sustained growth later. Both these outcomes, in fact, did emerge – deepened hardship and later robust recovery. While the conditions were imposed by the IMF and the US Treasury, there is no evidence that the measures were resisted by those making economic policy in Mexico, particularly President Zedillo and *Hacienda* secretary Ortiz.

Some actions to attain the fiscal and monetary targets did meet with considerable internal resistance. The fiscal measure that received most critical attention was an increase in the value added tax (VAT) rate on all goods from 10 percent to 15 percent. The stabilization program called for raising revenue and this was probably the most logical way to do this, by using a tax that is most easy to monitor and also would reduce consumption – and it was precisely these dual characteristics that made it so offensive. The size of the rate increase – 50 percent – remained a political issue in Mexico for years to come.

In addition, the March 9 program called for raising gasoline prices immediately by 35 percent and electricity rates to final consumers by 20 percent, and then raising these prices by an additional 0.8 percent each month of the year.

The stock of domestic credit (net domestic credit was defined as the difference between the monetary base and international reserves) from the Bank of Mexico declined substantially during the year. Nominal interest rates rose sharply. Using the average interbank interest rate (TIIP), the average for 1995, in nominal terms, was 54 percent, compared with the 1994 average of 18 percent. After factoring in inflation (the consumer price index or CPI) of 7 percent in 1994 and 52 percent in 1995, there was no real interest rate increase between the two years. The TIIP rose sharply after the March program was put in place and then followed a declining path starting in the third quarter. The consumer price index showed a similar path, rising by 8 percent in March when the austerity program was announced, and then continuing its upward path but at a declining rate for the rest of the year.

The floating exchange rate fell sharply in March – the peso depreciated by almost 18 percent in that month alone compared with the previous month – and then remained relatively stable during much of the remainder of the year. The rate at the end of December 1995 was 7.6 pesos to the dollar. As points of comparison, the peso at the end of December 1993 was 3.1 to the dollar and, at the end of December 1994, 5.3 to the dollar. There was thus a depreciation of 43.5 percent in nominal terms during 1995 but, because consumer prices rose by 52 percent, the peso actually appreciated in real terms during the year. This was a source of some complaint by exporters, many of whom called for a more managed depreciation to make their exports more competitive. These calls were not heeded. Guillermo Ortiz was quoted at the end of 1997 as saying that while the flexible exchange rate system was introduced as a temporary expedient, he thought it should remain because it turned out to be more stable than expected.[11]

The short-term measures put in place to deal with the crisis have persisted, with some modifications, over the medium term. The test of economic policies is how well they achieve their objectives over some reasonable time period. GDP growth bounded back up in 1996, but it can be argued that this should not be given too much weight because the increase was from the low base of 1995. Fair enough, except that there had been no similar rebound over many years after the 1982 debt fiasco. Real GDP rose again in 1997, this time by 6.8 percent (1993 base).

The economic growth rate for 1998 was anticipated to be between 5 and 6 percent and the final figure was 4.8 percent – but therein also lies a story that almost surely would not have been the case in 1994. Budgetary projections for 1998 were based on an average export price for oil of $15 a barrel. The price fell below that and three times during the first seven months, budgetary expenditures were reduced to minimize the fiscal deficit and thereby reduce inflationary pressures. During 1994, it should be recalled, the authorities deliberately used the development banks to increase public sector expenditures. The lesson of fiscal discipline had sunk in, at least for the time being.

Mexico also was buffeted in 1998 by contagion from the Asian and Russian exchange-rate and economic crises. Solving its 1995 problems obviously did not assure a rose-garden economy indefinitely. A few other figures can be given, but it is unwise to dwell on these because the time elapsed – three years or so since the débâcle – is too short. Consumer prices, which rose (December-over-December) by 52 percent in 1995, almost 28 percent in 1996, rose by less than 16 percent in 1997. This decline was accomplished without using the exchange rate as the anti-inflation anchor.[12] The average interbank exchange rate at the start of 1997 was 7.81 pesos to the dollar, and 8.11 per dollar at the end of the year – a nominal depreciation of 4 percent for the year and actually an appreciation in real terms. The Bank insists that the main reason for the real appreciation of the peso in 1996 and 1997 was the large inflow of direct investment.[13] The rate continued to depreciate in nominal terms in 1998, quite sharply in the latter half of the year. The Bank of Mexico let it be known in 1997 that it would buy and sell foreign exchange not to influence the peso to any predetermined rate but to moderate volatility that might emerge. This has resulted in an increase in foreign reserves from the low point after December 1994 devaluation to more than $30 billion by mid-1998 – an amount higher than the peak reached in early 1994.

Foreign investment, particularly direct investment, has been pouring into Mexico. This amounted to almost $11 billion in 1994, fell to about $9.7 billion in 1995 – a figure that was as high as it was because investors took advantage of the exchange-rate depreciation to invest in maquiladora industries – dropped to $7.5 billion in 1996, and then shot up to more than $12 billion in 1997. There is considerable sectoral diversification of foreign direct investment (FDI) in Mexico, although manufacturing dominates. Portfolio capital fled the country in 1995, picked up again in 1996, but was only $3.7 billion in 1997.

As the Mexican economy kept growing in 1996 and subsequently, the trade and current account positions reflected this. Starting in mid-1997, Mexico's merchandise trade balance started to turn negative – that is, imports exceeded exports. This continued into 1998. The key determinant of Mexico's import level is not its tariff rates or even its exchange rate, but rather the rate of economic growth – and the higher this gets, the greater imports are. The current account deficit – that is, after including trade in services as well as goods – jumped in 1997 to $7.4 billion, about 1.8 percent of GDP.

Mexico, to put it in slightly technical jargon, has a high income elasticity of imports and this could spell trouble in terms of a large current account deficit if GDP growth is high, year after year.

Strengths and weaknesses

The main strengths of the Mexican economy as it approaches the millennium are those already discussed: an exchange-rate system less subject to attack than the semi-fixed rate that existed earlier; relatively low reliance on volatile capital to finance a large current account deficit; demonstrated fiscal discipline; confidence of long-term investors, as demonstrated by the large inflows of direct investment; reduction of inflation, but not in the form of an incomes policy and a controlled exchange rate; and a vast, largely open, market next door for its exports.

None of these strengths is immutable. No exchange-rate system is invulnerable to every pressure. Fiscal discipline is not necessarily eternal. Market evaluation of Mexican performance can change as policies change. Inflation is not yet at a low, single-digit level. The fact that the United States now takes almost 85 percent of Mexico's merchandise exports means that a downturn in the US economy could be devastating to Mexico. Yet, the current economic structure is surely more solid than that which existed before 1995.

Just about all sectors of the Mexican economy plummeted in 1995. Construction headed the list of losers; according to the Bank of Mexico, it fell by more than 23 percent (using 1993 prices). Commerce fell by double digits, as did banking services. Manufacturing and transportation fell at lower rates. Some sectors continued to do badly even as the recovery started in 1996, such as retail sales. By the start of 1998, however, there was recovery across the board, both in sales and profits. The automotive industry, pharmaceuticals, electronic equipment, capital goods, steel, construction, and consumer goods such as shoes and clothing, all increased. Bancomer refers to a diffusion index designed to measure the general expansion of manufacturing, which showed that between 80 and 90 percent of manufacturing branches showed increases in production volume in the 22 months after mid-1996.[14] The diversity of its production is one of the strengths of the Mexican economy.

There are several other elements of strength. Domestic savings in Mexico in 1994 had dropped to 14.5 percent of GDP. President Zedillo, in the years before he became president, regularly pointed to this low rate of savings as perhaps Mexico's main vulnerability. It meant that Mexico had to rely excessively on foreign savings to maintain an adequate level of investment. As president, Zedillo acted to shore up the savings rate. The pension system, which now permits wage earners to invest in the private sector via independently managed accounts, was designed, in part, to raise the savings rate. A more stable peso could surely do the same once confidence exists that this will continue even when administrations change. In 1996, the savings rate was 20 percent of GDP, and it rose a few more points in 1997. This level, around 24 percent, may not be durable, but the early indications are that the new economic policies are having a positive effect on this important variable.

One of the most significant developments in Mexico during the past three decades has been a steady decline in population growth rates. These, some 30 years ago, were about 3 percent a year. Each woman, on average, had seven children as recently as 1970. The average number of children per woman is now around three. The population growth rate is now below 2 percent a year, and falling. The rule of thumb used to be that Mexico had to create upwards of 1 million jobs a year just to accommodate new entrants into the labor force. If the recent and current trends continue, this number may be only 650 000 in the year 2010.[15]

The Mexican economic structure also has many weaknesses, deriving generally from the reality that the country is a developing one. Focusing first on purely economic issues, the banking fragility that so sorely plagued the country during 1994 and which contributed to faulty Bank of Mexico decisions on interest-rate matters is not resolved. Indeed, it was much worse at the end of 1998 than it was in 1994. The handling of the bad loans accumulated over the years by Fobaproa is largely resolved, but not without controversy. The total cost of the rescue of a weak financial system has not yet been reckoned.

The decline in world oil prices in 1998 highlighted another fundamental weakness, namely, the over-representation of receipts from oil sales in public-sector tax revenue. Oil exports now constitute about 10 percent of all export sales, but they contribute between 30 and 40 percent of tax revenue. Consequently, the biggest hit from a decline in oil prices comes not in the balance of payments, but in the ability to pay for vital social services. The heavy taxes also deprive Pemex, the state-owned oil monopoly, of resources for exploration and exploitation of additional oil and gas fields. The tax structure that leads to these unfavorable outcomes is finally under discussion, but it took a serious fiscal shortfall for the government to address a problem that has long been evident. Constant decisions driven by crisis is not the ideal way to run economic policy. Altering tax structures is not easy in any country, but Mexico surely has had some horrid experiences in recent decades as evidence that a more prudent decision-making procedure is needed.

Apart from the immediate economic problems, other weaknesses were highlighted as a result of the austerity of 1995. A high incidence of poverty has long been a feature of Mexican society. In his fifth *Informe* to the nation on November 1, 1993, President Salinas made much of the fact that the level of extreme poverty had been reduced from 18.8 percent to 16 percent of the population between 1989 and 1992. This, as he put it, was a reduction of people living below the poverty line from about 15 million to 13.5 million. "Extreme poverty," as he defined it, refers to people with income below the level that permits them to buy a basic basket of goods. On other occasions, he referred to the number of Mexicans living in poverty, but not extreme, as an additional 20 percent of the population.[16] Poverty tends to be procyclical – that is, it gets worse as economic conditions worsen and diminishes when economic growth is strong.[17] Poverty worsened in Mexico as the economy plummeted in 1995 and while the incidence of poverty later diminished as the economy recovered, Mexico's overall level remains unacceptably high.

Those who suffered during the 1995 economic downturn included more than the very poorest. Home mortgages and consumer credit in Mexico tend to have adjustable interest rates and since these rose along with the monetary tightness, the fallout was widespread. The government introduced a number of programs to tide people over until the recovery, and while these undoubtedly helped, they could not alleviate all the pain. El Barzón, a debtors' group, was organized, to obtain relief from the high interest rates, and this became an important lobbying organization. Yet, in a country that has no safety net of consequence, those least able to cope with the austerity were the people whose lives were austere to start with.

In addition to poverty, whether measured below or just above the poverty line, Mexico's income distribution is highly unequal. The data for the early 1990s indicated that the 40 percent of families with the lowest income received 12 percent of total national income, while the richest 10 percent of families received 39 percent.[18]

There has been a marked increase in crime in many Mexican

cities in recent years. In Mexico City, public opinion polls during 1997 and 1998 regularly showed that the population considered the major problem of the city to be lack of security, even more than pollution, corruption, and unemployment.[19] There is no way to state definitively that this lawlessness is a result of the periodic economic decline of recent decades, particularly during the 1980s and 1990s, a reaction to official corruption, or the influence of the drug trade, or perhaps some of all of these. This fear for personal safety, even if the sole cause is not poverty, surely leads to its own economic problems. Foreigners are regularly warned not to hail cruising taxis for fear of robbery, or worse, and this make it harder for taxi drivers to earn a living. Tourists now think of Mexico as an unsafe place to visit. Residents do not walk aimlessly in the streets window shopping, as they once did. The sole beneficiaries of this rise in personal violence, other than the perpetrators, are those who are in the business of providing protection.

In commercial terms, Mexico is fortunate in being located next to the largest, open market in the world. The country's proximity to the United States stimulates US investment to cut down on transportation costs for sending goods back and forth. When Mexicans seek to escape the country for better economic opportunity, they go north and try to enter the United States. However, one disadvantage of being next door to the United States is that this makes Mexico a logical transit location for shipment of narcotics to the largest market in the world for these commodities. The billions of dollars generated for the drug dealers translates into massive, unavoidable, bribery. The slogan that is common is that for law officials of Mexico, it is either *plomo o pesos* (bullets or money), and there is much of both. President Zedillo has called the drug issue Mexico's most serious problem.

One final weakness that merits mention is the lack of a trusted and credible system of justice. Zedillo recognized this when he assumed office, but his plans for reform were sidetracked by the economic crisis. Yet, it is hard for an economy to function efficiently if the population is unconvinced that there is equal justice before the law.

Mexico has become stronger in recent years from its growing political diversity and solid economic policies. It is now a more solid country in these dimensions than it was before the 1994–5 economic collapse. Mexico, however, is still a country with serious economic and social weaknesses, some of which were worsened by the economic crash and the tribulations of the recovery. The lost gamble taken in 1994 to wait until 1995 to deal with the country's economic problems came with a high price tag.

The NAFTA connection

Opponents of NAFTA, both in Mexico and the United States, have seized on the events of 1994 and 1995 as the basis for renewed attacks on the agreement. One line of attack is technical, that free international capital mobility is incompatible with free multinational trade and full employment.[20] The corrective, according to these analysts, is to throw sand in the wheels of portfolio capital movement. This is not a purely US–Mexico issue, although the argument is applicable here. The suggestion to do something universal to complicate the movement of volatile capital is arguable, with supporters and critics, but it is not the what the NAFTA-haters in the United States have in mind. They are less concerned with portfolio capital than they are with the movement of goods and services and long-term direct investment moving out of the United States into Mexico.

A number of anti-NAFTA members of the US House of Representatives sent a "Dear Colleague" letter on July 14, 1998, to buttress support for legislation they submitted to prevent use of the Exchange Stabilization Fund to (ESF) "open credit lines to bail out banks and investors around the globe without the approval of Congress."[21] Appended to the letter was one dated July 9, 1998, signed by Carlos Heredia Z., a member of the Mexican Chamber of Deputies and coordinator of international relations for the PRD in the Chamber. Heredia said he was writing on behalf of 126 members of the congressional bloc of the PRD – that is, its full representation in the 500-member Chamber. It was obviously a solicited letter and it blamed the US–IMF rescue package for, among other things, the harsh adjustment program that went with the credit, business failures, growth in unemployment, reduced wages, bailout of bankers (the Fobaproa issue was what was cited), an increasing trade imbalance, and a high cost to service government bonds in order to pay the US and IMF credits. This is like blaming the surgeon for the pain and suffering from an operation to correct a self-inflicted wound. The letter did not confine itself to the 1995 situation, but went as far back as the suffering that followed the 1982 crisis.

It is a curious letter, apart from some inaccurate facts; after all,

Mexico's trade imbalance did not take place until *after* the economy recovered. The US–IMF credit did not deal with the later Fobaproa controversy. The letter was essentially an anti-IMF and an anti-PRI diatribe being displayed on the US legislative scene. It is an example of the left in the lower legislative houses of the two countries getting together. In each country, the two lefts have strong allies on the right who opposed both NAFTA and the US peso credit.

The anti-NAFTA argument in the United States in 1995 focused primarily on the turnaround in the US bilateral trade balance with Mexico from a modest surpluses in 1993 and 1994 (less than $2 billion each year) to a large US deficit in 1995 (almost $16 billion). This was then translated into the argument that a trade deficit means a loss of jobs. Apart from the primitive economics – exports are good and imports are bad – what was evident at the time was that the one bright spot in the Mexican economy was the big jump in exports. The decline in Mexico's GDP would have been much more severe without the export increase. NAFTA, to its credit, gave assurance to Mexican exporters that the US market would remain open and it is surprising that serious Mexicans deprecate this reality.

Bilateral trade performance between Mexico and the United States, to repeat what already has been stated, depends crucially on the level and change in economic activity. As the US economy grows, it sucks in imports; so, too, does the Mexican economy. As the Mexican economy contracts, it takes in fewer imports; so, too, would the US economy if it contracted. Increased imports are not the sign of a sick economy, but of a healthy one.

US exports to Mexico have increased substantially since NAFTA came into effect. The value in 1993, before NAFTA, was about $42 billion; in 1997, it was $86 billion.[22] Mexico now competes with Japan as the second largest market for US exports, after Canada. The US trade deficit with Mexico jumped to $17 billion in 1996, then declined to $14 billion in 1997, and rose slightly to $15 billion in 1998.

The bilateral trade balance with Mexico, which is not a meaningful figure in the global context of trade, is less relevant in analyzing the NAFTA connection than is the impact of the agreement on the financial and macroeconomic decisions Mexico took in 1994. NAFTA had two potentially "negative" effects: it probably encouraged portfolio investment in Mexico, mainly because Mexico popped up more frequently on the computer screens of money traders; and because of the uncertainty of congressional approval of NAFTA in late 1993, this would have prevented a peso devaluation at that time, even if one were under consideration – which was not the case.

All other relevant Mexican policy decisions leading to the December 1994 catastrophe were unrelated to NAFTA – on the exchange rate during 1994, lack of concern over the growing current account deficit, the use of tesobonos, catering to commercial bank weakness in managing interest rates, the lack of openness to foreign investment in the Mexican commercial banking structure, secrecy in the release of key financial and economic data, and the fact that political considerations played such a large role in economic policy prior to the August elections. NAFTA did not cause the Chiapas uprising on January 1, 1994, the day the agreement came into effect; and it did not cause the other political shocks Mexico suffered in 1994. The US Federal Reserve did not hold back on raising the federal funds rate because it would have a significant impact on Mexico, NAFTA notwithstanding.

With respect to Mexico's $18 billion trade deficit in 1994, almost $7 billion was with countries in Europe and $8 billion with countries in Asia. Mexico's trade deficit that year with the United States was only $3 billion.[23] The overall size of the deficit that year clearly cannot be attributed to NAFTA. One interesting point that I was told by a person close to Pedro Aspe was that Aspe, in 1994, had recommended to Jaime Serra Puche, then Secretary of Secofi, that Mexico should raise its tariffs against non-NAFTA countries, especially those in Asia. Mexico could do this and still conform to its GATT obligations and, in fact, did exactly this after the deluge.

The only argument that remains for connecting NAFTA with the economic collapse is that cited at the beginning, that Mexico should not have opened its economy to imports and to portfolio capital and to foreign borrowing by commercial banks as fully as it did with the sequencing that occurred. Mexico, it can be argued, should not have allowed commercial banks to borrow as freely as they did without a more thorough supervisory and oversight mechanism in place. The banks should not have been allowed to lend based on the kind of crony capitalism that existed in Mexico in the absence of a more rigorous regulatory framework. These are only peripherally NAFTA issues and, even if accepted as valid, deal more with internal policy actions than with the workings of NAFTA. Mexico, after all, was not the only country which received large amounts of portfolio capital flows.

Final comment

It is too soon with say with great confidence where Mexico is headed. A recovery that is only a few years old, and which followed on a devastating collapse, is not a solid basis for projection.

Its last three decades of history make the crucial time for assessing the solidity of the Mexican structure the transition from one government to the next, which will occur on December 1, 2000. Political considerations dominated economic decision-making in 1994 and there is some danger of this in 2000 when there will be a realistic chance that an opposition candidate will be elected president. While political opening undoubtedly has been healthy for the future of Mexico, political posturing and maneuvering can create short-term problems. Another peso collapse in 2000 would surely have profound effects on the nature of the Mexican polity and would lead to major shifts in the exchange-rate structure, such as the adoption of the dollar as the nation's currency, or a fixed dollar–peso relationship under a currency board system, as in Argentina. This kind of speculation can await the outcome of events in the year 2000 because Mexico may manage the transition without a currency collapse.

Investors, both foreign and domestic, were burned in 1994, as they were in earlier presidential transition years, and they will be sensitive to policy actions of the government and the Bank of Mexico. Cold-blooded investors must be convinced this time, in 2000, that past errors will not be repeated. That will be the critical time to decide just how much the Mexican government – the PRI – has matured politically to be able to carry out sensible economic policies even in the face of possible electoral loss.

9
To Bet a Nation

"Somebody said I was going to bet the farm – I said, I'm going to bet the country." (Robert Dole[1])

The fascination with the Mexican economic experience of 1994–5 has many facets. For economists and players in the financial markets, the speed with which capital left the country once confidence in Mexican policies was destroyed became an object lesson in the new and unsentimental world of vast capital movements. The Mexican experience was unique in its magnitude until 1997 but, after the repetition in countries in East Asia, it is now just Exhibit A. The cruelty of globalized capital movements spawned suggestions for "throwing sand" in the gears of this market, most notably a tax on currency transactions as advocated by James Tobin, Professor Emeritus at Yale and a Nobel Laureate in economics in 1981.[2] While some countries do inhibit short-term capital movements – Chile, most notably – the "Tobin tax" has not attracted widespread support.

For political scientists, the most noteworthy aspects of the Mexican experience were the evident domination of political over economic calculations during the fateful year 1994 and the damage caused by this priority. Yet, there has been a golden lining even to this in that the economic breakdown surely accelerated the political opening that was nascent in Mexico even earlier. The PRI may still dominate Mexican politics for some years, but its monopoly of power is over.

For the men and women in the street in Mexico, the experience of the meltdown was a tragedy. Incomes declined, unemployment rose, poverty increased, and lawlessness in large cities took on new intensity. The analysis of technicians can be quite cold-blooded but, for those caught up in the process, the experience is starkly personal. Nothing ever will be quite the same for the Mexican people; distrust of what the government says, and speculation about what it is keeping secret, has now become part of the national character. While not completely new, this skepticism is now deeply ingrained. Mexico now is the "show-me" country par excellence.

The reputations of erstwhile heroes have been destroyed. Carlos Salinas is correct; he is Mexico's *"villano favorito,"* whereas in 1993 he was seen as Mexico's most successful president in decades. Jaime Serra Puche might well have become the PRI presidential candidate in 2000, but this is now out of the question. This list could be extended, but the purpose of this analysis is not to characterize individuals as heroes or villains. The main assumption is, instead, that most of the decision-makers were men of good will and honest in their sincerity to do what was right for their country.

Many knowledgeable experts have commented on the lessons learned from the Mexican experience. For a time, indeed, this lesson listing became something of an international pastime. Some of the more notable contributions that deal with technical matters will be noted below. These generally look at Mexico from the outside and, for the most part, contain valuable, even if by now clichéd, advice about what countries should and should not do if they wish to avoid a Mexican-type crash. The purpose of this book is different. The objective here has been to understand why particular decisions were taken in the contemporary situation that existed. These can lead to lessons in an *ex post* context, but have their own logic at the time the decisions were made. The related and deeper purpose of the analysis here is to understand the main cultural features of Mexican society that consciously or unconsciously led to actions taken or not taken. What was there in the cultural formation of Mexican decision-makers that led them to do what they did? Explaining that is the main purpose of this book. The book is intended to be an analysis of important characteristics that Mexican policy officials brought to their positions – from their educational formation, governmental experience, historical antecedents, and sociological milieu – as viewed through a case study of decision-making on an issue of substantial importance to the Mexican people.

The technical lessons

Lawrence Summers, Deputy Secretary of the US Treasury and the US official most deeply involved in the peso rescue package, listed 10 lessons[3]: There is no substitute for sound economic policies; unsustainable policies cannot be sustained [sic]; officials in countries with emerging economies should treat capital outflows as permanent; high rates of domestic savings are essential for healthy development; current account deficits are dangerous if they are too big; transparency is essential to a well functioning international capital market; the international financial community must become better at surveillance; the international financial community must develop greater capacity to respond to financial emergencies; long-term investment must be promoted; and there is no substitute for continuing the work of economic integration.

Edwin M. Truman, the senior staff official at the US Fed regularly engaged in Mexican affairs, listed lessons based on what he called a three-by-three perspective – that of creditors; recipients of capital inflows; and the financial system as a whole.[4] Truman's analysis with respect to creditors is that their individual losses were marginal (and close to nil for holders of tesobonos) because there were so many of them and their Mexican investments were not a large portion of their total portfolios. This contrasts with the debt crisis of 1982, when the claims on Mexico of the top nine US commercial banks amounted to 50 percent of their capital. The main lesson he draws from this is that creditors, in the next liquidity crisis, should expect to take more extensive losses. This, in fact, is what happened in the East Asian and Russian financial breakdowns.

The main lesson for recipients of foreign portfolio investment is to take account of the size, scope, and speed of the crisis once it erupted. As Truman put it: "By the standards of the 1980s, this was a new world."[5] A second lesson is that if a country is going to run a large current account deficit financed by net private capital inflows, it must ensure that the funds are wisely invested. Truman lists three other "obvious" (his word) lessons: countries should not be tempted to try to sustain overvalued exchange rates for too long; they should avoid excessive reliance on short-term borrowing; and when a country is forced to change its exchange-rate regime, there should be compensating and complementary changes in other macroeconomic policies.

With respect to the international financial system, the main lesson Truman puts forward is that authorities must rethink how they interact with the market when a crisis emerges. There were, he said, differences of view about whether the Mexican crisis involved systemic risk, defined at four levels: the banking system in other countries; other financial institutions, such as stock and bond markets; economic activity around the world; and the trend that exists for market-oriented reforms. His conclusion is that risk existed in all these spheres, if one defines risk as a non-zero probability. Finally, Truman emphasizes the need for transparency of financial data.[6]

Michel Camdessus, Managing Director of the IMF, cited four lessons for countries, four for the IMF, and suggested a number of adaptations of the current international financial structure that flow from these.[7] The country lessons he gave are: the "unfailing obligation" to impose discipline on their economic policy; large external current account deficits are dangerous; sound and credible accompanying measures are essential to make a new exchange rate sustainable; the costs are high of failure to regularly publish information about key economic indicators. His lessons for the IMF are variations on the same theme: the development of standards for the publication of data (which has since taken place); continuous policy dialogue between the Fund and countries; more focused surveillance; and more candid policy dialogue. Camdessus concluded his discussion with the need for the IMF to have and to be able to mobilize resources more quickly because other crises will occur from time to time. This speech was delivered about two years before the chain of crises erupted in East Asia.

One other technical evaluation will be cited, that of Julio López G., who concluded that the main cause of the December 1994 crisis was the combination of the large current account deficit and the overvalued peso which stimulated imports and discouraged exports.[8] His lessons, therefore, fall into the mainstream of those cited by the critics concerning the pernicious effects when these two aspects of policy – the exchange rate and the size of the current account deficit – are allowed to get out of kilter.

I have no disagreement with these lessons, which by now are part of the conventional wisdom of what the Mexican experience has taught the world about the dangers of economic policy shortcomings.

The collapse of a number of economies in Northeast and Southeast Asia in 1997 had elements similar to those of Mexico in 1994, but also differences. Some similarities were weak banks with a growing level of non-performing loans, lack of transparency about the true situation of both the banks and the economy as a whole, large deficits in the current account of the balance of payments, and overvalued currencies. There was considerable bank lending to affiliated parties, what has come to be known as "crony capitalism," and lack of rigorous bank supervision both in Mexico and East Asia. Some East Asian countries had authoritarian leaders whose popular support vanished once the economic troubles began; Indonesia stands out in this respect.

There also were differences between East Asia and Mexico. Savings rates in East Asia were high, as was gross investment – although investment was not always in the most productive activities. The contagion from country to country in East Asia – "bahtulism" as it was called because the troubles originated in Thailand – was much more virulent than the "tequila effect" after the Mexican breakdown. Policy-makers in the Asian countries gave no indication from their behavior before the financial collapses that they considered the Mexican experience relevant to their situations.

Brazil, in 1998–99, faced an economic problem with elements eerily similar to those Mexico faced in 1994: an overvalued exchange rate pegged to the US dollar; sharp losses in foreign reserves to protect the currency; a large current account deficit, although smaller than in Mexico in 1994; and a public-sector deficit larger than that in Mexico, even taking into account Mexican spending through its development banks. The Brazil rescue package from the IMF and industrial countries of the Group of Seven (G-7) came before there was an economic collapse in exchange for measures to eliminate the fiscal deficit. The end of the Brazilian story was more benign than in Mexico. It is clear that the Mexican experience was very much on the minds of the Brazilian authorities; and on the minds of the management of the IMF and leaders of the industrial countries as they seek to take action of prevent a repeat of the Mexican débâcle. The G-7 members said they intended to put in place a facility in the IMF to mount preventive financial support before breakdowns occur rather than rescue countries after catastrophe has struck.

The most important financial lesson that has emerged from the Mexican, East Asian, Russian, and Brazilian experiences is the intolerance of markets to national policy weakness. This is likely to be an enduring lesson for serious economic policy-makers around the globe.

These *ex post* lessons, valid though they may be, do not tell us why technically capable Mexican policy-makers, educated largely in the same graduate schools as their critics, committed the errors that their counterparts now criticize so severely.

The cultural explanation

A number of revealing features of decision-making on economic policy during 1994 are manifest when the contemporaneous record is examined. These include the following:
1 The group making the decisions *deliberately was kept limited*. The "Club de Toby" phenomenon was in full play throughout. Indeed, when dissenting views did emerge within the government hierarchy, they were stifled; discordant voices were excluded from the inner circle of decision-makers.

   It is hard to say whether the small size of the decision group was conscious or the consequence of force of habit learned over years of experience. There undoubtedly was some of both, automatically keeping the group small and consciously excluding dissenters. This was not exactly secrecy, but a habit of *top-down decision-making* – and this amounted to the same thing. The cultural conditioning in Mexico dictated that this was the way to make major decisions.
2 There was *deliberate secrecy* as well in not sharing information with the public and not even with the congress which, for the most part, was held in contempt by the executive leaders. Central Bank officials again and again defended the periodic release of reserve figures only after long delays, using the argument that this was the way things always were done. For some reason, it never was evident to senior Bank officials that a practice that developed when Mexico was largely isolated from world capital markets and looked mostly within for its economic stimulus was not adequate after Mexico consciously sought long-term and portfolio capital, and after Mexico became part of the global marketplace.

   There was never a full public debate on the legitimacy of the model of using the exchange rate for as long as it was used to contain inflation. The pacto setup was a version of Mexico's long-standing corporatist way of doing business, of periodically bringing together a limited group of representatives of key sectors

– industry, finance, labor, the government – and substituting this for public discussion.

3 Strong leadership was taken to mean that *restricted groups made the key decisions*. Powerful corporate groups were brought in to promote an image of public consultation, but even then the decisions that ostensibly would be taken at the pacto meetings were mostly made in advance. The one major exception to this was the pacto meeting on December 19–20, 1994, when the consensus inside the government and the Bank of Mexico to float the peso was overridden because of the influence of a single, powerful interest group, the private bankers.

It is striking to non-Mexicans that interested parties could so decisively influence a change in exchange-rate policy that benefitted them and not necessarily the general interest. It is even more astounding that they would be given advance notice of the decision and not expect this to be seen as manifestly inappropriate – even dishonest. This mode of operation was Mexican to its core.

The word "leadership" in Mexico has an unstated adjective, the word "strong." Salinas was a leader in his first five years because he brooked little dissent. He was not in his last year. Zedillo was at first distrusted by the various elements of the corporate structure because he was not seen as strong; hence, he was not seen as a full-fledged leader.

4 This way of operating instilled considerable *arrogance in the behavior of key decision-makers*. The almost unlimited power of the Mexican president during his term of office – certainly until his designated successor was chosen and the incumbent increasingly became a lame duck – encouraged presidential arrogance. So did the secrecy. The attitude of many of the key decision-makers can be described as "We know best, and there really is no need to have open, national debates on economic policy." This arrogance was tolerated as long as the PRI and the key government decision-makers delivered high economic growth with modest inflation, but began to break down after there were financial collapses every six years or so. Mexican history encouraged official arrogance and then more recent history made this increasingly anachronistic.

5 Another anachronism was the *deliberate delay in true political reform*. PRI power was only marginally challenged during the years of steady prosperity. True, this prosperity did not reach the entire

population, probably not even a majority, but economic conditions were improving even for the majority. Once this improvement ceased, and once the growing middle class found itself adversely affected by the periodic collapses, the clamor grew for a greater public voice in choosing political leaders. Salinas erected walls to limit the full flowering of political democracy until he could bring about the structural economic changes he sought. This strategy worked, more or less, until the final year of his sexenio, but broke down completely that year. The arrogance of the leadership in limiting democratic participation could not withstand the débâcle.

The behavior of key decision-makers can be described using a number of descriptive words: exclusivity, arrogance, stubbornness, hegemony. The hegemony was of the leaders over the general population. It is no wonder that Mexican intellectuals were so fond of citing Gramsci. The stubbornness grew out of the conviction that policy-makers knew best and therefore did not need to heed outside voices, of the public through debate, of outside agencies like the IMF and the World Bank, and even of dissenting officials of lower rank. The arrogance was the result of years of experience in making decisions without second-guessing by those not directly involved in the process. Exclusivity meant the deliberate limitation of participants who might present alternative scenarios. Each of these traits grow out of Mexican history and experience. These traits are likely to change in the future because of the grief they have caused in more recent history, but old habits are not easily shed.

The kind of stubbornness demonstrated by Mexican officials in their refusal to alter the central features of economic policy – even as it was becoming clear that they were fighting a rearguard action that at best delayed the unavoidable devaluation – is not unique to Mexico. In writing about the continuation of the Vietnam War by the United States, one analyst said the following:

> How did men of superior quality, sound training, and high ideals – American policy-makers of the 1960s – create such costly and divisive policy?[9]

This is not the place to deal extensively with US history in Vietnam, but some of the same elements existed in the minds of policy-makers, such as "wishful thinking" and "persistent and repeated miscalculation."[10] Robert McNamara, the US Defense Secretary during the years of the US troop buildup in Vietnam, wrote the following many years later with respect to policy failings: "Worse, our government lacked experts for us to consult to compensate for our ignorance."[11] The assertion is inaccurate, and one must therefore conclude that those making policy did not want to hear the experts who were subordinate to them in the hierarchy.[12] This was the situation in Mexico as well where many, perhaps the majority, of subordinates in the key cabinet agencies had views different from their chiefs on exchange-rate and related policies.[13]

The persistence of pursuing a failing policy was more costly in Vietnam than it was in making economic policy in Mexico in that tens of thousands of people died as a result of Vietnam policy. But whatever it is that drives the architects of policy to continue despite the overwhelming evidence that the policy is not succeeding was at work in both places. The United States has been going through decades of catharsis as a consequence and Mexico must go through its own deep self-examination of why things went so devastatingly wrong in 1994. The issue is not just that faulty decisions were made, but rather the need for self-analysis of the elements that brought on these decisions.

The disproportionate bet

It is remarkable how many Mexican officials and observers used a gambling description to characterize the decision-making during 1994. Martín Werner, a Subsecretary of *Hacienda*, used exactly this phraseology: "It was a bet" that things would go back to normal.[14] From Guillermo Ortiz, the Senior Subsecretary and later Secretary of *Hacienda*: "We bet in 1994 that the shocks were temporary."[15] Agustín Carstens, General Director of economic research at the Bank of Mexico, when referring to the repeated shocks during 1994: "We took a calculated bet and lost".[16] One of the subheads in the articles that journalist Rossana Fuentes-Berain wrote for three successive issues of the newspaper *Reforma* was worded as follows: "Tesobonos: la apuesta" (Tesobonos: the bet).[17] One of the most sophisticated analyses of the 1994 experience, by Carlos Elizondo Mayer-Serra, reached the following conclusion: "The bets would have been less attractive if they [the policy-makers] had to pay a higher political costs for their errors."[18]

Elizondo's working paper has the title "Tres trampas," roughly three frauds, about the origins of the economic crisis in 1994. The three frauds he sets out were the behavior of policy-makers that foreign portfolio capital could be treated as if it was not volatile, that the key players in the government thought they could manipulate the fundamental price of the peso, and the lack of a democratic political culture. The value of Elizondo's essay to the work of this book is that it contains a holistic analysis, from a Mexican author, of the elements that led to the decisions that turned out so tragically for the Mexican people. Elizondo, in essence, is challenging the right of politicians elected in a less than democratic fashion to make the kinds of bets they made when, after all was said and done, their futures were affected less than were the destinies of millions of Mexicans.

When he was a candidate for the US presidency, Bob Dole was within his democratic rights when he said he was prepared, in his policy proposals, to bet the country. The electorate had a choice, and he was not elected. Yet, to continue with the bet analogy, it would have made no sense for a professional gambler to place a bet of the type made by Mexican policy-makers. If the bet had been won, we know from statements of the policy-makers themselves that all that would have been achieved was modest delay. Had the gamble succeeded, the necessary changes in the exchange rate and accompanying macroeconomic measures would have been taken early in the new year, in 1995. That was the upside – a few months of delay. That was understandable before the August elections, when action might have cost the PRI the presidency. This rationale no longer made sense once the succession for the next six years had been decided. To use technical jargon, the discounted present value of winning the bet was atrociously low.

The downside of the bet was far more consequential. The cost of betting wrong turned out to be a hastily arranged devaluation, without accompanying macroeconomic measures, that brought not only severe hardships, but set up a complicated presidential succession in the year 2000 when perhaps the most important consideration will be to avoid another crisis similar to those of the last 20 years. The bet, to put it simply, was disproportionate – with practically nothing to gain except to preserve Salinas' reputation of leaving office without an abrupt devaluation and with the stability of the country to lose.

Concluding comment

Mexico has changed much since 1994. The most important transformation is political, that the authoritarian monopoly on power that persisted so long under the PRI is no longer embedded in concrete. The full transformation to democracy will take more time, but elections – local, state, and federal – are now real contests. The federal legislature, and those of some states and the Federal District, are now dominated by non-PRI parties. This path toward democracy may be turbulent, but the executive secrecy inherent in the old system, and the certainty that the legislature would rubber stamp whatever was asked of it, is now obsolete. This inevitably will bring about a profound change in the way economic decisions are made. The avoidance of debate on key matters will not be possible if the federal legislature insists on being brought into the loop.

This greater sharing of the responsibility for specific actions does not necessarily mean that future decisions will be wiser than those of the past. They may just take more time and involve much more disorder. But the *trampas* or frauds about which Elizondo wrote will have to be shared. The decision-making circle will have to be widened. Executive arrogance will be tempered by legislative arrogance. Secrecy is destroyed if decision-makers must openly explain their actions. This means that the specific features of decision-making during 1994 will not be repeated. Future policy mistakes, assuming they will occur in Mexico as elsewhere, will be shared errors.

One important discovery I made in the course of many interviews was that younger officials, the professionals below the very top level in the economic agencies, already engage in much appraisal of policies. For the most part, they were willing in internal discussions to discuss problematic aspects of policies and point out shortcomings in information made available to the public. As often as not, however, these officials were reluctant to be publicly cited. Looking ahead, however, the formation of future policy officials will take place in a more open atmosphere than existed in 1994 and, consequently, ingrained habits are likely to change. The next generation of economic policy-makers may even thrive on public debate.

It would be naive, however, to expect rapid change in old habits of how Mexico should be governed. There is too much history behind what now exists and many practices are deeply ingrained in the character of the Mexican population. But too much has changed in the domestic and international scenery for traditional habits to remain completely intact. This includes a more democratic Mexico, which has begun and surely will deepen; a Mexico that looks outward, which already is fact; a major trading nation in place of one that was highly pessimistic about its ability to export; a country that seeks foreign direct investment instead of one shunning this; a country with an activist federal legislature rather than a useless appendage to the executive; and a country in which increasing numbers of policy-makers are being trained in leading graduate schools outside of Mexico – all these realities presage lasting changes in the country's decision-making processes.

Notes and References

1 The Cultural Setting

1. The technical–political backgrounds of the senior officials making economic policy in Mexico are discussed in Stephanie R. Golob, "'Making Possible What is Necessary': Pedro Aspe, the Salinas Team, and the Next Mexican 'Miracle'," in Jorge I. Dominguez (ed.), *Technopols: Freeing Politics and Markets in Latin America in the 1980s* (University Park, PA: Pennsylvania State University, 1997), 95–143.
2. This argument is set out forcefully in the annual report of the Bank for 1994, *Informe Annual 1994* (México, DF: Banco de México, 1995), and in a meticulously documented article by two high-level Bank officials, Francisco Gil-Díaz (then a vice governor) and Agustín Carstens (the chief economist), "Some Hypotheses Related to the Mexican 1994–95 Crisis," presented at the annual meeting of the American Economic Association (San Francisco) (January 5–7, 1996).
3. Enrique Krauze, *Mexico: Biography of Power: A History of Modern Mexico, 1810–1996*, trans. Hank Heifets (New York: HarperCollins, 1997), xiii. The Spanish version is in three volumes, published between 1994 and 1997.
4. Octavio Paz, *The Labyrinth of Solitude: Life and Thought in Mexico* (New York: Grove Press, 1961), from the revised Spanish version of 1959.
5. Ibid., p. 20.
6. Samuel Ramos, *El perfil del hombre y la cultura en México* (México, DF: Colección Austral Espasa Calpe Mexicana, 1980), 9th edn; originally published in 1934.
7. Enrique Krauze, *La presidencia imperial: Ascenso y caída del sistema político mexicano (1940–1996)*, (México, DF: Tusquets, 1997), 417.
8. Rolando Cordera Campos, "La reforma del estado como necesidad," in Jorge Alonso, Alberto Aziz and Jaime Tamayo (eds), *El nuevo estado mexicano: Tomo I, estado y economía* (Guadalajara: Universidad de Guadalajara, 1992), 295.
9. See Antonio Gramsci, *Selections from the Prison Notebooks*, trans. and ed. Quintin Hoare and Geoffrey Nowell Smith (New York: International Publishers, 1971).
10. This is not the place to get into the kind discussion with which practically all Mexicans are familiar, whether *malinchismo*, or the relationship of the Indian women with Cortés is best depicted as betrayal of one's fatherland or the beginning of *mestizaje*.
11. Krauze, *Mexico: Biography of Power*, 135.
12. Michael C. Meyer and William Sherman, *The Course of Mexican History* (New York: Oxford University Press, 1983), 2nd edn, 552.
13. Krauze, *Mexico: Biography of Power*, p. 271–2, cites a message that

Ambassador Wilson sent to Washington on February 19, 1913: "General Huerta asked my advice about whether it would be better to send the ex-president out of the country or to place him in a mental asylum. I replied that he should do what would be best for the peace of the country."

14 A good discussion of the background to the nationalization can be found in Lorenzo Meyer, *Mexico and the United States in the Oil Controversy: 1917–1942* (Austin, TX: University of Texas Press, 1977).

15 A report of the Asamblea Nacional Indígena Plural por la Autonomía indicated that of the 20 million indigenous people in Mexico, 56 percent are illiterate, including 53 percent of the children aged 6–14, and 43 percent have incomes below one minimum wage. *Reforma* (September 12, 1997), via internet.

16 Roger Bartra, *The Cage of Melancholy: Identity and Metamorphoses in the Mexican Character* (New Brunswick, NJ: Rutgers University Press, 1992), 175, trans. C. Hau from the original Spanish book, *La jaula de la melancolía* (México, DF: Grijalbo, 1987).

17 Jonathan Heath, "Economic Sovereignty in Mexico," in Joyce Hoebing, Sidney Weintraub and M. Delal Baer (eds), *NAFTA and Sovereignty: Trade-Offs for Canada, Mexico, and the United States* (Washington, DC: Center for Strategic and International Studies, 1996), 86.

18 Bartra (n. 16) makes this point, 3.

19 This insight comes from Roderic Camp, one of those outside experts whose opinion on internal Mexican events is frequently sought.

20 Reuters' report, March 22, 1998.

21 Personal conversation, April 9, 1997.

22 Krauze, *Mexico: Biography of Power*, 212.

23 Ibid., 735, emphasis in the original.

24 Enrique Alduncin Abitia, *Los valores de los mexicanos: México en tiempo de cambio*, tomo II (México, DF: Banco Nacional de México [Banamex], 1991), 200.

25 Ibid., p. 216. Alduncin and his colleagues at Banamex published three volumes dealing with surveys of Mexican values, in 1989, 1991, and 1993. In addition, the bank has published yearly volumes on social issues and these also involve extensive surveying.

26 *Por una democracia sin adjetivos* (México, DF: Joaquín Mortiz/Planeta, 1986).

27 Ronald F. Inglehart, Mark Nevitte and Miguel Basañez, *The North American Trajectory: Cultural, Economic, and Political Ties among the United States, Canada, and Mexico* (New York: Aldine de Gruyter, 1996).

28 *Este País*, 88 (July 1998), 18.

29 Krauze, *Mexico: Biography of Power*, 775.

30 Ibid., 772 and 773.

31 Ibid., xv.

32 Daniel Cosío Villegas, *El estilo personal de gobernar* (México, DF: Joaquín Mortiz, 1974).

33 Pablo Arredondo Ramírez, "El estado y la comunicación: Dilemas frente a un proyecto modernizador," in J. Alonso, A. Aziz and J. Tamayo (eds), *El nuevo estado mexicano: Tomo IV, estado y sociedad*, 39–66.

34 See letter of June 6, 1997, to President Ernesto Zedillo from the Committee to Protect Journalists, which provides considerable detail on recent "disturbing" actions (that is the word used in the letter) that limit press freedom in Mexico.
35 See Sidney Weintraub, "The Interplay between Economic and Political Opening in Mexico," *Proceedings of the American Philosophical Society*, 137 (1) (1993), 64–78.
36 A discussion of the July 1997 elections can be found in Armand B. Peschard-Sverdrup, "The 1997 Mexican Midterm Elections: Post-election Report" (Washington, DC: Center for Strategic and International Studies, August 1997). The newly elected head of government of Mexico City, as he is called, is Cuauhtémoc Cárdenas, an ex-PRI leader who twice has run for president on an opposition ticket.
37 Gabriel Zaid, *La economía presidencial* (México, DF: Vuelta, 1987), 155. ("La mentira oficial no es consequencia de la corupción (para ocultarla): es su condición de orígen.")
38 Ibid., p. 161. ("La corupción no es una característica desagradable del sistema político mexicano: es la sistema.")
39 Jacques Rogozinski, *La privatización en México: Razones e impactos* (México, DF,: Editorial Trillas, 1997), 73, states that central government transfers to state-owned enterprises were by themselves 26.9 percent of GDP in 1982.
40 Nora Lustig, *Mexico: The Remaking of an Economy* (Washington, DC: Brookings Institution, 1992), 105. The precise number of government enterprises is not, in itself, a significant figure in that major ones, like Pemex, are more important than hundreds of others combined.
41 Rogozinski, *La privatización en México*, 111.
42 James Q. Wilson, *Bureaucracy: What Government Agencies Do and Why They Do It* (New York: Basic Books, 1989), 295–334.
43 Lorenzo Meyer, *Liberalismo autoritario: las contradicciones del sistema político mexicano* (México, DF: Oceano, 1995), 154. ("Es posible que el déficit más importante que haya tenido el gobierno mexicano, no sea con el exterior, sino interno. Y entre ellos destaca el de la credibilidad.")
44 *Reforma* article, "Amenaza el PAN vetar presupuesto" (The PAN threatens to veto the budget) (October 3, 1997), from the internet.
45 Arnaldo Córdova, *La política de masas del cardenismo* (México, DF: Ediciones Era, 1974), 164.
46 See George W. Grayson, *Mexico: From Corporatism to Pluralism?* (Fort Worth, TX: Harcourt Brace College Publishers, 1998).
47 Germán Pérez Fernández del Castillo, "La democracia mexicana: sus problemas actuales," in Luis Rubio and Arturo Fernández (eds), *México a la hora del cambio* (México, DF: Cal y Arena, 1995), 315–54.
48 In an article in the *Wall Street Journal* (September 10, 1998, 1), under the headline "Mum's the Word: Mexico Isn't Free With Information," the reporter Jonathan Friedland emphasizes the official secrecy that still prevails.

2 Antecedents to the Decisions of 1994

1. Nora Lustig, *Mexico: The Remaking of an Economy* (Washington, DC: Brookings Institution, 1992), 15.
2. It is not easy to define what is the "middle class." One way to do this is to include families in the fifth to the ninth deciles of the income distribution pattern – that is, excluding the poorest 40 percent and the richest 10 percent of the population. By this definition, the middle class constituted 43 percent of families in 1950 and 51.8 percent in 1977. See Sidney Weintraub, *A Marriage of Convenience* (New York: Oxford University Press, 1990), 35.
3. The cost-of-living data are compiled by the Bank of Mexico and the figures cited here were provided by INEGI, Mexico's statistical agency. They are December-over-December data, using an index with 1978 as 100. Because the method for calculating the consumer price index (CPI) has been revised since then, it is hard to directly compare data of those years with current statistics.
4. The figures are from Salvador Kalifa-Assad, "Income Distribution and Poverty in Mexico: A Reconsideration of the Distribution Problem," PhD dissertation (Cornell University, 1977), 56 ff.
5. These years are described in Sidney Weintraub, "Case Study of Economic Stabilization: Mexico," in William R. Cline and Sidney Weintraub (eds), *Economic Stabilization in Developing Countries* (Washington, DC: Brookings Institution, 1981), 271–96.
6. As quoted in Carlos Elizondo Mayer-Serra, "Tres trampas: sobre los orígenes de la crisis económica mexicana de 1994," Centro de Investigación y Docencia Económicas, *Working Paper*, 46 (1996), 5.
7. The 1982 crisis is discussed in Lustig, *Mexico: The Remaking of an Economy*; and in Nora Lustig, "Mexico in Crisis, the US to the Rescue: The Financial Assistance Packages of 1982 and 1995," *Discussion Paper* (Brookings Institution, June 1996).
8. Paul A. Volcker and Toyoo Gyohten, *Changing Fortunes: The World's Money and the Threat to American Leadership* (New York: Times Books, 1992), 180.
9. These relationships on the import content of Mexico's exports in the chemical and automotive industries are analyzed in Kurt Unger, *Las exportaciones mexicanas ante la reestructuración industrial internacional: La evidencia de las industrias química y automotriz* (México, DF: El Colegio de México y Fondo de Cultura Económica, 1990). The same author, based on a national survey in 1992, found that the 1991 import content of foreign firms exporting from Mexico was 86 percent of the export value, compared with only 20 percent for national exporting firms. In the maquiladora, the import content of exports was between 98 and 99 percent for all firms.
10. All the inflation figures are December-over-December.
11. See George W. Grayson, *Mexico: From Corporatism to Pluralism?* (Fort Worth, TX: Harcourt Brace College Publishers, 1998).
12. Conversation with the author in Mexico City, April 9, 1997.
13. This, in my view, was an unforgivable form of official theft.

14 "Articulo de Portada: Salario Minimo," *Expansión* (November 5, 1997), 20.
15 Bureau of Labor Statistics, "International Comparisons of Hourly Compensation Costs for Production Workers in Manufacturing, 1995," *Report*, 909 (September 1996).
16 The Mexican Congress, in early 1998, conducted hearings on precisely this matter, to try to clarify what happened in 1968. The Mexican weekly news magazine *Proceso*, 1109 (February 1, 1998), 6–11, has a series of commentaries on the need to open the official archives on the events of 1968 to get at the truth. The following issue of *Proceso*, 1110 (February 8, 1998), 15–20, has a discussion of the 1968 events that includes pictures of Díaz Ordaz and Echeverría with the caption: "1968 – mentiras y mentirosos" (lies and liars).
17 Enrique Krauze, *Mexico: Biography of Power: A History of Modern Mexico, 1810–1996*, trans. Hank Heifets (New York: HarperCollins, 1997).
18 Banco de México, *The Mexican Economy 1997* (México, DF: Banco de México, 1997), 270.
19 These books, all published by the Fondo de Cultura Económica, a government-owned publishing house, included the following: Guillermo Ortiz Martínez, *La reforma financiera y la desincorporación bancaria* (1994); Gabriel Martínez and Guillermo Fárber, *Desregulación económica 1989–1993* (1994); Herminio Blanco Mendoza, *Las negociaciones comerciales de México con el mundo* (1994); and Jacques Rogozinski, *La privatización de empresas paraestatales* (1993).
20 Pedro Aspe, *Economic Transformation: The Mexican Way* (Cambridge, MA: MIT Press, 1993).
21 Banco de México, *The Mexican Economy 1997*, 256.
22 This included me.
23 Carlos Salinas de Gortari, "VI Informe de Gobierno" (November 1, 1994) (*El Mercado de Valores, año LIV*, December 1994).
24 David Ibarra, *¿Transición o crisis?* (México, DF: Aguilar Nuevo Siglo, 1996).
25 Ortiz, *La reforma financiera*.
26 Gary C. Hufbauer and Jeffrey J. Schott, *NAFTA: An Assessment* (Washington, DC: Institute for International Economics, 1993) 61–6.
27 *Reforma* (October 7, 1997). ("Ni los administradores de los bancos estatales, ni las autoridades y ni los propios compradores, fueron lo suficientemente profundos en sus análisis como para percibir que se tendrían problemas.")
28 Banco de México, *Informe Anual 1994* (México, DF: Banco de México, 1995), 240.
29 Generally Accepted Accounting Principles, or GAAP.

3 The First Quarter of 1994

1 The data in this paragraph come from Banco de México, *Exposición sobre la política monetaria para el lapso 1°de abril de 1994–31 de diciembre de 1994* (México, DF, May 1994).
2 Many informants preferred not to be named and these requests are being honored.

3 This issue will be taken up later.
4 On September 5, 1993, in Puerto Vallarta, to the First Banking Convention. The Bank of Mexico published and made available all of Mancera's speeches during this period.
5 These included speeches on October 27, 1993, in Mexico City; November 27, 1993, in Puerto Vallarta; and March 8, 1994 in Mexico City.
6 Speech of July 16, 1993, in Chihuahua.
7 This was on September 5, 1993, at the same banking convention in Puerto Vallarta at which Mancera spoke. ["Estos elementos permitan afirmar que a fines de año la economía mexicana estará en recuperación."]
8 Speech of January 20, 1994, in Tlaxcala.
9 Speech of February 4, 1994, in Campeche.
10 Rudiger Dornbusch and Alejandro Werner, "Mexico: Stabilization, Reform, and No Growth," *Brookings Papers on Economic Activity*, 1 (1994), 253–315. In the discussion that followed the presentation of the article, Stanley Fischer, later the Deputy Managing Director of the IMF, also argued for a devaluation within the pacto but, if this were not forthcoming, he recommended an acceleration of the daily crawl.
11 Francisco Gil-Díaz and Agustín Carstens, "Some Hypotheses Related to the Mexican 1994–95 Crisis," Banco de México, research paper presented to the annual meeting of the American Economic Association (San Francisco, January 5–7, 1996), 17.
12 Banco de México, *Informe Anual 1993* (México, DF, 1994), 226.
13 On a personal note, when my book *Free Trade between Mexico and the United States?* (Washington, DC: Brookings Institution, 1984) was published, the dominant reaction of the reviewers was that I was hopelessly naive, that I did not understand the innate political resistance in Mexico to an embrace of the United States in this way.
14 Banco de México, *Informe Anual 1993* (México, DF: Banco de México, 1994), 229.
15 Ibid., 229–30, for this and subsequent data in this paragraph.
16 Bertrand de la Grange and Maite Rico, *Marcos, la genial impostura* (México, DF: Nuevo Siglo Aguilar, 1997), which has been a best-seller in Mexico, deals extensively with the character and actions of Marcos. Andres Oppenheimer, *Bordering on Chaos* (Boston: Little, Brown, 1996) contains much discussion of Marcos and the *Zapatistas*.
17 The minimum wage varies by region of the country, depending on living costs.
18 This and other reserve figures come from Banco de México, *Informe Anual 1994* (México, DF, 1995), 192–9.
19 Ibid., 180–1.
20 The data presented in this section come from various publications of the Bank of Mexico.
21 Enrique Krauze, "Nuestra Glasnost," essay dated March 12, 1995, reprinted in *Tiempo Contado* (México, DF: Oceano, 1996), 164–8.
22 "Sexto Informe de Gobierno, Carlos Salinas de Gortari," November 1, 1994. The cited sentence comes from the English-language version distributed by the Mexican Embassy in Washington, DC.

23 *El Financiero International* (March 23–29, 1998), article by Dolia Estévez, 4.
24 Translation by author from various parts of the speech.
25 Córdoba was then living in Washington, DC, and he returned for the interview out of concern over a letter by Colosio's father, Luis, that had been published in *Reforma* a few days before, making various allegations about his son's murder.
26 Text of letter obtained from the website of Infosel Financiero.
27 This is in Article 82:VI of the constitution.
28 Gil-Díaz and Carstens, "Some Hypotheses," 22.
29 In a conversation with me on March 11, 1996.

4 The Second Quarter of 1994

1 Peter H. Smith, "Political Dimensions of the Peso Crisis," in Sebastian Edwards and Moisés Naím (eds), *Mexico 1994: Anatomy of an Emerging-Market Crash* (Washington, DC: Carnegie Endowment for International Peace, 1997), 32.
2 Jeffrey A. Frieden, "The Politics of Exchange Rates," in Edwards and Naím (eds) (1997), 82.
3 Sylvester C.W. Eijffinger and Jakob De Haan, *The Political Economy of Central-Bank Independence* (Princeton: Princeton University, International Finance Section, 1996) conclude that countries with independent central banks, all other things being equal, have lower inflation than in countries where politicians steer central bank policy (54). They add an important caveat that this independence may not enhance growth and employment. The anti-inflation priority of Mexico's central bank, even before the law was changed, had this dual outcome – reduced inflation and modest growth in GDP–during the Salinas years.
4 The exchange-rate data are from the Bank of Mexico, *The Mexican Economy 1995* (México, DF: Banco de México, 1995), 221.
5 President Zedillo, in 1998, submitted legislation to give the decisive vote on exchange-rate changes to the governor of the Bank of Mexico instead of the Secretary of *Hacienda*. This was still pending in the Congress when this was written.
6 Intervention data are from Banco de México, *Informe Anual 1994* (México, DF: Banco de México, 1995), 192–9.
7 "Some Hypotheses Related to the Mexican 1994–95 Crisis," Banco de México, research paper presented to the annual meeting of the American Economic Association (San Francisco, January 5–7, 1996). The summary explanation of the crisis they give in the abstract of their paper is that "the real causes are to be found on [sic] the combination of a semi-fixed exchange rate, the explosive availability of short-term capital, and the cumulative effect of the repeated political shocks that affected the Mexican scene during 1994."
8 Ariel Buira, "Reflections on the Mexican Crisis of 1994," in Guillermo Calvo, Morris Goldstein and Eduard Hochreiter (eds), *Private Capital Flows to Emerging Markets After the Mexican Crisis* (Washington, DC: In-

stitute for International Economics for the Austrian National Bank, 1996), 307–19.
9 See p. 60.
10 Editorial entitled "Don't Blame Monetary Policy."
11 Interview with Salinas reported in *Reforma* (February 5, 1997), by Ramón Alberto Garza, under the heading "La cosigna a Aspe: No devaluar," <Internet www.infosel.com.mx>.
12 *Reforma* (May 17, 1995), 21A; (May 18), 21A; and (May 19), 19A.
13 These statements are based on many interviews with government officials, some close to Salinas.
14 Leonardo Leiderman, Nissan Liviatan and Alfredo Thorne, "Shifting Nominal Anchors," mimeo (November 1995). The authors thank Bank of Mexico officials for their comments on the paper, and in particular, Agustín Carstens, General Director of economic research, and Moisés Schwartz, then Director of analysis and measurement of the financial sector.
15 Leonardo Leidermann and Alfredo Thorpe, "Mexico's 1994 Crisis and its Aftermath: What are the Main Lessons?," in Calvo, Goldstein and Hochreiter (eds), *Private Capital Flows to Emerging Markets*, 15.
16 Ibid., 17.
17 Stephany Griffith-Jones, "Causes and Lessons of the Mexican Peso Crisis," United Nations University/World Institute for Development Economics Research, *Working Paper*, 132 (May 1997).
18 *Informe Anual 1994*, 47.
19 Steven B. Kamin and John H. Rogers, "Monetary Policy in the End-Game to Exchange-Rate Based Stabilizations: The Case of Mexico," Federal Reserve System, *International Finance Discussion Paper*, 540 (February 1996).
20 This definition was taken roughly from Guillermo Ortiz Martínez, *La reforma financiera y desincorporación bancaria* (México, DF: Fondo de Cultura Económica, 1994), 145.
21 See ibid., 156–7 for a list of main development banks and funds.
22 *Mexico: OECD Economic Surveys 1994–1995* (Paris: Organization for Economic Cooperation and Development, 1995), 27–8.
23 Ibid.
24 Presidencia de la República, "Criterios generales de política económica para 1993," *Comercio Exterior* (December 1992), 1185. This reasoning breaks down when the commercial banks are in trouble and either default on their debts or the bad debts are taken over by the government, which is precisely what happened in Mexico.
25 Ortiz, *La reforma financiera*, 152.
26 Secretaría de Hacienda y Crédito Público, *Informe Hacendario* (April–June 1994), 2 (6), 34.
27 Jonathan E. Heath, "The Devaluation of the Mexican Peso in 1994," Center for Strategic and International Studies (June 1995).
28 See the *Diario Oficial de la Federación* for December 7, 1988.
29 This information comes from Roderic Ai Camp, *Mexican Political Biography 1935–1993* (Austin, TX: University of Texas Press, 1995), 3rd edn.
30 *Reforma* (August 29, 1997), column by Sergio Sarmiento, "Asesor incómodo," via internet.

31 *Reforma* (October 31, 1996), column by Sarmiento, "Córdoba y el PRD," via internet. This may have been the only public speech in the sense that reporters were present, but Córdoba did give off-the-record speeches to selected groups visiting Mexico, as I know from one I heard in just such a circumstance.
32 The book was published in Mexico City by Oceano (1997). Sarmiento, in the column cited above entitled "Asesor incómodo" (inconvenient advisor), trashes both the book and its author for having personal animosity against Córdoba.
33 Interview in Mexico City, July 5, 1996.
34 See column "Asesor incómodo."
35 Interview in Mexico City, June 6, 1996.
36 *Reforma* (December 11, 1996), 12A, article submitted by Córdoba which appeared under the heading "Que ahora hablen los jueces."
37 Interview in Mexico City, March 12, 1996.
38 Interview in Mexico City, July 4, 1996.
39 Interview in Mexico City, July 3, 1996.
40 This was the view of Jaime Serra Puche, then the Secretary for International Trade and Industrial Development and later the Secretary of *Hacienda* when the December devaluation occurred. Interview with Serra in Princeton, New Jersey, April 16, 1996.
41 The existence of the Weston Forum was first reported in an article in the *Wall Street Journal* (June 14, 1994), 1, by Craig Torres and Thomas T. Vogel, Jr., under the headline "Wield Growing Clout in Developing Nations," and a more directed subhead, "Late Night Call to Mexico." A more tendentious article on the Weston Forum appeared about nine months later in the *New Republic* (March 13, 1995), 20 ff., by Douglas W. Payne, with the more sensational title "How Investment Bankers Ruined Mexico."
42 Smith, "Political Dimensions of the Peso Crisis," in Edwards and Naím (eds), *Mexico 1994*, 41.

5 The Third Quarter of 1994

1 John Bailey, *The 1994 Mexican Presidential Elections: Post-Election Report* (Washington, DC: Center for Strategic and International Studies, October 8, 1994).
2 Denise Dresser, "Falling from the Tightrope: The Political Economy of the Mexican Crisis," in Sebastian Edwards and Moisés Naím (eds), *Mexico 1994: Anatomy of an Emerging-Market Crash* (Washington, DC: Carnegie Endowment for International Peace, 1997), 55.
3 Sebastian Edwards, "Bad Luck or Bad Policies? An Economic Analysis of the Crisis," in Edwards and Naím (eds), *Mexico 1994*, 113.
4 Both Guillermo Ortiz and Martin Werner, than an advisor in *Hacienda* and later Subsecretary himself, said this to me in separate conversations.
5 Banco de México, *Informe Anual 1994* (México, DF: Banco de México, 1995), 69–70.
6 Interview at the Bank, July 1, 1997.

7 Interview at the Bank, April 12, 1996.
8 Jonathan E. Heath, "The Devaluation of the Mexican Peso in 1994" (Washington, DC: Center for Strategic and International Studies, June 1995), 11.
9 The quoted question is the way it is phrased in a sub-head in Moisés Naím, "Mexico's Larger Story," in Edwards and Naím (eds), *Mexico 1994*, 298.
10 Shahid Javed Burki, "A Fate Foretold: The World Bank and the Mexican Crisis," in Edwards and Naím (eds), *Mexico 1994*, 252.
11 Ibid., 253.
12 Interview in Mexico City, March 12, 1996. Fernández also told me that, during the presidential campaign, he had chaired a group in the PRI think-tank – then called the Institute of Economic, Political, and Social Sciences (IEPES in its Spanish initials) and since renamed Fundación Nacional Colosio – which recommended that an exchange-rate change would be desirable.
13 Interview in Mexico City, July 4, 1996.
14 Interview in Mexico City with Luis Tellez K., July 15, 1996. Tellez was chief of staff when Zedillo assumed the presidency and later was secretary of energy.
15 Zedillo's position, as stated to *ABC*, was the subject of a commentary in the Mexico City newspaper *El Economista* (September 6, 1994), which is critical of the entire debate between those who favored using the exchange rate to reduce inflation even at the price of low economic growth and those who proposed a devaluation to stimulate growth even at the cost of a little more inflation. Competitiveness, the commentary argues, is not accomplished by means of the exchange rate.
16 Interview with President Zedillo in Los Pinos, the presidential residence in Mexico City, July 10, 1996. The November 20 date refers to a meeting held in Salinas' house at which key persons from the existing and incoming administrations discussed the exchange-rate issue.
17 US General Accounting Office, *Mexico's Financial Crisis: Origins, Awareness, Assistance, and Initial Efforts to Recover*, GAO/GGD-95-96 (February 1996), 92. More detail about Fed thinking is contained in Chapter 7 where the concerns that were developing in Washington during 1994 are discussed.
18 Interview in US embassy in Mexico City, April 9, 1996.
19 Other than the effect on capital flight, which coincided in November with the charge of obstruction made by Mario Ruiz Massieu, this story of fraternal relations will not be discussed here. There is some preliminary discussion of this case in Andres Oppenheimer, *Bordering on Chaos* (Boston: Little, Brown, 1996), 193–4. The story of Mario's actions are still unfolding as this is written, many years later.
20 I did meet with Pedro Aspe in Mexico City on June 4, 1996, and while he was most gracious, as I have always found him to be, he said there were no differences in his public and private attitudes. If I wished to know his thinking, he said, I should read his public statements and written materials, which are considerable. I have read them, of course. Aspe has said nothing to anybody that conflicts with the position he

took with me. I did not meet with Salinas, although on several occasions I sent written questions to him to Dublin, where he was living. I never received a response. I must rely, therefore, largely on second-hand sources of people who worked with and knew the two men.

21 Interview in Mexico City, July 3, 1996.
22 The word "small" is part of a longer phrase that has quotation marks in Aspe's column in the *Wall Street Journal* (July 14, 1995), A13, under the heading "Mexico's Ex-Finance Minister Sets the Record Straight."
23 The *comisión de cambios* (exchange commission) had six members, three each from *Hacienda* and the Bank of Mexico, and in the event of a tie, the deciding vote was that of the chair, normally the secretary of *Hacienda*.
24 Nora Lustig, "The Mexican Peso Crisis: The Foreseeable and the Surprises," Brookings Institution, *Discussion Paper* (June 1995). The word "tricked" is in quotes in the original.
25 The data used in the previous section come from the Bank of Mexico, *The Mexican Economy*, various years.
26 Interview in Mexico City, June 6, 1996.
27 This quotation is from Dornbusch, "The Folly, the Crash, and Beyond: Economic Policies and the Crisis," in Edwards and Naím (eds), *Mexico 1994*, 127. The more technical criticism of the policy came before the crash, in Rudiger Dornbusch and Alejandro Werner, "Mexico: Stabilization, Reform, and No Growth," *Brookings Papers on Economic Activity*, 1 (1994), 253–315.
28 Maurice Obstfeld and Kenneth Rogoff, "The Mirage of Fixed Exchange Rates," *Journal of Economic Perspectives*, 9 (4) (Fall 1995), 73–96.
29 Ibid., 84.
30 Ibid, chart on p. 82.
31 Jeffrey Sachs, Aarón Tornell, and Andrés Velasco, *The Mexican Peso Crisis: Sudden Death or Death Foretold?*, mimeo (November 1995), 1.
32 Arnold C. Harberger, "Mexico's Exchange Rate Crisis," executive summary, *Grupo Financiero Bancomer*, May 1996, xvii.
33 International Monetary Fund, *International Capital Markets: Developments, Prospects, and Policy Issues* (Washington, DC: IMF, August 1995), 7–8 and 53–79.
34 Background discussion of this issue can be found in Liliana Rojas-Suárez and Steven R. Weisbrod, "Financial Fragilities in Latin America: The 1980s and 1990s," *Occasional Paper*, 132 (Washington, DC: International Monetary Fund, October 1995), 36–9.
35 The 17 percent figure comes from Grupo Financiero Bancomer, *Economic Report*, May 1998, 26. The precise percentage may be anywhere between 15 and 30 percent of GDP.
36 Heath, "The Devaluation of the Mexican Peso in 1994," 13.

6 The Fourth Quarter of 1994 and Beyond

1 Agustín Carstens, Research Director at the Bank of Mexico, said precisely this to me in an interview at the Bank on May 8, 1996.

2   The size of the support package to Mexico was unprecedented in order to correct an economic meltdown that was both rapid and itself unprecedented. The world has since seen other rapid and tragic economic meltdowns in East Asia, starting in 1997. The circumstances in Asia and Mexico differ, but there are some comparable elements. Mexico was first and we now know it was not the last.
3   Texts of their remarks can be found in *El Mercado de Valores*, a publication of Nacional Financiera (December 1994), 11–32.
4   Ibid., 12.
5   Ibid., 24.
6   Ibid., 32.
7   The annual *Informe* is required under the Mexican constitution. The Spanish version was provided by the office of the president and an English translation by the Mexican embassy in Washington, DC. Extensive documents are prepared to provide details of the contents of the speech. A summary of the economic aspects of the speech is contained the same issue of *El Mercado de Valores* cited above, 3–10.
8   Data in this discussion come from Banco de México, *Informe Anual 1994* (México, DF: Banco de México, 1995).
9   The attendee list comes from Pedro Aspe's op-ed article in the *Wall Street Journal* (July 14, 1995), A13, under the heading "Mexico's Ex-Finance Minister Sets the Record Straight." I was told by a number of the people I interviewed – Santiago Oñate, then Salinas' chief of staff, and Luis Rubio, the head of an independent think tank – that Farell was widely respected for his political acumen. Farell had been secretary of labor under three presidents, López Portillo, De la Madrid, and for a time Salinas, and therefore had much influence with labor leaders. He was also trusted by Aspe. Oñate was not present at the November 20 meeting; it is hard to conceive that José Córdoba, the previous chief of staff, would not have been present had he still been in his old position.
10 Interview at Princeton, New Jersey, April 16, 1996.
11 In his interview with me in Mexico City on June 4, 1996, Aspe was insistent on this point, presumably because he wanted it made clear that he was speaking first to his own countrymen and women and not just to the foreign financial community.
12 I was told this by Serra and again by Sergio Sarmiento in my interview with him on May 8, 1996. I do not know Sarmiento's source.
13 This was the general judgment, and mine as well. I heard it live.
14 Interview in Mexico City, July 3, 1996.
15 *Reforma* (December 16, 1994), 9A, by cartoonist Francisco Calderon.
16 Andres Oppenheimer, *Bordering on Chaos* (Boston: Little, Brown, 1996), 215 ff. contains fascinating material on the reactions of Serra and Mancera to the reported news of the Zapatista takeovers.
17 Ibid, 219. Silva Herzog expressed the same sentiments to me in an interview at the Mexican embassy in Washington, DC, on June 11, 1996
18 Interview in Mexico City on July 3, 1996.
19 Every person with whom I spoke in the Bank, other than Mancera, told me this. Mancera did not say what his pre-pacto position was in

his meeting with me on July 1, 1997, but one of the Vice Governors, Jesús Marcos Yacamán, said in an interview at the Bank on April 12, 1996, that the unanimous position of the Bank *junta* was to float.
20 I tried on three occasions to obtain an interview with Madariaga, but with no success.
21 Interview at ITAM, March 12, 1996. The peso depreciated much more; it was 5.3 to the dollar at the end of December 1994, and then depreciated further during the first quarter of 1995.
22 Interview at the Bank of Mexico, July 1, 1997.
23 Interview at Los Pinos, July 10, 1996.
24 Arnold C. Harberger, "Mexico's Exchange Rate Crisis," executive summary, *Grupo Financiero Bancomer* (May 1996), xviii.
25 Interview at ITAM, March 12, 1996.
26 Jeffrey Sachs, Aarón Tornell, and Andrés Velasco, *The Mexican Peso Crisis: Sudden Death or Death Foretold?*, mimeo (November 1995), 2.
27 This became clear in my interviews with investment houses in New York.
28 For example, see *Reforma* (May 17, 1995), 21A, article by Rossana Fuentes-Berain under the heading "Detrás de la escena" (Behind the scenes).
29 Interviews April 9, 1996, in Mexico City, and May 30, 1998, in Westchester County, New York.
30 Interview on April 16, 1996, in Princeton, New Jersey.
31 P. 6 of survey.
32 *Economist* (November 11, 1995), 8. When it printed Serra's letter, the *Economist* added an editor's note: "Our survey disagreed with Mr. Serra's interpretation of events, but intended no slur on his integrity."
33 The discussion that follows is based on the full text of the statement as it appeared in the Mexico City newspaper *La Jornada* (December 4, 1995).
34 The statement also brought out the animosity between Salinas and another ex-president, Luis Echeverría, and a number of other political figures, which is not relevant to the story of this book.
35 *Wall Street Journal* (December 20, 1996), A17, under the heading " Mexico's Money Theorists Need a Tip from Hong Kong."
36 Robert L. Bartley, "The Peso Folklórico: Dancing Away from Monetary Stability," in Sebastian Edwards and Moisés Naím (eds), *Mexico 1994: Anatomy of an Emerging Market Crash* (Washington, DC: Carnegie Endowment for International Peace, 1997), 162.
37 Interview in Mexico City, March 13, 1996.
38 Interview with Raúl Ramos at the Secretariat for Trade and Industrial Development (Secofi), May 7, 1996.
39 *El Financiero International* (August 10–16), 8. The four controlled by foreign capital were Mercantil–Probursa, Mexicana, Inverlat, and Confía; the five still controlled by the original owners were Banamex, Banorte, Bancomer, Serfin, and Bital; the eight merged or closed were Banpaís, Unión, Promex, Bancen, Banorie, Cremi, Banoro, and Atlántico; and the one seeking a foreign partner was Bancrecer.
40 See Rogelio Ramírez de la O., "The Mexican Peso Crisis and Recession of 1994–1995: Preventable Then, Avoidable in the Future?," in Riordan

Roett (ed.), *The Mexican Peso Crisis* (Boulder, CO: Lynne Rienner, 1996), 23–4.

7 Back in Washington and New York

1. The chronology draws heavily on Patricia C. Wertman, "Mexico: Chronology of a Financial Crisis," Congressional Research Service, Library of Congress (September 27, 1995).
2. Conversation with Lawrence Summers, October 9, 1996.
3. Philip Zelikow, "Treasury and the Mexican Shock," Kennedy School of Government, Harvard College, case study (1998), recounts the same story of this inaccurate estimate made by Treasury officials.
4. In its discussion of the peso crisis, the US General Accounting Office (GAO), *Mexico's Financial Crisis: Origins, Awareness, Assistance and Initial Efforts to Recover*, GAO/GGD-95-96 (February 1996), reached this same conclusion, that the Treasury saw no compelling need in 1994 for a change in Mexican financial and economic policy.
5. This memorandum and others cited subsequently, unless they are otherwise identified, are from the US Senate Banking Committee, "Chronology of the Mexican Economic Crisis," documents released by Senator Alfonse D'Amato (June 29, 1995).
6. GAO, *Mexico's Financial Crisis*, 14.
7. Ibid., 8.
8. My view is that Guillermo A. Calvo came closest to this in Calvo, Leonardo Leiderman and Carmen Reinhart, "Capital Inflows and Real Exchange Rate Appreciation in Latin America," *IMF Staff Papers*, 40 (1) (March 1993), 108–51, but he and his colleagues never really laid out the dangers from heavy use of dollar-indexed, short-term public liabilities.
9. Nora Lustig, "Mexico in Crisis, the US to the Rescue: The Financial Assistance Packages of 1982 and 1995," Brookings Institution, *Discussion Paper* (June 1996), contains a thorough exposition of the differences between the two incidents.
10. *Wall Street Journal* (September 19, 1997), A2, article by David Wessel under the heading "Rubin Says Global Investors Don't Suffer Enough.
11. The short-lived financial consequences are a different matter from the long-term impact on Mexican politics of the Colosio assassination. Sergio Sarmiento, a widely read columnist and popular television commentator in Mexico, repeatedly made the point that Colosio's murder was a seminal event in modern Mexican history, one that thoroughly changed the course of Mexican politics for the worse.
12. Pedro Aspe gave his account of what happened at what he called the "famous" meeting of November 20 to the Mexican press and in an editorial comment in the *Wall Street Journal* (July 14, 1995). This account is practically the only explanation that Aspe has given about the events of mid- to late 1994, other than what is contained in the public record.
13. Sidney Weintraub, "Case Study of Economic Stabilization: Mexico," in William R. Cline and Sidney Weintraub (eds), *Economic Stabilization*

188 Notes and References

in Developing Countries (Washington, DC: Brookings Institution, 1981), 271–96.
14. Rogelio Ramírez de la O., "The Mexican Peso Crisis and Recession of 1994–1995: Preventable Then, Avoidable in the Future?," in Riordan Roett (ed.), *The Mexican Peso Crisis* (Boulder, CO: Lynne Rienner, 1996), 13, makes the same point, that resources were misallocated to increase consumption and housing and not production.
15. On p. 92.
16. Greenspan is normally elliptical in his public pronouncements. However, the word "blunt" was repeated several times during the interviews.
17. Interview reported on February 5, 1997, in *Reforma*, by Ramón Alberto Garza, under the heading: "La cosigna a Aspe: No devaluar." Internet version: <www.infosel.com.mx>.
18. *Latin American Weekly Report* (May 4, 1995), 191.
19. Wolf Grabendorff, "Repercussions of the Mexican Monetary Crisis Across the Atlantic: Ripples, Breakers, or a Sea Change in European Perspectives?," in Riordan Roett (ed), *The Mexican Peso Crisis*, 96, refers to the resentment of the EU about the IMF's heavy involvement and inadequate consultation in the peso rescue package.
20. Miguel de la Madrid, in a conversation with me on another subject on April 9, 1997, said that he felt there were no feasible options other than to alter Mexican development policy in light of the economic crisis he faced when he entered office at the end of 1982.
21. I published a modest piece expressing concern about the growing current account deficit at about this time. Sidney Weintraub, "Evaluación de la balanza de la cuenta corriente en México," *Economía Mexicana*, 1 (1) (January–June 1992), 249–51.
22. Shahid Javed Burki, "A Fate Foretold: The World Bank and the Mexican Crisis," in Sebastian Edwards and Moisés Naím (eds), *Mexico 1994: Anatomy of an Emerging-Market Crash* (Washington, DC: Carnegie Endowment for International Peace, 1997), 247–58.
23. Ibid., 248.
24. Manuel Suárez-Mier, an official of the Bank of Mexico who served for a number of years in the embassy in Washington, noted in a paper in early 1996 that "For the most part Mexico's policies received not only the approval but rave reviews from the multilateral agencies involved." He was referring mainly to the IMF, but the paper also dealt with the roles of the World Bank and the Inter-American Development Bank. "The Role of International Agencies in the Management of the World Economy: The Point of View of a LDC Member Country," paper presented at a program on the Role of International Agencies, Alamos, Sonora (February 23–25, 1996).
25. International Monetary Fund, *International Capital Markets: Developments, Prospects, and Policy Issues* (Washington, DC: International Monetary Fund, August 1995), 53–79.
26. This argument is supported by interviews with private-sector participants engaged in pacto discussions with the Mexican financial and monetary authorities.
27. *Wall Street Journal*, op-ed column (December 20, 1996), A16. Malpass

wrote an earlier column for the *Wall Street Journal* in which he argued that Mexico should reverse the devaluation and restore the exchange rate to 3.5 pesos per dollar ("The Mexican Peso: 3.5 or Bust," January 11, 1995, A14).
28 Alan Greenspan, testimony before the House Committee on Banking and Financial Services, January 25, 1995.
29 See Banco de México, *Indicadores Económicos*, various issues. *Indicadores Económicos* is a monthly statistical publication.
30 The existence of this group was first reported in articles from the Mexico bureau of the *Wall Street Journal* during 1994. The first of these, by Craig Torres and Thomas Vogel, Jr., which contained considerable detail, appeared on June 14, 1994, A1. The most complete reporting was an article in the *New Republic*, by Douglas W. Payne (March 13, 1995). Payne reported that the consortium included Fidelity Investments; Trust Company of the West; Scudder, Stevens & Clark; Oppenheimer Management; Putnam Funds Management; Soros Fund Management; Salomon Brothers; Nomura Securities International; and the Weston Group.
31 *Wall Street Journal*, op-ed column (January 26, 1995), "Why Alarm Bells Didn't Ring Over Mexico."
32 Council on Foreign Relations, *Lessons of the Mexican Peso Crisis*, report of an independent task force (New York: Council on Foreign Relations, 1996), 26–8.
33 *Wall Street Journal* (July 6, 1995), A1, "Peso Surprise: How Mexico Crisis Ambushed Top Minds in Officialdom, Finance," by David Wessel and others.
34 The quoted words come from statements by Rubin and Christopher, respectively.
35 See Sidney Weintraub, *NAFTA at Three: A Progress Report* (Washington, DC: Center for Strategic and International Studies, 1997) for a discussion of job loss and creation from NAFTA.
36 Alan Greenspan, see n. 28.
37 I know this from queries I received from a number of senators after I testified before the Senate Foreign Relations Committee in favor of the guarantee proposal. These senators, even though they were skeptical, were not prepared to dismiss out of hand Greenspan's statements about possible financial damage to the United States in the event of a Mexican debt default.
38 Hearing before US Senate Foreign Relations Committee, "Mexico's Economic Situation and US Efforts to Stabilize the Peso," 104 congress, session 1, US Government Printing Office (January 26, 1995), 12 and 14.
39 His op-ed column was on January 23, 1995, and his testimony before the Senate Foreign Relations Committee was three days later, on January 26, 1995.
40 GAO, *Mexico's Financial Crisis*, 109–32, contains a discussion of the nature of and conditions on US and IMF assistance to Mexico. Treasury Secretary Rubin laid out the details of the US credit to Mexico in a signing ceremony on February 21, 1995.
41 The US Treasury issued monthly reports on the situation in Mexico and on compliance with the loan conditions pursuant to the Mexican

Debt Disclosure Act of 1995. The Congress also was provided with semi-annual reports under this act.
42 These were Germany, Great Britain, Denmark, the Netherlands, Belgium, and Switzerland. See *New York Times* (February 13, 1995), article by Nathaniel C. Nash, "Western Allies Rebuff Clinton in Mexico Vote."
43 I, for one, have made this argument in Sidney Weintraub, "The Interplay between Economic and Political Opening in Mexico," *Proceedings of the American Philosophical Society*, 137 (1) (1993).
44 Nora Lustig, "Mexico in Crisis, the US to the Rescue."
45 I know this because I was in the office of an editor of the *Los Angeles Times* who told me about the phone call he had received that day from Larry Summers.
46 Allan H. Meltzer, *Wall Street Journal*, op-ed article (February 2, 1996), A11, "Clinton's Bailout Was No Favor to Mexicans."
47 David Felix, *Washington Times*, op-ed article (February 14, 1995), A19, "NAFTA and the Mexican Peso Crisis." Felix later wrote another article in which he argues that unrestricted capital mobility is incompatible with free multilateral trade and full employment. See "On Drawing General Policy Lessons from Recent Latin American Currency Crises," *Journal of Post-Keynesian Economics*, 20 (2) (Winter 1997–8), 191–221.
48 Bradford DeLong, Christopher DeLong and Sherman Robinson, "The Case for Mexico's Rescue," *Foreign Affairs*, 75 (3) (May–June 1996), 8–14.
49 David Hale, *Washington Post* (June 2, 1996), C4, "Such a Deal! The Much Maligned Mexico Bailout Is Looking Smart – and Not Just for Mexico." David Hale has made this same argument since then, for example, "The Markets and Mexico: The Supply-side Story," in Edwards and Naím (eds), *Mexico 1994*, 201–45.
50 Thomas L. Friedman, *New York Times* (January 25, 1995), A21, "Helping Mexico Help Us."

8 The Aftermath

1 Data from the Bank of Mexico, *The Mexican Economy 1996*, English version (México, DF: Banco de México, 1996).
2 Both these percentages were calculated from tables in ibid, 289–90.
3 Article "Artículo de portada: Salario mínimo," *Expansión* (November 5, 1997), 18–30.
4 US Embassy, Mexico City, *Mexico: Economic and Financial Report* (January 1997), 31.
5 OECD, *Mexico: OECD Economic Surveys 1994–1995* (Paris: Organization for Economic Cooperation and Development, 1995), 93.
6 Mexico's statistical office (INEGI in its Spanish initials) changed the base for measuring GDP from 1980 to 1993 and the 1995 growth figure given in the text uses the new base. When the 1995 GDP decline is measured using the 1993 base, it comes to 6.2 percent and not the 6.9 percent using the 1980 base.
7 Several informants stressed the insistence to pay the external debt. They included José Julian Sidaoui Dib, a Vice Governor of the Bank of Mexico

who had been in *Hacienda* in the previous administration, in an interview at the Bank on July 1, 1997; and two other senior Bank officials, Armando Baquero and Roberto Merino, in a joint interview with them on April 9, 1996. The point they made was that it was important not to repeat the Mex-dollar experience of 1982, when Mexico reneged on what was a clear commitment on these accounts by paying Mex-dollar holders in pesos that had just been devalued rather than in dollars.

8   Bank of Mexico, *The Mexican Economy 1996*, 112–13. The first placements were for $274 million by Nacional Financiera in May and the National Bank for Foreign Trade (Bancomext) for $105 million in June. Total placement of public-sector debt instruments in 1995 was $2.6 billion in markets in Germany, Japan, Switzerland, and the United States.

9   Bank of Mexico, *The Mexican Economy 1997* (México, DF: Banco de México, 1997), 102.

10 Speech of May 22, 1995, before the 25th Washington conference of the Council of the Americas, "Staying the Course: Forging a Free Trade Area in the Americas."

11 *Financial Times*, survey on Mexico Finance and Investment (December 16, 1997), I, article by Stephen Fidler under the heading "On the Crest of a Wave."

12 As a matter of interest to the reader, most of the data for the most recent year comes from the web sites of various Mexican government agencies.

13 See Bank of Mexico press release of September 22, 1997, entitled "Informe sobre la política monetaria en el lapso 1°de enero de 1997 al 30 de junio de 1997."

14 *Grupo Financiero Bancomer, Economic Report* (June 1998), 39.

15 Binational Study on Migration, *Migration Between Mexico and the United States* (US Commission on Immigration Reform and Secretaría de Relaciones Exteriores of Mexico, printed in Mexico, 1997), 29.

16 Drawing the poverty line is not a precise procedure. Nora Lustig in the "Introduction" to Lustig (ed.), *Coping with Austerity: Poverty and Inequality in Latin America* (Washington, DC: Brookings Institution, 1995), 49, notes that in Latin America the line is normally set at twice the cost of the food component of the basic basket.

17 Ibid., 54.

18 World Bank, *World Development Report 1996* (New York: Oxford University Press, 1996), 196–7.

19 *Este Pais*, 88 (July 1998), 18 gives a time series of polls taken by MORI de México since December 1997.

20 David Felix, "On Drawing General Policy Lessons from recent Latin American Currency Crises," *Journal of Post-Keynesian Economics*, 20 (2) (Winter 1997–8), 191–221.

21 The signatories of this letter were Representatives Bernard Sanders, George Miller, Marcy Kaptur, Peter DeFazio, Dennis Kucinich, and Major Owens. This was not the first time Representative Sanders (an independent from Vermont) made known his distaste for financial support to Mexico. On July 19, 1995, the House of Representatives voted 245 to 183 to approve a rider he included in the appropriations bill for the treasury,

postal service, and other agencies, to halt US support for the peso effective October 1, 1995. See *Washington Post* (July 20, 1995), A6, article by Alan Fram, "House Votes to Block More Loans to Mexico."
22 US data are from the web site of the US Department of Commerce.
23 Mexico's trade data are from Secofi. Bilateral trade figures are not identical from US and Mexican sources.

9 To Bet on a Nation

1 *New York Times* (August 4, 1996), 1, article by Katharine Q. Seelye, "As Dole Seeks a Verb."
2 Tobin has written both technical and popular articles on this subject. See *Washington Post* (December 21, 1997), C3, under the heading "Why We Need Sand in the Market's Gears."
3 Lawrence Summers, "Ten Lessons to Learn," *Economist* (December 23, 1995–January 5, 1995), 46–8.
4 Edwin M. Truman, "The Risks and Implications of External Financial Shocks: Lessons from Mexico," *International Finance Discussion Paper*, 535, Board of Governors of the Federal Reserve System, January 1996.
5 Ibid., 16.
6 Truman's language is worth quoting: "It was inappropriate that until early 1995 an important country like Mexico announced its international reserve position only three times a year *or* when it was otherwise convenient." (28 Truman's emphasis)
7 Michel Camdessus, speech of May 22, 1995, before the 25th Washington conference of the Council of Americas, "Staying the Course: Forging a Free Trade Area in the Americas."
8 Julio López G., "Mexico's Crisis: Financial Modernization and Financial Fragility," *Quarterly Review*, Banca Nazionale del Lavoro, 50 (201) (June 1997), 165–85.
9 James C. Thomson, Jr., "How Could Vietnam Happen? An Autopsy," in G. John Ikenberry (ed.), *American Foreign Policy* (New York: HarperCollins, 1996), 2nd edn, 502. Thomson's piece was published originally in the *Atlantic Monthly* (April 1968).
10 Ibid., 508, 509.
11 Robert S. McNamara, *In Retrospect: The Tragedy and Lessons of Vietnam* (New York: Times Books, 1995), 32.
12 If I may be permitted to be personal, I was in the State Department at that time and those of us on the inside knew that there were experts whose knowledge was not exploited and whose advice presumably was not wanted.
13 Irving L. Janis, *Victims of Groupthink: A Psychological Study of Foreign-Policy Decisions and Fiascos* (Boston: Houghton Mifflin, 1972) analyzes how critical, independent thinking was replaced by "groupthink" in a number of US foreign policy disasters, such as Vietnam and the Bay of Pigs. I mention this because faulty decisions from mindsets that policy-makers bring to the table is by no means an exclusive Mexican problem.
14 Interview in Mexico City, July 3, 1996.

15 Interview in Mexico City, July 4, 1996.
16 Interview in Mexico City, May 8, 1996.
17 *Reforma* (May 17, 1995), 21A.
18 Carlos Elizondo Mayer-Serra, "Tres trampas: sobre los orígenes de la crisis económica mexicana de 1994," Centro de Investigaciones y Docencia Económicas, *Working Paper* 46 (1996), 19. ("Las apuestas resultarían menos attractivas, si estós tuvieron que pagar un mayor costo político por sus decisiones equivocados.") Elizondo directs CIDE, which is a combined university–research center on the outskirts of Mexico City.

Bibliography

Albo Márquez, A. (ed.). *México Social 1994-1995* (México, DF: Banco Nacional de México [Banamex], 1996).
Alduncin Abitia, E. *Los valores de los mexicanos: México – entre la tradición y la modernidad* (México, DF: Banamex, 1989).
Alduncin Abitia, E. *Los valores de los mexicanos: México en tiempos de cambio*, tomo II (México, DF: Banamex, 1991).
Alduncin Abitia, E. *Los valores de los mexicanos: En busca de una esencia*, tomo III (México, DF: Banamex, 1993).
Alonso, J., Azis, A. and Tamayo, J. (eds). *El nuevo estado mexicano: Tomo I, estado y economía* (Guadalajara: Universidad de Guadalajara, 1992).
Arredondo Ramírez, P. "El estado y la communicación: Dilemas frente a un proyecto modernizador," in J. Alonso, A. Aziz and J. Tamayo (eds), *El nuevo estado mexicano: Tomo IV, estado y sociedad* (Guadalajara: Universidad de Guadalajara, 1992), 39–66.
"Articulo de portada: Salario minimo." *Expansión* (November 5, 1997), 18–30.
Aspe, P. *Economic Transformation: The Mexican Way* (Cambridge, MA: MIT Press, 1993).
Aspe, P. *Discursos, 1993-1994* (México, DF: Secretaría de Hacienda y Crédito Público, 1994).
Aspe, P., Speech before the 58th National Banking Convention, Cancún (October 19, 1994), *El Mercado de Valores, año LIV* (December 1994).
Aspe, P. "Mexico's Ex-Finance Minister Sets the Record Straight," *Wall Street Journal* (July 14, 1995), A13.
Bailey, J. *The 1994 Mexican Presidential Election: Post-Election Report* (Washington, DC: Center for Strategic and International Studies, October 8, 1994).
Baliño, T., Enoch, C. and others. *Currency Board Arrangement: Issues and Experiences* (Washington, DC: International Monetary Fund, 1997).
Banco de México. *Informe Anual 1993* (México, DF: Banco de México, 1994).
Banco de México. *Indicadores Económicos*, monthly compilation of economic data in print form and on the Bank's web site.
Banco de México. *Exposición sobre la política monetaria para el lapso 1° de abril de 1994, 31 diciembre 1994* (México, DF: May 1994).
Banco de México. *Informe Anual 1994* (México, DF: Banco de México, 1995).
Bank of Mexico. *The Mexican Economy 1995* (México, DF: Banco de México, 1995).
Bank of Mexico. *The Mexican Economy 1996* (México, DF: Banco de México, 1996).
Bank of Mexico. *The Mexican Economy 1997* (México, DF: Banco de México, 1997).
Bartley, R. "The Peso Folklórico: Dancing Away from Monetary Stability," in S. Edwards and M. Naím (eds), *Mexico 1994: Anatomy of an Emerging-*

Market Crash (Washington, DC: Carnegie Endowment for International Peace, 1997).

Bartra, R. *The Cage of Melancholy: Identity and Metamorphosis in the Mexican Character* (New Brunswick, NJ: Rutgers University Press, 1992), trans. C. Hall, from the original Spanish book, *La jaula de la melancholía* (México, DF: Grijalbo, 1987).

Beltrán, U. and others. *Los mexicanos de los noventa* (México, DF: Instituto Sociales, Universidad Nacional Autónoma de México, 1996).

Binational Study on Migration. *Migration Between Mexico and the United States* (México, DF: US Commission on Immigration Reform and Secretaría de Relaciones Exteriores de México, 1997).

Blanco Mendoza, H. *Las negociaciones comerciales de México con el mundo* (México, DF: Fondo de Cultura Económico, 1994).

Buira, A. "Reflections on the Mexican Crisis of 1994," in G. Calvo, M. Goldstein and E. Hochreiter (eds), *Private Capital Flows to Emerging Markets After the Mexican Crisis* (Washington, DC: Institute for International Economics for the Austrian National Bank, 1996), 307–19.

Buira, A. "Financial Crisis: Towards an Alternative Approach," paper delivered at a conference on Coping with Financial Crises in Developing and Transition Countries: Regulatory and Supervisory Challenges in a New Era of Global Finance (Amsterdam: Nederlandsche Bank, March 16–17, 1998).

Burki, S. J. "A Fate Foretold: The World Bank and the Mexican Crisis," in S. Edwards and M. Naím (eds), *Mexico 1994: Anatomy of an Emerging-Market Crash* (Washington, DC: Carnegie Endowment for International Peace, 1997), 247–58.

Calvo, G., Leiderman, L. and Reinhart, C. "Capital Inflows and Real Exchange Rate Appreciation in Latin America," *IMF Staff Papers*, 40 (1) (March 1993), 108–51.

Calvo, G. and Mendoza, E. "Mexico's Balance of Payments Crisis: A Chronicle of Death Foretold," *International Finance Discussion Paper*, 545, Board of Governors of the Federal Reserve System (March 1996).

Camdessus, M. "Staying the Course: Forging a Free Trade Area in the Americas," speech before the 25th Washington Conference of the Council of the Americas (May 22, 1995).

Camp, R. A. *Mexican Political Biography 1935–1993* (Austin, TX: University of Texas Press, 1995), 3rd edn.

Committee to Protect Journalists. Letter to President Ernesto Zedillo (June 6, 1997).

Cordera Campos, R. "La reforma del estado como necesidad," in J. Alonso, A. Aziz and J. Tamayo (eds), *El nuevo estado mexicano: Tomo I, estado y economía* (Guadalajara: Universidad de Guadalajara, 1992), 281–301.

Córdova, A. *La política de masas del cardenismo* (México, DF: Ediciones Era, 1974).

Cosío Villegas, D. *El estilo personal de gobernar* (México, DF: Joaquín Mortiz, 1974).

Council on Foreign Relations. *Lessons of the Mexican Peso Crisis*, report of an independent task force (New York: Council on Foreign Relations, 1996).

D'Amato, A. "Report on the Mexican Economic Crisis," presented by the

Chairman of the Senate Banking Committee (June 29, 1995).
De la Grange, B. and Maite, R. *Marcos, la genial impostura* (México, DF: Nuevo Siglo Aguilar, 1997).
DeLong, B., DeLong, C. and Robinson, S. "The Case for Mexico's Rescue," *Foreign Affairs*, 75 (3) (May–June 1996), 8–14.
Domínguez, J. (ed.). *Technopols: Freeing Politics and Markets in Latin America in the 1980s* (University Park, PA: Pennsylvania State University Press, 1997).
Dornbusch, R. "The Folly, the Crash, and Beyond: Economic Policies and the Crisis," in S. Edwards and M. Naím (eds), *Mexico 1994: Anatomy of an Emerging-Market Crash* (Washington, DC: Carnegie Endowment for International Peace, 1997), 125–40.
Dornbusch, R. and Werner, A. "Mexico: Stabilization, Reform, and No Growth," *Brookings Papers on Economic Activity*, 1 (1994), 253–315.
Dresser, D. "Falling from the Tightrope: The Political Economy of the Mexican Crisis," in S. Edwards and M. Naím (eds), *Mexico 1994: Anatomy of an Emerging-Market Crash* (Washington, DC: Carnegie Endowment for International Peace, 1997), 55–79.
Economist, The. "A Survey of Mexico" (October 25, 1995).
Edwards, S. "Bad Luck or Bad Policies? An Economic Analysis of the Crisis," in S. Edwards and M. Naím (eds), *Mexico 1994: Anatomy of an Emerging-Market Crash* (Washington, DC: Carnegie Endowment for International Peace 1997), 95–124.
Edwards, S. and Naím, M. "Introduction: Anatomy and Lessons in Mexico, 1994," in S. Edwards and M. Naím (eds), *Mexico 1994: Anatomy of an Emerging-Market Crash* (Washington, DC: Carnegie Endowment for International Peace, 1997), 1–30.
Eijffinger, S. C. W. and De Haan, J. *The Political Economy of Central-Bank Independence* (Princeton: Princeton University, International Finance Section, 1996).
Elizondo Mayer-Serra, C. "Tres trampas: sobre los orígenes de la crisis económica mexicana de 1994," Centro de Investigación y Docencia Económicas, *Working Paper*, 46 (1996).
Felix, D. "NAFTA and the Mexican Peso Crisis," *Washington Times*, op. ed. article (14 February, 1995), A19.
Felix, D. "On Drawing General Policy Lessons From Recent Latin American Currency Crises," *Journal of Post-Keynesian Economics*, 20 (2) (Winter 1997–8), 191–221.
Fidler, S. "On the Crest of a Wave," *Financial Times*, Survey on Mexico Finance and Investment (December 16, 1997).
Fram, A. "House Votes to Block More Loans to Mexico," *Washington Post* (July 20, 1995).
Frieden, J. A. "The Politics of Exchange Rates," in S. Edwards and M. Naím (eds), *Mexico 1994: Anatomy of an Emerging-Market Crash* (Washington, DC: Carnegie Endowment for International Peace, 1997), 81–94.
Friedland, J. "Mum's the Word: Mexico Isn't Free with Information," *Wall Street Journal* (September 10, 1998).
Friedman, T. L. "Helping Mexico Help Us," *The New York Times* (May 23, 1995), A21.

Fuentes-Berain, R. "Crónicas de peso," *Reforma* (May 17, 18, 19, 1995).
García Alba Iduñate, P. *Testimonio de política económica, 1982–1988* (México, DF: Universidad Autónoma Metropolitana, 1993).
Gil Díaz, F. "Don Rodrigo Gómez, Visionario de la Economía," in *Rodrigo Gomez: Vida y Obra* (México, DF: Banco de México y Fondo de Cultura Económica, 1991).
Gil-Díaz, F. and Carstens, A. "Some Hypotheses Related to the Mexican 1994–95 Crisis," Banco de México, research paper presented to the annual meeting of the American Economic Association (San Francisco, January 5–7, 1996).
Gil-Díaz, F. and Carstens, A. "Pride and Prejudice: The Economics Profession and Mexico's Financial Crisis," in S. Edwards and M. Naím (eds), *Mexico 1994: Anatomy of an Emerging-Market Crash* (Washington, DC: Carnegie Endowment for International Peace, 1997), 165–200.
Golob, S. "Making Possible What is Necessary: Pedro Aspe, the Salinas Team, and the Next Mexican Miracle," in J. Dominguez (ed.). *Technopols* (University Park, PA: Pennsylvania State University Press, 1997), 95–143.
Grabendorff, W. "Repercussions of the Mexican Monetary Crisis Across the Atlantic: Ripples, Breakers, or a Sea Change in European Perspectives?," in R. Roett (ed.), *The Mexican Peso Crisis* (Boulder, CO: Lynne Rienner, 1996), 93–112.
Gramsci, A. *Selections from the Prison Notebooks*, trans. and ed. Q. Hoare and G. Nowell Smith (New York: International Publishers, 1971).
Grayson, G. W. *Mexico: From Corporatism to Pluralism*? (Fort Worth, TX: Harcourt Brace College Publishers, 1998).
Greenspan, A., Testimony before the House Committee on Banking and Financial Services (January 25, 1995).
Griffith-Jones, S. "Causes and Lessons of the Mexican Peso Crisis," United Nations University/World Institute for Development Economics Research, *Working Paper*, 132 (May 1997).
Grupo Financiero Bancomer. *Economic Report* (May 1998).
Grupo Financiero Bancomer. *Economic Report* (June 1998).
Hale, D. "Such a Deal! The Much Maligned Mexico Bailout Is Looking Smart – and Not Just for Mexico," *The Washington Post* (June 2, 1996), C4.
Hale, D. "The Markets and Mexico: The Supply-Side Story," in S. Edwards and M. Naím (eds), *Mexico 1994: Anatomy of an Emerging-Market Crash* (Washington, DC: Carnegie Endowment for Interational Peace, 1997), 201–45.
Harberger, A. C. "Mexico's Exchange Rate Crisis," executive summary, *Grupo Financiero Bancomer* (May 1996).
Heath, J. E. "The Devaluation of the Mexican Peso in 1994" (Washington, DC: Center for Strategic and International Studies, June 1995).
Heath, J. E. "Economic Sovereignty in Mexico," in J. Hoebing, S. Weintraub and M. D. Baer (eds), *NAFTA and Sovereignty: Trade-Offs for Canada, Mexico, and the United States* (Washington, DC: Center for Strategic and International Studies, 1996), 86–106.
Hernández Ramírez, R. Speech before 58th National Banking Convention (October 19, 1994), Cancún (*El Mercado de Valores, año LIV*, December 1994).

Hufbauer, G. and Schott, J. J. *NAFTA: An Assessment* (Washington, DC: Institute for International Economics, 1993).
Ibarra, D. *¿Transición o crisis?* (México DF: Aguilar Nuevo Siglo, 1996).
Inglehart, R. F., Nevitte, N. and Basañez, M. *The North American Trajectory: Cultural, Economic, and Political Ties among the United States, Canada, and Mexico* (New York: Aldine de Gruyter, 1996).
International Monetary Fund. *International Capital Markets: Developments, Prospects, and Policy Issues* (Washington, DC: International Monetary Fund, August 1995), 7–8 and 53–79.
Janis, I. L. *Victims of Groupthink: A Psychological Study of Foreign-Policy Decisions and Fiascos* (Boston: Houghton Mifflin, 1972).
Kalifa-Assad, S. "Income Distribution and Poverty in Mexico: A Reconsideration of the Distribution Problem," PhD dissertation (Cornell University, 1977).
Kamin, S. B. and Rogers, J. H. "Monetary Policy in the End-Game to Exchange-Rate Based Stabilizations: The Case of Mexico," Federal Reserve System, *International Finance Discussion Paper*, 540 (February 1996).
Kaufman, H. "Why Alarm Bells Didn't Ring Over Mexico," *Wall Street Journal* (January 26, 1995).
Krauze, E. *Por una democracia sin adjectivos* (México, DF: Joaquín Mortiz/ Planeta, 1986).
Krauze, E. *Tiempo Contado*, (México, DF: Oceano, 1996).
Krauze, E. *Mexico: Biography of Power: A History of Modern Mexico, 1810– 1996*, trans. Hank Heifets (New York: HarperCollins, 1997).
Krauze, E. *La presidencia imperial: Ascenso y caida del sistema político mexicano (1940–1996)* (México, DF: Tusquets, 1997).
Leiderman, L. and Thorne, A. "Mexico's 1994 Crisis and its Aftermath: What are the Main Lessons?," in G. Calvo, M. Goldstein and E. Hochreiter (eds), *Private Capital Flows to Emerging Markets After the Mexican Crisis* (Washington, DC: Institute for International Economics for the Austrian National Bank, 1996), 1–43.
Leiderman, L., Liviatan, N. and Thorne, A. "Shifting Nominal Anchors: The Experience of Mexico," mimeo (November 1995).
López, G. J. "Mexico's Crisis: Financial Modernization and Financial Fragility," *Quarterly Review, Banca Nazionale del Lavoro*, 50 (201) (June 1997), 165–85.
López Moreno, J. *Reformas constitucionales para la modernización* (México, DF: Fondo de Cultura Económica, 1993).
Lustig, N. *Mexico: The Remaking of an Economy* (Washington, DC: Brookings Institution, 1992).
Lustig, N. "Introduction," in N. Lustig (ed.), *Coping with Austerity: Poverty and Inequality in Latin America* (Washington, DC: Brookings Institution, 1995), 1–41.
Lustig, N. "The Mexican Peso Crisis: The Forseeable and the Surprises," Brookings Institution, *Discussion Paper* (June 1995).
Lustig, N. "Mexico in Crisis, the US, to the Rescue: The Financial Assistance Packages of 1982 and 1995," Brookings Institution, *Discussion Paper* (June 1996).
Malpass, D. "The Mexican Peso: 3.5 or Bust," *Wall Street Journal*, op-ed column (11 January 1995), A14.

Malpass, D. "Currency Stability on the March," *Wall Street Journal*, op-ed column (20 December 1996), A16.
Mancera Aguayo, M. Speech before 58th National Banking Convention, Cancún (October 19, 1994), *El Mercado de Valores, año LIV* (December 1994).
Mancera Aguayo, M. "Don't Blame Monetary Policy," *Wall Street Journal* (January 31, 1995).
Martínez, G. and Fárber, G. *Desregulación económica, 1989-1993* (México, DF: Fondo de Cultura Económica, 1994).
McNamara, R. S. *In Retrospect: The Tragedy and Lessons of Vietnam* (New York: Times Books, 1995).
Meltzer, A. "Clinton's Bailout Was No Favor to Mexicans," *Wall Street Journal*, op-ed article (February 2, 1996), A11.
Meyer, L. *Mexico and the United States in the Oil Controversy: 1917-1942* (Austin, TX: University of Texas Press, 1977).
Meyer, L. *Liberalismo autoritario:las contradicciones del sistema político mexicano* (México, DF: Oceano, 1995).
Meyer, M. C. and Sherman, W. *The Course of Mexican History* (New York: Oxford University Press, 1983), 2nd edn.
Naím, M. "Mexico's Larger Story," in S. Edwards and M. Naím (eds.), *Mexico 1994: Anatomy of an Emerging-Market Crash* (Washington, DC: Carnegie Endowment for International Peace, 1997), 295-311.
Nash, W. C. "Western Allies Rebuff Clinton in Mexico Vote," *New York Times* (February 13, 1995).
Obstfeld, M. and Rogoff, K. "The Mirage of Fixed Exchange Rates," *Journal of Economic Perspectives*, 9 (4) (Fall 1995), 73-96.
OECD. *Mexico: OECD Economic Surveys, 1994-1995* (Paris: Organization for Economic Cooperation and Development, 1995).
Oppenheimer, A. *Bordering on Chaos* (Boston: Little Brown, 1996).
Ortiz Martínez, G. *La reforma financiera y desincorporación bancaria* (México, DF: Fondo de Cultura Económica, 1994).
Ortiz Martínez, G. Speech before the 58th National Banking Convention, Cancún (October 19, 1994), *El Mercado de Valores, año LIV* (December 1994).
Payne, D. "How Investment Bankers Ruined Mexico," *New Republic* (March 13, 1995).
Paz, O. *The Labyrinth of Solitude: Life and Thought in Mexico* (New York: Grove Press, 1961), from the revised Spanish version of 1959.
Paz, O. "Dos décadas de Vuelta," *Vuelta 242* (January 1997), 42-3.
Pérez Fernández del Castillo, G. "La democracia mexicana: sus problemas actuales," in L. Rubio and A. Fernández (eds), *México a la hora del cambio* (México, DF: Cal y Arena, 1995), 315-54.
Peschard-Sverdrup, A. "The 1997 Mexican Midterm Elections: Post-election Report" (Washington, DC: Center for Strategic and International Studies, August 1997).
Ramírez, C. *El asesor incómodo: Joseph-Marie Córdoba Montoya* (Mexico City: Oceano, 1997).
Ramírez de la O, R. "The Mexican Peso Crisis and Recession of 1994-1995: Preventable Then, Avoidable in the Future?," in R. Roett (ed.), *The Mexican Peso Crisis* (Boulder, CO: Lynne Rienner, 1996), 11-32.

Ramos, S. *El perfil del hombre y la cultura en México* (México, DF: Collección Austral Espasa Calpe Mexicana, 1980), 9th edn; originally published in 1934.

Roett, R. "The Mexican Devaluation and the US Response: Potomac Politics, 1995-Style," in R. Roett (ed.), *The Mexican Peso Crisis* (Boulder, CO: Lynne Rienner, 1996), 33–48.

Roett, R. (ed.). *The Mexican Peso Crisis* (Boulder, CO: Lynne Rienner, 1996).

Rogozinski, J. *La privatización de empresas para estatales* (México, DF: Fondo de Cultura Económica, 1993).

Rogozinki, J. *La privatización en México: Razones e impactos* (México, DF: Editorial Trillas, 1997).

Rojas-Suárez, L. and Weisbrod, S. R. "Financial Fragilities in Latin America: The 1980s and 1990s," *Occasional Paper*, 132 (Washington, DC: International Monetary Fund, October 1995), 36–9.

Rubio, L. "El sistema político mexicano: ¿cambio y evolución?," in L. Rubio and A. Fernández (eds), *México a la hora del cambio* (México, DF: Cal y Arena, 1995), 385–408.

Sachs, J., Tornell, A. and Velasco, A. *The Mexican Peso Crisis: Sudden Death or Death Foretold?*, mimeo (November 1995).

Salinas de Gortari, C. Speech before 58th National Banking Convention, Cancún (October 19, 1994), *El Mercado de Valores, año LIV* (December 1994).

Salinas de Gotari, C. "VI Informe de Gobierno" (November 1, 1994), *El Mercado de Valores, año LIV* (December 1994).

Salinas de Gortari, C. Message to various media outlets dated December 3, 1995, version used taken from *La Jornada* (December 4), via internet.

Seelye, K. Q. "As Dole Seeks a Verb," *New York Times* (August 4, 1996).

Seidman, W. "Block the Bailout: Let Market Solve Mexico's Woes," *Wall Street Journal*, op-ed column (January 23, 1995).

Smith, C. "International Perspectives on the Mexican Peso Crisis: An Introduction," in R. Roett (ed.), *The Mexican Peso Crisis* (Boulder, CO: Lynne Rienner, 1996), 1–9.

Smith, P. H. "Political Dimensions of the Peso Crisis," in S. Edwards and M. Naím (eds), *Mexico 1994: Anatomy of an Emerging-Market Crash* (Washington, DC: Carnegie Endowment for International Peace, 1997), 31–53.

Storrs, L. "Mexico and the US Financial Support Package: Summary of Congressional Actions," Congressional Research Service, Library of Congress (May 3, 1996).

Suárez-Mier, M. "The Role of International Agencies in the Management of the World Economy: The Point of View of an LDC Member Country," paper presented at a program on The Role of International Agencies, Alamos, Sonora (February 23–25, 1996).

Summers, L. "Ten Lessons to Learn," *Economist* (December 23, 1995–January 5, 1996), 46–8.

Thomson, J. C., Jr. "How Could Vietnam Happen? An Autopsy," in G. Ikenberry (ed.), *American Foreign Policy* (New York: HarperCollins, 1996), 2nd edn., 502–11, originally published in *Atlantic Monthly* (April 1968).

Tobin, J. "Why We Need Sand in the Market's Gears," *Washington Post* (December 21, 1997).

Torres, C. and Vogel, T., Jr. "Wield Growing Clout in Developing Nations," *Wall Street Journal* (June 14, 1994), A1.

Truman, E. M. "The Risks and Implications of External Financial Shocks: Lessons from Mexico," *International Financial Discussion Paper*, 535, Board of Governors of the Federal Reserve System (January 1996).

Truman, E. M. "The Mexican Peso Crisis: Implications for International Finance," *Federal Reserve Bulletin* (March 1996), 199–209.

Unger, K. *Las exportaciones mexicanas ante la reestructuración industrial internacional: La evidencia de las industrias química y automotriz* (México, DF: El Colegio de México y Fondo de Cultura Económica, 1990).

US Bureau of Labor Statistics. "International Comparisons of Hourly Compensation Costs for Production Workers in Manufacturing," *Report 1996* (September 1996).

US Embassy, Mexico City. *Mexico: Economic and Financial Report* (January 1997).

US General Accounting Office. *Mexico's Financial Crisis: Origins, Awareness, Assistance, and Intitial Efforts to Recover*, GAO/GGD-95-96 (February 1996).

US Senate Banking Committee. "Chronology of the Mexican Economic Crisis," documents released by Senator A. D'Amato (June 29, 1995).

US Senate Foreign Relations Committee, hearing on "Mexico's Economic Situation and US Efforts to Stabilize the Peso," 104th congress, session 1, US Government Printing Office (January 26, 1995).

Velasco Márquez, J. "The Mexican Viewpoint on the War with the United States," *Voices of Mexico*, 41 (Center for Research on North America of the National Autonomous University of Mexico, October–December 1997), 49–57.

Volcker, P. and Gyohten, T. *Changing Fortunes: The World's Money and the Threat to American Leadership* (New York: Times Book, 1992).

Weintraub, S. "Case Study of Economic Stabilization: Mexico," in W. R. Cline and S. Weintraub (eds), *Economic Stabilization in Developing Countries* (Washington, DC: Brookings Institution, 1981), 271–96.

Weintraub, S. *Free Trade Between Mexico and the United States?* (Washington, DC, Brookings Institution, 1984).

Weintraub, S. *A Marriage of Convenience* (New York: Oxford University Press, 1990).

Weintraub, S. "Evolución de la balanza de cuenta corriente en México," *Economía Mexicana* 1 (1) (January–June 1992), 249–51.

Weintraub, S. "The Interplay between Economic and Political Opening in Mexico," *Proceedings of the American Philosophical Society*, 137 (1) (1993), 64–78.

Weintraub, S. *NAFTA at Three: A Progress Report* (Washington, DC: Center for Strategic and International Studies, 1997).

Wertman, P. "The Mexican Support Package: A Survey and Analysis," Congressional Research Service, Library of Congress (September 19, 1995).

Wertman, P. "Mexico: Chronology of a Financial Crisis," Congressional Research Service, Library of Congress (September 27, 1995).

Wertman, P. "Mexico's Recent Economic Performance: A 'Snapshot'," Congressional Research Service, Library of Congress (October 11, 1995).

Wertman, P. "The Mexican Support Package: An Issue Overview," Congressional Research Service, Library of Congress (December 14, 1995).

Wessel, D. "Rubin Says Global Investors Don't Suffer Enough," *Wall Street Journal* (September 19, 1997).

Wessel, D. and others. "Peso Surprise: How Mexico Crisis Ambushed Top Minds in Officialdom, Finance," *Wall Steet Journal* (July 6, 1995), A1.

Wilson, J. Q. *Bureaucracy: What Government Agencies Do and Why They Do It* (New York: Basic Books, 1989).

World Bank. *World Development Report 1996* (New York: Oxford University Press, 1996).

Zaid, G. *La economía presidencial* (México, DF: Vuelta, 1987).

Zelikow, P. "Treasury and the Mexican Shock," Kennedy School of Government, Harvard College, case study (1998).

Index

Alduncin, Enrique Abitia, 12
Alemán, Miguel, 15
Aspe, Pedro, 33, 41–3, 63, 69, 85–6, 98–9
　meeting with Federal Reserve officials (October 1994), 125–6
　opposes peso devaluation (November 1994), 126
　relations with Weston Group, 87
　remarks at Mexican national banking convention (1994), 95
authoritarianism
　in East Asian nations, 166
　historical, 14
　Mexican preference for, 12–14
　political, 17
　of *porfiriato* (1876–1910), 6
　of PRI, 15
　of Salinas administration, 11–12
　of single-party dominance, 3–4
　weakened, 39

bailout (1995), *see* rescue loans
balance of payments
　capital account liberalization, 70
　capital inflow financing of current account, 71
　deficit with European and Asian countries, 160
　merchandise trade and current account (1994), 51, 80, 93
　Mexican–U.S. bilateral, 159
Banco Nacional de Comercio Exterior (Bancomext), 71
Banco Nacional de Crédito Rural (Banrural), 72
Banco Nacional de Obras y Servicios Públicos (Banobras), 71–2
Bank for International Settlements (BIS), governments financing support to Mexico through, xi, 110, 113, 142

Bank of Mexico, *see* central bank
banks
　current weakness of, 37–8, 155
　nationalization of (1982), 24, 26, 29, 35
　reprivatization under Salinas, 32, 35–8
　weakness of commercial banks, 91–2, 131
　see also development banks
Bartley, Robert L., 109
Beltran, Ulises, 76
Bentsen, Lloyd, 116–17, 127
Brady Plan debt agreement, 29, 130
Brazil, IMF and G-7 rescue package to (1999), 166
budget deficit
　accounting related to, 71–3
　during De la Madrid administration, 28
　related to shift from cetes to sale of dollarized tesobonos, 80–1, 132
　during Salinas administration, 32
　see also development banks
Buira, Ariel, 57–8, 66
Burki, Shahid Javed, 131
Bush, George, 44

Camacho Solis, Manuel, 49, 55–7, 75
Camdessus, Michel, 116, 127, 151
　on lessons of Mexican peso crisis, 165
capital account, *see* balance of payments
capital flows
　central bank sterilization of in- and outflows, 65
　inflows (1993–4), 43, 50–1, 64
　inflows following Colosio assassination, 58, 64

203

capital flows – *continued*
  inflows from tesobonos sales
    (4th quarter, 1994), 93
  outflows after Colosio
    assassination, 58, 64
  post-devaluation outflows
    (January 1995), 117–18,
    133–4, 162
  Tobin tax, 162
capital markets
  Mexican access after peso crisis
    (1995), 149
  opening (1989–95), 45–6
Cárdenas, Cuauhtémoc, 30, 60, 76
Cárdenas, Lázaro, 6, 19
Carpizo, Jorge, 66
Carstens, Agustin, 43, 58, 66, 170
Carter, Jimmy, 9
central bank
  assigning blame for reserve
    losses, 98
  data on web pages, 20
  intervention and sterilization in
    foreign reserves (1993), 130
  intervention and sterilization of
    foreign reserves (1994), 51,
    63–8, 116
  intervention (November 1994),
    97
  intervention (December 1994),
    102, 105, 138
  intervention within exchange
    rate band, 65–6
  justification for its actions,
    97–100
  monetary policy to prevent
    interest rate rise, 66–71
  nominal independence of, 61, 63
  policy reaction to Colosio
    assassination, 57–9, 62–71
  recommendations for economic
    policy of, 70
  see also exchange-rate band;
    exchange-rate policy; foreign
    reserves
cetes (peso-denominated debt
  instruments)
  foreign investment in, 45
  interest rate on, 51, 67
  shift to tesobonos from (1994),
    78, 132–3
Chiapas uprising
  causes of, 160
  economic effect of, 50–1
  effect on government, 49
  questions raised by, 52–3
  Salinas's preoccupation with,
    47–8, 59
  Zapatista rebellion (1994), x, 1–2,
    46–8
Christopher, Warren, 139
Clavijo, Fernando, 48, 76, 83
Clinton, Bill, 117, 118, 139, 146
Colosio, Luis Donaldo, 42, 49, 50
  assassination of, x, 1–2, 54–8, 64,
    74, 116
  campaign of (1994), 52–6
  as PRI candidate for president,
    41
consumer price index (CPI), 151–2
contagion
  effect in Mexico of Asian and
    Russian crises, 153
  from Mexican peso crisis (tequila
    effect), 166
  from Thai baht crisis
    (Bahtulism), 166
Cordera, Rolando, 4
Córdoba Montoya, José, 48, 55,
  61
  as adviser to C. Salinas, 74–7
  departure of (April 1944), 74–7
  recommends peso devaluation
    (1992), 75
corruption, in PRI-dominated
  government, 16–17
Cosío Villegas, Daniel, 14
crony capitalism, East Asian
  nations, 166
currency
  peso devaluation (1954), 22–3,
    123
  peso devaluation (1976), 90, 123
  peso devaluation (1987), 32, 88
  peso devaluation and depreciation
    (December 1994), x–xi, 33,
    62–5, 70, 94, 102, 104–6,
    110, 124, 133, 152, 171

peso's daily slide (*desliz*), 64, 84
World Bank recommends peso
  depreciation (1992, 1994),
  130–2
see also exchange rate
currency board concept, 89
currency crisis
  East Asian (1997–8), xi, 153,
    165–6
  systemic risk in, 165
currency crisis, Mexican (1994–5)
  non-NAFTA-related decisions, 160
  potential effect of NAFTA on
    decisions related to, 159–60
  see also debt crisis, Mexican
    (1982)
current account, *see* balance of
  payments

debt, external
  borrowing practices (1970s–80s),
    24–5
  growth during López Portillo
    administration, 27
  Mexico's liquidation of US/IMF
    loan, 142
  Salinas's rejection of reliance on,
    10
  Zedillo's insistence on paying, 148
debt crisis, Mexican (1982)
  effect of, 15–16, 28–9
  effect on nationalistic thinking,
    10
  financial claims related to, 164
  onset of, 24
  see also currency crisis, Mexican
    (1994–5)
decision-making
  after Colosio assassination, 57–9,
    62–71
  behavior and characteristics of
    key decision-makers, xii, 1,
    8, 169
  centralization and secrecy of,
    18–19
  with changes (early 1994), 50–1
  Club de Toby joke, 48–9, 167
  concerning going to floating
    exchange rate, 168

following 1994–5 débâcle, 20–1
influence of bank weakness on
  (1994), 38
making bets as basis for, 170–1
Mexican nationalism shaping,
  4–8
top–down, 167
see also central bank; economic
  policy; exchange-rate policy;
  pactos (agreements)
De la Madrid Hurtado, Miguel, 10,
  19
  economic policy of, 27–8, 31–2
  as president (1982–8), 27
democracy
  incomplete, 39
  opinions about Mexican, 12–13
  transition to, 172–3
deposit insurance fund (Fobaproa),
  37, 91
development banks
  deficit (1994), 71–3
  off-budget spending from (1994),
    41, 61, 71–3
  subsidies to, 72
Díaz, Porfirio, 6, 14
Díaz Ordas, Gustavo, 12, 29
Dole, Bob, 116, 139, 171
Dornbusch, Rudiger, 43, 89, 116
Dresser, Denise, 80

Echeverría, Luis, 14, 23–4, 29
economic crisis, Russia (1998), 153
economic performance, Mexico
  after 1982 debt crisis, 88
  contagion effects from other
    crises (1998), 153
  during De la Madrid and Salinas
    administrations, 27–8, 33–4,
    40–4
  effect of peso crisis (1995),
    147–8
  following 1995 bailout, 13–14,
    120, 153–8
  during import-substitution
    period, 22–3
  during López Portillo
    administration, 27
  under PRI-led governments, 15–16

economic policy
  after December 1994 devaluation, 150
  after Zedillo's election, 82–8
  anti-inflation model adopted (1987), 88–9
  central bank officials in government policy meetings, 63
  Chiapas issue distracts Salinas, 48–52
  criticism of incomes policy, 43
  of De la Madrid administration, 31
  designed to assure Zedillo election victory, 61–2
  of Echeverría administration, 23–5
  elements before 1994 crisis in, 150
  following 1995 bailout, 10
  justification by Salinas administration for, 94–7
  of López Portillo administration, 24–6
  Mexican officials refusing to alter, 169–70
  misleading statements about (1993), 42–3
  new Mexican program (January 1995), 111
  pressures from foreign investors, 77–81, 86–7
  of Salinas administration, 10–12, 31–2
  statist, 17
  see also decision-making; exchange-rate policy; inflation; pactos (agreements)
Edwards, Sebastian, 80
Ejército Zapatista de Liberación Nacional (EZLN), 1, 46–8
  see also Chiapas uprising
elections, democratic, 172
Elizondo Mayer-Serra, Carlos, 170–1
ESF, see Exchange Stabilization Fund (ESF)
exchange-rate band
  analysis of Mexican policy, 89
  central bank intervention to protect upper limit (1994), x, 19–20
  criticism of, 89
  peso depreciation within (early 1994), 51, 64–5
  peso (first quarter, 1994), 64
  post-June 1992 narrower, 123
  raising of (December 1994), 65, 105–7, 112, 114–15, 117, 129, 135
  recommended shift from, 70
exchange-rate policy
  after Zedillo's election, 82–8
  criticism in United States of, 118
  debate (1993), 40–1
  decision not to float peso (December 1994), 105–6
  foreign investors influence, 77–81, 86–8
  see also exchange-rate band
exchange rates
  as anchor for 1987 anti-inflation policy, x, 32–3, 88–9
  pacto as vehicle to make decision related to (December 1944), 103–4
Exchange Stabilization Fund (ESF), United States
  loan to Mexico from (1995), 118, 129, 140–1
  restrictions on future use of, 141
EZLN, see Ejército Zapatista de Liberación Nacional (EZLN)

Federal Reserve Board
  concerns about Mexican exchange-rate policy, 83–4, 124–5
  officials meeting with Mexican authorities (October 1994), 125–6
  raises interest rates (1994), 63–4, 93
  tracking events in Mexico, 122–7
Felix, David, 144
Fernández, Arturo, 82, 106
Fernández, Eduardo, 37
Fernández de Cevallos, Diego, 60
financial markets
  criticism of timing of privatization, 70

Index 207

effect of Mexican experience on business of, 112
liberalization under Salinas, 32
tracking events in Mexico, 133–7
fiscal policy
  after peso devaluation (1994), 151–2
  current fiscal discipline, 154
  of De la Madrid administration, 28, 31–2
  development banks removed from budget, 41, 61, 71–3
  effect of tax structure, 155–6
  of Salinas administration, 31–2
  see also budget deficit
Fobaproa, *see* deposit insurance fund (Fobaproa)
Forbes, Malcolm (Steve), Jr., 135, 140
foreign direct investment (FDI)
  into Mexico (1995–7), 153
  in Mexico (1st quarter 1994), 50
foreign reserves, Mexican
  dollars sold to buy pesos, 66–7, 66–71, 78, 94
  levels (early 1994), 50–1, 57–8, 60, 64, 66
  levels (2d, 3d and 4th quarters 1994), 57, 60, 81, 97–8, 102, 116
  levels (December 1994), 104–6, 138–9
  levels (December 1994–8), 153
  net reserve concept, 121
  used as sterilized intervention (1994), x, 51, 65–8
Friedman, Thomas L., 145
Fuentes-Berain, Rossana, 69, 170

Gadsden Purchase, 6
García Alba Iduñate, Pascual, 102
General Agreement on Tariffs and Trade (GATT)
  Mexico as contracting party in, 28
  Mexico's participation in Uruguay Round, 31
Ghigliazzi García, Sergio, 110
Gil-Díaz, Francisco, 43, 66, 89

Gingrich, Newt, 117, 139
Greenspan, Alan, 107, 136
  on effect of potential Mexican default, 140
  view of Mexican financial situation (October 1994), 126
Griffith-Jones, Stephany, 70–1
gross domestic product (GDP)
  decline (1995), 142, 147
  growth (1996), 142, 148
  post-1982 growth in Mexico, 88

Hacienda (Treasury Department)
  Ortiz as secretary, 110, 132, 149, 170
  policy reaction to Colosio assassination, 57–9
  relations of secretary with foreign investors, 86–7
  Serra as secretary, 99–108
  tesobonos sales of, 65
  see also cetes (peso-denominated debt instruments); tesobonos (dollar-indexed debt instruments)
Hapsburg, Maximilian von, 6
Harberger, Arnold, 90, 105–6
Heath, Jonathan, 8, 72–3
Heredia Z., Carlos, 158
Hernández Ramírez, Roberto, 96
host countries, lessons about receiving foreign portfolio investment, 164–5

Ibarra, David, 35
import-substitution
  breakdown of model, 22–35
  motive and rationale in Mexico, 44
inflation
  anti-inflation policy, x, 35, 63, 88–91
  during De la Madrid administration, 27
  during Echeverría and López Portillo administrations, 27, 32–3
  following 1994–5 débâcle, 27–8, 33, 147, 151–2

inflation – *continued*
 reduction under Salinas, 32–3
 see also exchange rate; pactos
  (agreements)
information
 misleading statements about
  economic policy, 42–3
 not sharing, 167
 see also secrecy
interest rates
 intervention as alternative to rise
  in, 66–71
 levels in Mexico (1994), 51, 67, 80
 raised in United States (1994),
  63–4, 93, 116–17, 126
 for U.S. rescue package to
  Mexico, 143
 see also real interbank rate (tasa
  de interes interbancaria
  promedio [TIIP])
International Monetary Fund (IMF)
 conditions linked to rescue loan,
  151
 endorsement of Mexican
  economic program (1995), 111
 financial support package
  (January 1995), xi, 94, 110,
  113, 127, 129, 141
 Fundspeak in interviews related
  to Mexico (early 1994), 127–8
 lessons of Mexican peso crisis
  for, 165
 pre-crisis consultations with
  Mexico, 128–9
 response to Mexican experience,
  112–13
 tracking events in Mexico, 127–9
investment, foreign
 in equity market (1989), 45
 in government debt (1990), 45
 Mexico's restrictions on, 44
 in tesobonos, 45–6
investors, foreign
 differing views of Mexican
  policies, 133–7
 pressures on Mexican economic
  policies, 77–81, 86–7, 133–7
 role in policy to issue tesobonos,
  136–7

Iturbide, Agustín de, 5

Jones, James, 53, 84, 107
Juárez, Benito, 6

Kaufman, Henry, 137
Kemp, Jack, 135
Krauze, Enrique, 3–5, 12–14, 31, 53
Kuznets, Simon, 23

López G., Julio, 165
López Portillo, José, 9–10, 11, 14, 30
 criticism of, 30
 economic policies of, 24, 28–9

McNamara, Robert, 170
macroeconomic policy
 funneling money through
  development banks, 73
 pacto meeting to discuss
  (December 1994), 103–4
Madariaga Lomelín, José, 104
Madero, Francisco, 6
Malpass, David, 135
Mancera, Miguel, 36, 41–2, 61, 63,
  68, 69, 81, 86
 remarks at Mexican national
  banking convention (1994), 95
Marcos, Subcomandante, 46
Marcos Yacaman, Jesús, 61, 81
Mariscal, Jorge, 135
Maroni, Yves, 123
Meltzer, Allan H., 144
mestizaje (joining of national
 races), 4, 7
mestizo culture, Mexican, 7
Mexico
 character of rebellions in, 7, 47
 independence from Spain (1821), 5
 losing territory to United States,
  5–6
 as member of OECD, 52, 95
 mestizaje/mestizo culture, 4–5, 7
 nationalism of, 4–8
 porfiriato (1876–1910), 6
 relations with United States, 9, 11
 Revolution (1910), 6
 unequal economic growth and
  opportunity, 46–7

Meyer, Lorenzo, 18
monetary policy
   Weston Forum suggestions, 78, 87, 137
   see also exchange-rate policy
moral hazard
   of investors seeking high returns, 113
   Rubin's view, 120
   Seidman's view, 140
   Summers's view, 120

Nacional Financiera (Nafin), 71
nationalism, Mexican
   of Echeverría administration, 29
   to entrench privilege, 8
   following 1995 bailout, 11
   to limit United States economic influence in Mexico, 3–10, 44
   in reprivatization of commercial banks, 36
   shaping decision-making, 4–10
   using myth as substitute for democracy, 8
nationalization
   of foreign oil properties (1938), 6–7
   of Mexican-owned commercial banks, 24, 26, 29, 35
North American Framework Agreement (NAFA), swap line to Mexico under, 110, 117, 125–6, 139
North American Free Trade Agreement (NAFTA)
   anti-NAFTA argument in United States, 159
   approval by United States Congress, 43
   conclusion of, ix–x
   effect in Mexico of entry into, 51
   effects on Mexican decisions (1994), 159–60
   factors influencing implementation of, 31
   Mexico's entry into, 9

   opponents of, 45, 158–60
   uncertainty in Mexico about U.S. acceptance of, 43–5

Obstfeld, Maurice, 89
oil industry, Mexico, effect of lower oil prices (1998), 155
Oñate, Santiago, 48, 76–7, 85, 104
Oppenheimer, Andres, 104
Organisation for Economic Cooperation and Development (OECD), 52, 95
Ortiz Martínez, Guillermo, 35–6, 63, 69, 72, 74, 75, 83
   on making bets in decision-making, 170
   on retention of flexible exchange rate, 152
   succeeds Serra at Hacienda, 110, 132

pactos (agreements)
   adoption of technique of (1987), 88
   anti-inflation (1987), 19–20, 32, 41–2
   to bring down inflation, 32–3
   debate about peso devaluation (1993), 40–3
   GDP growth during anti-inflation policy, 88
   pacto meeting (December 1994), 103–4, 168
   pacto meeting (September 1994), 83, 124
   as part of economic policy, 27
Partido de Acción Nacional (PAN), 11
   Fernández de Cevallos as presidential candidate (1994), 60, 79
   winning some elections (1980s), 16
Partido de la Revolución Democrática (PRD), 11
   C. Cárdenas as presidential candidate (1994), 60, 79
   concerns of Chamber of Deputies members of, 158–9
   election wins (1997), 16

Partido Revolucionario
    Institucional (PRI)
  adherence to closed political
    system, 13
  assassinations of principals in
    (1994), 1–2
  challenges to power of, 168–9
  Colosio as presidential candidate
    (1994), 52–3
  corporatist structure of control
    of, 19
  as dominant party, 3–4, 15, 47
  end of political monopoly
    (1994–5), 16
  ideology shift during Echeverría
    administration, 29
  weakened monopoly (1980s), 16,
    30
  weakened power position, 162
  Zedillo as candidate (1994), 56–7,
    60, 79
Partido Revolucionario Mexicano
    (PRM), see Partido
    Revolucionario Institucional
    (PRI)
Paz, Octavio, 3, 8
Pemex, see oil industry, Mexico
Perot, Ross, 45, 140
political system
  delayed reforms in, 168–9
  post-1994 transformation, 172
population levels, Mexico
    (1970s–1990s), 155
porfiriato, 6
portfolio capital flows
  increased size and mobility, ix
  inflows (1st quarter-1994), 50–1
  outflows, ix, x–xi
poverty
  in Chiapas state, 47
  in Mexico, 7
  post-1995 levels, 156
  pre-1994–5 levels, 156
PRI, see Partido Revolucionario
    Institucional (PRI)
privatization
  beginning of process (1982), 17–18
  criticism of timing of financial
    sector privatization, 70

reprivatization of banks in
    Salinas administration, 32,
    35–8, 111
Programa de Capacitación
    Temporal (Procapte), 37

Ramírez, Carlos, 75–6
Ramos, Samuel, 3, 9
real interbank rate (tasa de interes
    interbancaria promedio [TIIP]),
    67, 80, 151–2
Rebolledo, Juan, 76
rescue loans
  Bank for International
    Settlements (BIS), xi, 110,
    113, 142
  International Monetary Fund
    (IMF), 151
  United States, xi, 94, 110, 113,
    117, 129, 140–1, 144–6, 149,
    151
Rogoff, Kenneth, 89
Rubin, Robert, 118, 120, 125, 146
  advocates proposed loan
    guarantee program, 139
Rubio, Luis, 75–6
Ruiz Massieu, José Francisco, 2, 74,
    84, 85, 116
Ruiz Massieu, Mario, 84, 97–8
ruling class, Mexico, 8

Sachs, Jeffrey, 90
Salinas administration
  criticism of, 35
  inflation reduction policy, 32–3
  liberalised trade policy under, 10,
    18, 31
  privatization program, 18, 31–2
  reprivatization of commercial
    banks, 35–8
Salinas de Gortari, Carlos
  attention to problem of Chiapas
    uprising, 47–8
  as candidate to lead WTO, x, 34,
    49, 69, 85
  change in public opinion toward,
    30–31
  concern about his reputation, 33,
    69, 84–5

as darling of investment
community, ix, 33, 114
describes accomplishments of his
administration, 108–9, 118
distractions related to 1994
election, 49–50, 59–61, 69
economic policies of, 10–12, 16,
33–5
effort to change Mexican–U.S.
relationship, 9
leaves Mexico, 94
legacy of, 13–14
opposition to peso devaluation
(November 1994), 126
perception in Mexico of
leadership, 34–5, 168
political policy of, 11–13, 53
popularity of, 3, 33, 52
proposes US–Mexican free-trade
agreement, 31, 43–4
remarks at Mexican national
banking convention (1994), 95
social policy of, 34–5
statements citing
accomplishments of his
sexenio, 96–7, 108–9
strategy related to economic
policies of, 52–3, 169
as *villano favorito*, 26, 31, 108, 163
Salinas de Gortari, Raúl, 17
Santa Anna, Antonio López de,
5–6, 14
Sarmiento, Sergio, 55, 75–6
secrecy
distrust as outcome of, 18, 163
effect of deliberate, 167–8
effect of practice of, 20, 138
in Mexican policy-making, xii, 8,
18–19, 138
in multilateral financial
institutions, 138
of Salinas administration
decision-making, 18
Segovia, Rafael, 30
Seidman, William, 140–1
Serra Puche, Jaime, 48, 65, 62, 87, 98
announcement of widened
exchange rate band
(December 1994), 135

at pacto meeting (December
1994), 104
resigns (December 1994), 107
Shafer, Jeffrey, 115–17
Smith, Peter, 61
social conditions, Mexico, pre- and
post 1994–5, 154–8, 162–3
Solidarity (Programa Nacional de
Solidaridad [Pronasol]), 34–5
speculative attack, against peso
(1994–95), 105
state-owned enterprises
privatization, 17–18, 34
of statist economic philosophy,
17
statism, 17, 23
Suárez, José María Pino, 6
Summers, Lawrence H., 114–16,
118
on Mexico's macroeconomic
policy errors, 139
ten lessons of Mexican peso
crisis, 164
on warnings related to tesobonos
buildup, 124–5
swap lines, Mexico–Canada–United
States, 110, 117, 122, 125–6,
139

Tellez, Luis, 126
tequila effect, xi, 146
tesobonos (dollar-indexed debt
instruments)
auction canceled (December
1994), 110
effect of large-scale (liquidation
of (late 1994), 46, 65
foreign investors' pressures
related to, 136–7
Greenspan on role of, 136
growing levels of sales, 2, 20,
45–6, 61, 80–1, 124
history of issuance of, 136–7
IMF concern about increasing
issues of, 128–9
sales and value (1994), 50, 65,
132
shift in public debt from cetes
to, 132–3

TIIP, *see* real interbank rate (tasa de interes interbancaria promedio [TIIP])
Tobin, James, 162
Tobin tax, 162
trade, Mexican–U.S., 159
trade policy
  import-substitution, 22–35
  liberalization, 31
  nationalism as justification for protectionism, 8
  to restrict United States economic influence, 44
  Salinas' idea of free trade with the United States, 44
  see also balance of payments; import-substitution; North American Free Trade Agreement (NAFTA)
Treaty of Guadalupe–Hidalgo (1848), 5–6
Trigueros, Ignacio, 82, 105
Truman, Edwin M. (Ted), 125, 164–5

United States
  Mexican relations with, 9, 11
  rescue loan (January 1995), xi, 94, 110, 113, 117, 129, 140–1, 151
  U.S. Treasury, tracking events in Mexico (1994), 114–22

Volcker, Paul, 25

Werner, Alejandro, 43
Werner, Martin, 170
Weston Forum, 77–8, 87, 137–8
Wilson, Henry Lane, 6
Wilson, James Q., 18

World Bank
  misgivings about and mission to Mexico (1992, 1993), 130–3
  post-1982 loans to Mexico, 129–30
  recommendations (summer 1994), 82
  relationship with Mexico, 129
  tracking events in Mexico, 129–33
World Trade Organization (WTO)
  C. Salinas as candidate to lead, 49, 85
  formation of, 49
  see also General Agreement on Tariffs and Trade (GATT)

Zaid, Gabriel, 16–17
Zedillo, Ernesto
  criticism of, 13
  economic accomplishments, 14
  elected as president (1994), 79, 128
  exchange-rate policy decision as president-elect, 83
  insistence on crash correction, 148–9
  letter to Colosio (1994), 55–6
  perception in Mexico of leadership, 168
  policy to reinforce savings rate, 155
  as replacement PRI candidate, 56–7, 60
Zedillo administration
  bailout gave credibility to, 149
  economic growth during, 13–14
  tension between central bank and *Hacienda*, 63